WILL WILLIMON'S

LECTIONARY SERMON RESOURCE

WILL WILLIMON'S

YEAR
B
PART 2

LECTIONARY
SERMON
RESOURCE

Abingdon Press
Nashville

WILL WILLIMON'S LECTIONARY SERMON RESOURCE,
YEAR B PART 2

Copyright © 2017 by Abingdon Press

This book is printed on acid-free paper.

ISBN 978-1-5018-4725-7

17 18 19 20 21 22 23 24 25 26—10 9 8 7 6 5 4 3 2 1

MANUFACTURED IN THE UNITED STATES OF AMERICA

Contents

Introduction   vii

SEASON AFTER PENTECOST

Trinity Sunday—God in Three Ways   1
May 29 to June 4—Troubled Sleep   11
June 5 to June 11—Out of His Mind   23
June 12 to June 18—The Mystery of God's Growth   33
June 19 to June 25—Salvation, Now!   43
June 26 to July 2—The Spirit of Generosity   53
July 3 to July 9—Power in Weakness   63
July 10 to July 16—The Perils of Power   71
July 17 to July 23—The New Household   81
July 24 to July 30—What Are You Looking For?   91
July 31 to August 6—Making Sense of Jesus   101
August 7 to August 13—Bread of Life   111
August 14 to August 20—Projection   121
August 21 to August 27—The Joy of Self-Forgetfulness in Christ   131
August 28 to September 3—Work Righteousness   139
September 4 to September 10—Expect a Miracle   147
September 11 to September 17—The Journey   157
September 18 to September 24—Does God Have a Plan
    for Your Life?   167
September 25 to October 1—Don't Go to Hell   177
October 2 to October 8—The Power of Positive Thinking   187
October 9 to October 15—The Good Teacher   197
October 16 to October 22—Christianity: Following Jesus   207

October 23 to October 29—On the Way 217

October 30 to November 5—Ordinary People 225

All Saints Day—Talking to the Dead 233

November 6 to November 12—Money and How to Manage It 239

November 13 to November 19—Our Future with God 247

November 20 to November 26—Overwhelmed 255

PREACHING WORKSHOPS

Preaching Miracles 267

On *Not* Reaching Our Culture through Our Preaching 271

Poetic Preaching 275

Postmodern Preaching: Peculiar Truth 279

Prophets All 283

Taking the Truth 289

The Biblical Word 295

The Theological Significance of Preaching 299

The Wonderful Thickness of the Text! 303

Scripture Index 309

Introduction

For over three decades *Pulpit Resource* has been helping preachers prepare to preach. Now, in this volume, some of the most helpful resources have been brought together to help you faithfully preach your way through the second half (Season after Pentecost) of Year B of the Common Lectionary. This *Lectionary Sermon Resource* doesn't claim to be the sole resource needed for engaging, faithful biblical preaching, but it does give you, the pastor who preaches, accessible, easy-to-use help on your way to a sermon.

No sermon is a solo production. Every preacher relies on inherited models, mentors in the preacher's past, commentaries on biblical texts by people who have given their lives to such study, comments received from members of the congregation, last week's news headlines, and all the other ways that a sermon is communal. Using this resource is equivalent to sitting down with a trusted clergy friend over a cup of coffee and asking, "What will you will preach next Sunday?"

In the sermons that follow, I give you just what you need to begin the journey toward a sermon. I hope that this *Lectionary Sermon Resource* stokes, funds, and fuels your imagination. Rarely do I give you a full sermon in the Proclamation section that can be preached verbatim. I've left plenty of room to insert your own illustrations, to make connections that work within your congregational context, and to speak the word in your distinctive voice. Sermons are occasional: God's word spoken in a particular time and place to a particular people. Only you can speak God's word in your distinctive voice to your distinctive context. All I try to do in this volume is to give you my insights and ideas related to a specific biblical text and then leave you free to allow the Holy Spirit to work within you and your particular congregation.

From what pastors have told me, the value of this guide is its simplicity, its un-varying format. Every Sunday you are given the following sections: "Theme" (I still think the time-honored practice of using a theme sentence to begin sermon preparation is a good practice, enabling the sermon to have coherence and unity); "Introduction to the readings" (that can be used as preparation for listening to the texts read in corporate worship); and "Prayer" (because every sermon is a gift of the Holy Spirit). The sections "Encountering the text" (listening to the biblical text, engagement with its particular message, is the first essential step on the way to a faithful sermon), "Proclaiming the text" (my sketch of ideas and movements for developing what I hear in the assigned text), and "Relating the text" (copious illustrative material that helps the sermon hit home) are given on different Sundays.

I'm honored that you have invited me to be a partner in your preaching. It's a demanding, challenging, joyful vocation to which God has called us. Let's work together to make sure God's word is offered in a lively, engaging way to God's people. Onward in the great adventure of preaching!

WILL WILLIMON

Trinity Sunday
First Sunday after Pentecost

Isaiah 6:1-8

Psalm 29

Romans 8:12-17

John 3:1-17

God in Three Ways

Selected reading
John 3:1-17

Theme
The Trinity is a name for the multifaceted and dynamic God who is with us as Father, Son, and Holy Spirit. Our God is a present, revealing God, but God is also incomprehensibly, uncontainably complex. God is resourceful, persistent, and richly loving. A Christian is someone who tries, with God's help, to do that which is very difficult—that is, to be faithful in our thinking and in our living to the triune God who has been so faithful to us.

Introduction to the readings
Isaiah 6:1-8

The young man Isaiah is called to be a prophet.

Romans 8:12-17

Paul contrasts life in the flesh with life in the Spirit.

John 3:1-17

Nicodemus comes to Jesus at night and is told he must be born of the Spirit. Jesus also tells Nicodemus that God's Son comes into the world as a gift of love.

Prayer

Almighty God, you come to us as Father, Son, and Holy Spirit, having given us the gift of your presence in our lives and hearts. Now give us the grace to love you with our minds as fully as we ought. Cast aside in us our puny, inadequate, and too simplistic views of your majesty and power. Stir up in us a fresh awareness of the richness of your being, the worldwide diversity of your work, and the wide wonder of your love, that we might more perfectly love you in order to more faithfully serve you all our days. Amen.

Encountering the text

All of this Sunday's texts are testimonies to the nature of God. Note that we will again this Sunday, as every Sunday, read three texts from three very different times and places and from three very different parts of the Bible.

Why don't we just settle in and read from only one text? Why confuse people and run the risk of distraction by reading from three texts?

Blame it on the nature of God. Christians are those who have encountered (or should we say, those who have been encountered by) the triune God—God is Father, Son, and Holy Spirit. And this Sunday is when we make a "raid upon the articulate" (as T. S. Eliot said of his poetry) and attempt to bring to speech a complex, multifaceted God.

I suggest that we not focus on any one of today's lessons but rather that we focus upon all of them together as a collective, as three foci testimonials from the one Holy Bible, to the joyful complexity of the one God who is with us in three ways.

Proclaiming the text

Today is Trinity Sunday. Why on earth did we come up with a so complex and difficult-to-talk-about doctrine of God as the Trinity? Well, note that it's not enough for us to read one lesson from scripture; we read one from the Old Testament, one from one of Paul's epistles, and one from the New Testament. Today we read of God opening the heavens and coming to and calling young Isaiah in the temple. Then Paul speaks about the ever-present power of the Holy Spirit and the new life it brings. Then Jesus pays a visit to Nicodemus, engaging him in a mysterious conversation about Spirit and birth. Why can't matters between us and God be simpler?

Because in Jesus Christ we have found that God's rich, relentless love for us is not simple.

Christians believe that in the life, death, and resurrection of Jesus Christ we have seen as much of God as we ever hope to see. As 1 John says, "No one has ever seen God" (1 John 4:12). God is unfathomable, beyond reach of our thinking and perceiving.

Christians admit that it may be of the nature of God to be beyond human visibility or comprehension. Until Jesus Christ. Jesus Christ is the full, perfect, sufficient revelation of who God is and what God does. Everything we believe about God flows from what we've seen of God in Jesus Christ.

In his first advent among us, Jesus as "God's Son," the Messiah (that is, "anointed one of God"), challenged how people thought about God. Lots of people looked at Jesus, listened to his teaching, witnessed his work, saw his death, and said, "That's not God. God is powerful, distant, high, and lifted up. God is _____." (Fill in the blank with whatever high and noble attribute God simply must have if God is to be worthy of your worship.) Jesus failed to measure up to their preconceptions of who God ought to be and how God is to act if God is really God.

Especially today, to stand and affirm with the Apostles Creed, "I believe in God the Father Almighty . . . and in Jesus Christ, God's only begotten Son . . .

– 3 –

[and] I believe in the Holy Spirit," is to assert a considerably more complex and challenging view of God than that which prevails among most Americans.

Most people in our society appear to want God to be generic, abstract, vague, distant, and arcane. "God? Oh, can't say anything too definite about God. God is large, indistinct, vague." God for many of us is this big, blurry concept that we can make to mean about anything we like, something "spiritual," someone (if we have any distinct notions about God) whom we can make over so that God looks strikingly like us.

In Jesus of Nazareth, God got physical, explicit, and peculiar, and he came close—too close for comfort for many. Jesus Christ is God in action, is God refusing to remain a general idea or a high-sounding principle. Jesus Christ is God in motion toward us, is God refusing to stay enclosed in God's own divinity. Many people think of God as a vaguely benevolent being who never actually gets around to doing anything.

It is as if we are threatened by the possibility that God might truly be an active, intervening God who shows up where we live. We've designed this modern world, controlled by us, functioning rather nicely on its own, thank you, with everything clicking along in accord with natural laws, served on command by technological wonders of our creation. So who needs a God who relishes actually showing up and doing something? We modern people are loath to conceive of a God who is beyond our control or a world other than the one that is here solely for our personal benefit.

This is the deistic God of the philosophers, a minimalist, inactive, unobtrusive, noninvasive, detached God who is just about as much of a God as we moderns can take. There's a reason why many thoughtful modern people seem so determined to sever Jesus from the Trinity, to render Jesus into a wonderful moral teacher who was a really nice person who enjoyed lilies and was kind to children and to people with disabilities. To point to a peripatetic Jew from Nazareth who wouldn't stay confined within our boundaries for God and say, "Jesus is not only a human being but also God," well, it's just too unnerving for us enlightened, modern people to handle. Note how frequently many people refer to *God* and how seldom they refer to *Christ* and you will know why the statement "God was reconciling the world to himself through Christ" (2 Cor 5:19) is a threatening disruption to many people's idea of a God who stays put.

With all orthodox Christians at all times and places, we have maintained that God is one; but not simply one, not merely one. We baptize in the name of the Trinity, signifying that baptism relates us to the fullness of God. We are monotheists (belief in one God) but not mere monotheists. We believe that the God who is present to us as Father, Son, and Holy Spirit is one. Father, Son, and Holy Spirit are three distinct yet unified and interactive, relational, and loving ways in which God is one. The Trinity is God in three ways being the same God.

If all this talk of three-in-one seems a bit overwhelming to you, you are not alone. Unitarianism is always a bit easier on the brain than trinitarianism. Still, there is no way for us to do justice to the God whom we have met in Jesus Christ without believing three ways in one God.

To say with the Hebrew scriptures, "Israel, listen! Our God is the LORD! Only the LORD!" (Deut 6:4), is to say not simply that there is just one God but also that the God of Israel is singular, the one and only God, the true God, whereas lots of our idolatrous god-substitutes are not.

Here again, in my experience, the Wesleyan view of God challenges many modern folk. In order to keep God distant, vague, and irrelevant, many people want to keep God simple, uncomplicated, and abstract. These are the dear folk who say, "Well, I'm not sure that I'm very religious, but I do believe in God; and, after all, isn't that what it's all about?"

The problem is that once we discovered that "God was in Christ," things got complicated, not because the church wanted to make the simple faith of Jesus complex and confusing, but rather because we discovered in Jesus that God was at once much more demanding and much more interesting than we had first thought. In Christ, God was reiterated in ways that meant that we were forced to expand our notions of God. We could have gotten along quite nicely without the Trinity had John the Baptist not intruded into our settled arrangements with God by shouting, "Look! The Lamb of God who takes away the sin of the world" (John 1:29). Once Jesus showed up—the one "conceived by the Holy Spirit," born of a poor peasant woman in Judea, who is God in the flesh, teaching, working wonders among us in the "power of the Spirit," suffering and dying at our hands, rising after three days, returning to the very people who crucified him, breathing his Holy Spirit upon us—well, we had to talk about God in a way that only complex, dynamic trinitarian theology could do justice. After being met by Jesus, we could never again think of God in the simple, uncomplicated way as we had before.

1. God is the creative, caring Father, but not simply at the beginning of creation. And God is not only the maker of the world but also the sustainer of the world. The same darkness-to-light, nothing-into-something of Genesis 1 continues every day of our lives. God keeps creating, bringing something out of nothing, making a way when there was thought to be no way. God keeps caring, keeps reaching out to us in active love, constantly watching over us in vigorous providential care.

2. God is the redeeming, loving, seeking Son. He ventures forth like some prodigal son (Luke 15) to search out and to save lost humanity in the "far country" where we live. When God decisively, revealingly came to us, God came to us as one of us. God got incarnate as a Jew from Nazareth who was born in a most embarrassing way to a young peasant woman, grew up to be a man about whom we know next to nothing save his three years as a young adult in ministry, and was tortured to death by the government. That one is God among us.

The name Jesus (or Joshua) means "God saves," and the Gospels depict Jesus as God's answer to what's wrong between us and God, God saving the world: "God so loved the world . . ." (John 3:16).

It is one thing to have a belief in God; it is quite another thing to have a personal experience of the living, seeking God. It is one thing to believe that

God is there; it is quite another matter to believe that God is there for you. It's fine to believe that God in Christ reconciles the world to himself; it's quite another thing to believe that God has stepped in and actually reconciled you.

Our story with God begins, in the Bible, with two new human beings, fresh, vulnerable, at home, and at peace in a lush garden. In just a couple of chapters things quickly go bad as humanity rebels against God's good intentions for us and disobeys God's minimal demands ("don't eat from the tree of knowledge of good and evil" [Gen 2:17]), and the first child becomes the first murderer, bashing in the head of his own brother (Gen 4:1-12). Alienation from God is the result of our lust to be gods unto ourselves. Listen to the news on any given day and you will hear what fresh outrage we have perpetrated, the latest proof that we have a serious neighbor problem and an even more serious God problem. What righteous, holy God would have anything to do with humanity—the embarrassingly inept supposed summit of God's creation and the defaced image of God?

Our sin and rebellion make all the more remarkable that the Bible says God refused to give up on us. God kept returning to us, in constant loving guidance, in the words of the law, the testimony of the prophets, the apocalyptic visions of a better future, finally coming to us as God's own Son. Because we couldn't come to God, because we demonstrated time and again that we were powerless to do something about our God problem, God came to us and solved our God gap as only God could.

The same Father who created the world, the God who kept returning to Israel in mercy and graciousness, is one with the Son who came to us, sought us, and died for us.

3. God is the present, dynamic Holy Spirit who is God near to us. It is God empowering us to do those things that we could never do on our own, God constantly revealing God to us, and God talking to us about God. There are things that God wants us to know, things that we cannot know except as revelation—that is, as gift of God working through the Holy Spirit. And there

are things that God wants us to do that we cannot do except through the empowerment of God's Holy Spirit.

The Holy Spirit is not an exotic third kind of God or some strange phenomenon that is somewhat similar to God. The Holy Spirit is more than some impersonal force, psychic energy, or indistinct power. The Holy Spirit has a personality because it is the spirit of the Father and of the Son; it is God in action, the God who not only loves, not only redeems, but also now, presently, all the time, convinces the world of sin, leads us into the church, then comforts, sustains, and empowers us all along the way of discipleship. In other words, the Holy Spirit is God in action, God revealed, God present.

We believe in the Trinity because we have been encountered by the Trinity, transformed by a power greater than ourselves, loved by a love greater than our love, embraced by a God who is so large, so rich, so close to us that we could have never thought this God up by ourselves.

Relating the text

You will note that all three scripture lessons today—the call of young Isaiah, Paul's testimony to the power of life in the Holy Spirit, and Jesus's nocturnal visit to Nicodemus—demonstrate a God who intrudes, who calls, who acts, who reaches and empowers.

When the far-off one who has been brought near is you, when the wall that has been kicked down is the wall that you built in a vain attempt to keep God out of your life and off your back, then you are believing in the Trinity.

Much of the theology that I hear in our church (and, alas, much that I preach!) tends to stress the first person of the Trinity—God the creative, ordering, providential Father—rather than God the actively redeeming Son or God the relentlessly reaching Holy Spirit. The more chaotic and confusing our world becomes, it seems the more we need to stress God the creator, the God who "has a plan for your life"!

I wonder if we are due for a revitalized stress upon Christology. Jesus, second person of the Trinity, is our experience of the active, reaching, seeking, redeeming Son. God in Jesus Christ is not only love embodied but also the active savior of the world. Today, when many speak of the "sovereignty of God," they seem usually to speak of God the creator of the world. But let us be reminded, by the work of the second and third persons of the Trinity, that divine sovereignty is not only in God's creation of the world but also in God's continuing, constant redemption of all people and all things to God.

We discovered, in Jesus Christ, that God is love, but not simply love as an inclination or disposition. An often-repeated criticism of Jesus was that he "welcomes sinners and eats with them" (Luke 15:2). Jesus constantly intruded where he was not invited, sometimes where he was not wanted. The thing that got Jesus's critics (at least those in Luke 15) was not that Jesus loved people but that Jesus received, ate with, and thereby loved the wrong people. Thus, Jesus showed us not only that God is love but also that God's love was considerably more interesting, active, expansive, and determined than most of what passes for either "God" or for "love" around here.

Sunday between May 29 and June 4 inclusive
(if after Trinity Sunday) [Proper 4, Ordinary/Lectionary 9]

1 Samuel 3:1-10, (11-20)
Psalm 139:1-6, 13-18
2 Corinthians 4:5-12
Mark 2:23–3:6

Troubled Sleep

Selected reading

1 Samuel 3:1-10, (11-20)

Theme

Sometimes God bypasses the religious professionals, the tenured experts, the wise and experienced leaders, and goes directly to younger, ordinary people, calling them into God's service. The church must be supple and open to God's ways, surprised and delighted when God moves outside our expectations and conventions and speaks and calls, surprising people to speak God's word and do God's work in the world.

Introduction to the readings

1 Samuel 3:1-10, (11-20)

The boy Samuel is called by God to be a prophet, to speak God's truth to Israel, even though that truth may be troubling for God's people to hear.

2 Corinthians 4:5-12

Paul, writing to the church at Corinth, speaks of the gospel as "treasure in clay pots." Christ has chosen thoroughly human agents (us) and a thoroughly human institution (the church) to bear his great treasure into the world.

Mark 2:23–3:6

Jesus heals on the Sabbath, and immediately a bitter controversy breaks out. As a result, Jesus's critics begin to conspire to destroy him.

Prayer

Jesus, we give thanks that you have called us together this morning. Help us during this time of worship to praise you as we ought, to listen carefully for your word, to be courageous in applying your word to ourselves, and to be bold in living out your word after this service of worship.

Loving savior, we don't know why you elected to call us to be your disciples. We know for sure that you didn't call us because we were the best people in town or had the highest moral standards or were the most successful in obeying and serving you.

However, we know wherefore you called us. You have summoned us to be your lights in the world, to enable people to see some of your love and glory through our little lives. Strengthen us in our vocations so that your realm might spread to every corner of the world, so that others might also hear you calling them and have the grace to follow. Amen.

Encountering the text

Today's first lesson is the story of the call of the little boy, Samuel, to become a prophet of the Lord. As is typical of the narratives of 1 Samuel, this is an exceedingly well-crafted story with colorful, dramatic elements. In our explication and proclamation of this story we will need hope to be as vivid as the story as 1 Samuel presents the episode. This lesson appears on the Second

Sunday after Epiphany as well it should, for it is a memorable divine revelation. However, it is also good that we have it on this Sunday as preparation for the great divine disclosure on Pentecost.

The story begins on an ominous note: "The LORD's word was rare at that time." The high priest, Eli, has made a mess of things. His family has been leading the religious rites of Israel in corrupt ways. It is a time of widespread corruption in Israel.

And though the word of the Lord was rare, the word of the Lord intrudes, coming not to old Eli but to the little boy Samuel. The new age for Israel comes as a voice intruding into the night, calling, "Samuel, Samuel!" That call leads to a response, "Speak. Your servant is listening."

Old Eli is Samuel's mentor, and thus there is tension between the older servant of God, Eli, and the young boy, Samuel, to whom the vision comes. The author sets up a wordplay between "visions" that are rare and Eli's being "unable to see." There is thus a hint that though God is offering visions, the visionless leaders are not able to discern God's communication with them.

God turns toward the untutored young child who hears the voice of God while the older, experienced spiritual leader fails to hear the voice. Eli's career is doomed because of his poor performance as a spiritual leader. Eli's children will pay dearly for their father's failures, whereas Samuel, Eli's surrogate child, will be elevated. Samuel's "Speak. Your servant is listening" is the model for any faithful person's response to the address by God.

Young Samuel will be burdened with a divine message and the message will be one of judgment. Even though Samuel is young, he does not shirk his prophetic responsibility to speak, no matter the cost of his speaking up for God.

In the Bible, this is so often how God makes a new beginning—with a voice in the night. We hear in this voice that spoke to Samuel an echo of that primal voice that spoke into the darkness so long ago, "Let there be light!" Many times, fresh beginnings, new life, and new worlds begin with God's voice intruding into the night. So it is for us as well.

Proclaiming the text

It is night. Everybody is asleep up at the temple. Old Eli and his sons have finished their religious duties for the day. The throngs of faithful people are gone. The religious rituals are ended, and all is quiet.

But not everyone sleeps peacefully. The boy Samuel is made restless. I am told that the expression "sleeping like a baby" is not accurate. In truth, young brains are quite active during sleep; rapid eye movement appears to be more pronounced among the very young, and therefore their sleep is full of dreams, imaginings, and restlessness.

For the little boy, Samuel, this night will be memorably restless. Into the child's night there is a voice, "Samuel, Samuel!" The voice is none other than the voice of God calling Samuel to become a prophet.

The context of this divine visitation, this divine vocation, is important. It was dark not only during night up at the temple but also at this time in the history of Israel. There was great moral confusion. Many were following "the devices and desires" of their own hearts (as we used to say in the prayer of confession) rather than the ways of God. Or, as scripture puts it vividly, the word of the Lord was "rare at that time." Not too many visions or revelations. Few memorable sermons. Not many hearing their names called and coming forth to live faithful lives for God.

But the silence did not last forever. There was in the night a voice of God. God did not leave God's people without a witness. The word of God came to a little boy, catapulting him to the head of the religious leadership in Israel.

Perhaps because I am growing older, but I seem to have increasing difficulty sleeping through the night. I fall asleep well enough, but then my sleep is disturbed. I wake up.

I, therefore, find myself perusing the magazine advertisements for "sleep aids," wondering if I need a little chemical help to enable me to sleep peacefully through the night.

Funny thing, I also seem to be having more vivid and often disturbing dreams. I don't remember dreaming much when I was young. At breakfast in my college days, people would sometimes report having had vivid dreams. But I never seemed to have anything much to report.

These days it is different. I find myself waking, sometimes in the middle of the night, with a sudden jerk, from a strange dream.

Most of the dreams that I can remember are often dreams of frustrating experiences. I am standing before some sort of door, struggling to get the door open. But the door will not open. In desperation, I look for another entrance. I find a door, but that one is locked, too. I spend what seems like the entire night, frustratingly going from door to door, rattling the locks.

After a night of these frustrations, I wake up tired.

As I remember, from days in college psychology, this particular sort of dream is called a "performance dream." As I recall, the dream betrays an inner sense of inadequacy, failure to perform in life as well as one might like.

I don't know. But I do know that these dreams are disturbing. Here I am, needing my rest, all prepared for a peaceful night, only to have these thoughts intrude uncontrollably, disturbingly into my consciousness while I am trying to sleep. That is frustrating.

Sometimes, when I go to bed, preparing to sleep, in that time between being awake and being asleep, as I close my eyes, suddenly I recall various events that have happened throughout the day. I hear a word that someone spoke to me many hours ago. I recall something that happened. The recollection is often of an event that happened much earlier in the day that I have put out of my mind. But while I am attempting to drift off into sleep, the event comes back into my consciousness. I become disturbed.

An hour or so later, there I lie in bed, still thinking about this event, going over in my mind what was said, what should have been said, what was done or left undone.

Psychologists say that one of the functions of dreams is to process material that has been incompletely processed in our brains during the day. We think of sleep as a time when we lose consciousness and drift off into peaceful, thought-free sleep. But perhaps sleep may be a time when things that have been suppressed or forgotten spring back into consciousness. Sleep may be a time not when we cease all thinking but rather when we move to a different level of thinking. Perhaps, in dreams and restless sleep we are being given access to that which we have attempted—during our conscious, waking hours—to put out of our minds.

Maybe that is why in scripture God seems to get to people in dreams. I think of Pharaoh's dreams that required Joseph's interpretation. Then there's Joseph and Mary being warned in a "dream" to flee as refuges to Egypt, fleeing the murderous wrath of King Herod and taking the baby with them.

Perhaps, with all of the distractions that come our way during the middle of the day, night provides a great occasion for God finally to sneak in, to get to us, to speak to us, to reveal something to us when our defenses are down. At night, in the quiet, perhaps we at last can hear that word of God that can't get through to us during the day.

Remember that restless night that Jacob spent on the banks of the river, where he wrestled with that mysterious night visitor. As dawn broke, Jacob realized that it was if he had been wrestling with God. In the Old Testament, the Hebrew words for *dream* and *vision* are often mentioned together (Job 20:8; Isa 29:7). And the roots of both of these words in Hebrew mean "to see."

Let's be honest about dreams and visions. Something about us wants simply to be left alone. We want to sleep in silence and peacefulness. As a young man, John F. Kennedy wrote a book on the factors leading to World War II. He focused on England in the days before the outbreak of World War II, when England thought it was enjoying a kind of perpetual peace. The title of Kennedy's book was *While England Slept*.

The other day when I was driving down the highway, I passed a large billboard that read, "Do you want Peace? Let us introduce you to Jesus Christ, who will bring you peace." The billboard was sponsored by a local congregation.

I know that Jesus is the Prince of Peace and that Jesus often brings peace to our troubled souls. But what I thought, driving past that billboard, is that in my experience Jesus is often the disturber of the peace! Something in me really wants to be left alone, to live my life as I please, to take responsibility for no one but myself. I try to get my life together—that is, living my life on my own terms, doing what I want to do, and heading in the direction that I have determined. And then somehow, someway, there is a word or a vision or a sense of being summoned to walk in a different direction. My sleep is shattered. I wake up with a start.

And I find, to my surprise, that my uneasy sleep is not due to some event during the day or something I ate for dinner. It's Jesus disturbing my sleep. Just as God disturbed the sleep of little Samuel, who then disturbed the sleep of old Eli, God is able even yet to disturb my sleep and your sleep.

I hear a lot of talk these days about the need "to achieve more balance in our lives." Many apparently crave a well-balanced life in which there is a feeling of right proportion and serenity. But then I remember that psychiatrist in one of my congregations who said, "Balance is what you feel when you have the illusion that your life is really under your control." Ouch.

And that is sometimes how God moves among us. Just when we want to close our eyes and peacefully drift off into sleep, just when we think that we have got everything in balance, just when we think our lives are solely under our control, God intrudes. There is a word in the night. Or a disarming dream, an unsought vision. We are summoned. We awaken. Our eyes open. We see something that is more than that which we could have come up with on our own, a thought that is not self-derived. That is what happened to little Samuel that night. While everybody else was asleep, he awoke with a start, hearing his name called, "Samuel, Samuel!"

So for today, let's define a Christian as the sort of person who knows that the life you are living is not your own. You believe we live in a world in which there is more going on than what you can control. You actually believe that not all the voices you hear come from within you. Sometimes, perhaps in the dark of night, a voice comes from outside you.

Sometimes—when everything is quiet after the singing of a song just before I rise to speak, and the congregation settles down—I hear something deep within myself that is more than just me talking to myself. Or maybe in the middle of the sermon you hear more than what the preacher is saying in the sermon. Or when the household is silent at the end of the day and all is dark and you are alone with your thoughts, you discover that your thoughts are not exclusively your thoughts. It's little Samuel and old Eli all over again.

I know a woman who, after all the hustle and bustle of the Christmas holidays, decided that she would take some time away at the beach, just sunbathing, dosing, and recovering from all of the busyness of the Yuletide.

I saw her back in town awhile back.

"How was your great vacation down in Florida?" I asked her.

"Well it was fine, mostly. I did a lot of recuperation, but I also found it a bit disturbing. When I got down there, out of my accustomed routine, away from family and friends and responsibilities, I had a lot of time simply to be by myself."

"That sounds very restful," I said.

"Not exactly," she replied. "As it turned out, I wasn't really alone. While I was down there, it was like God finally got my attention. It was as if God said to me that I need to reorganize my life. To start doing some things differently. I got down there, expecting to rest, and all I did was enable God to give me another assignment."

Lord Jesus, don't leave us alone in the dark. Keep disturbing our peace. Keep coming to us, especially when we don't know how to come to you. Keep enlightening us. Show us your will for our lives. Give us a job to do that we wouldn't have given ourselves. Disturb our sleep. Amen.

Relating the text

Recently at a civic club gathering I was introduced as "heading up one of the largest volunteer organizations in the state."

No, Christians don't volunteer for anything; we get summoned, enlisted, recruited, and called. Nobody present this morning worshipping this God, is here on your own. You got called.

Our scripture is the beloved story of the call of Samuel. I say "beloved" story but not loved by people of my age. I used to love this story when I was a kid, the way God called little boy Samuel to be a prophet. "Samuel, Samuel!" (sometimes God has to call you repeatedly before you get the point!). And the lad replied, "Speak. Your servant is listening," and then, "I'm here."

I used to like this story. But then I aged out of it. That is, at some point, say after my fortieth birthday, I came to the unwanted realization that I wasn't the boy Samuel. I was the old, professionally trained, experienced, credentialed, ordained Eli. A few years ago, I had to have cataract surgery in both eyes. I am Eli of the bad sight.

Question: Why did God call the kid? Why on that vocational night did God bypass the experienced, credentialed, ordained Eli and go to the ignorant, untrained, immature kid? The Bible says the "LORD's word was rare at that time," you couldn't find a good sermon for love or money. So why, when God finally stirred and spoke, did God speak to the kid? There was old Eli, working for the Lord for six decades, full time at the temple, waiting for a word from the Lord; and there was the Lord, bypassing Eli, jumping over two generations, and going to the child, Samuel, who didn't even know who the Lord was.

It reminds one of other Bible stories: of God calling little David to save the nation (when the hosts of Israel shook in their boots before Goliath), or of the little boy Jesus wowing the professors at the department of religion with his youthful wisdom: "God chose what the world considers low-class and low-life—what is considered to be nothing—to reduce what is considered to be something to nothing," Paul told his low, trashy, foolish congregation in Corinth.

Sometimes God seems to bypass religious officials and go directly to the kids.

A preacher whom I know told me that at her first meeting with the leaders of her new congregation, an elderly man arose and said, "Nothing against you personally, but I don't think this congregation is ready for a woman preacher. You seem like a nice person, but I just can't believe that the bishop would send you here."

She replied, "Well that makes at least two of us. Friend, I can tell that you and I are going to hit it off just fine, since we think alike. I fought God for twenty-two years. I told the Lord he must have lost his mind, calling somebody like me into the ministry. If you don't want me as your pastor, let me assure you that I've already told God that I don't want to be your pastor. But friend, sometimes the Lord just won't take no for an answer."

My prayer for our church is that we will listen to God, that we will get better in our ability to notice the work that God is doing in raising up a new generation of Christians. I hope that us older folk will be like old Eli and patiently instruct the young, saying, "Go and lie down. If he calls you, say, 'Speak, LORD. Your servant is listening.'" I pray that the young will be brash and bold enough to risk saying, "I'm here." I pray that the aging (in more ways than one) mainline church will be welcoming, open, and hospitable to those whom God is calling to this ministry, that it will step aside and let God jump over vision-impaired senior citizens like me and go to the kids.

To brag of ourselves and our lives, "I did it my way," is to reveal the folly of attempting to take your life into your own hands, to live the uncalled, unsummoned life. This is a prejudiced Christian comment, but I think it very sad that some venture forth on their own, oblivious to any command-ing, demanding external claim (such as the voice that disturbed the sleep of Samuel and Eli).

Google tells me that the word *vocation* is used today in print less than at any time since the mid-nineteenth century. The vocational assertion, "Know that the LORD is God—he made us; we belong to him. We are his people, the sheep of his own pasture" (Ps 100:3), sounds odd to most Americans, schooled as we are in the fiction that our lives are our possessions to use as we choose.

When we ask, "Who am I?" or "What am I here for?" the officially sanc-tioned, widely held, governmentally subsidized creed answers:

I am self-fabricated. Autonomous. My life is mine to live as I please. I am my personal possession, the sum total of my astute choices and my heroic acts of detachment from anyone more important than me. I bow to no claim other than that which I have freely chosen. I did it my way. I'm the captain of my fate, the master of my soul. I'm the sole author of the story that is me.

The church offers a countercultural answer to "Who am I?" This faith as-serts that God likes nothing better than to weave an interesting tale using someone as plain as me. I did not think myself up on my own. I am not self-constructed. God thought me up before I thought about God.

The same God who had the brilliant idea to breathe life into mud (Gen 2:7), making humanity out of nothing, breathed forth you. Both of us live on bor-rowed breath (David Kelsey).

There are all sorts of diversions and outright lies abroad to keep us from knowing the truth of our contingency and dependency, the truth of voca-tion. A fully functioning capitalist economy loves the lie that our powers of choice and self-possession are boundless. The myth of self-invention is a fiction produced by the market that gave us fifty different kinds of pizza and four hundred TV channels and calls the resulting wasteland "freedom." Never before have we had so much freedom to get what we want with so little to tell us what is worth wanting.

Augustine charged that our boasts of Promethean, unbounded human freedom of choice are little more than the rattling of our chains, a failure truthfully to acknowledge our masters. In this supermarket of desire, what I choose is less significant than that I choose. Endless, never really satisfied consumption is my fate. I tell myself that I am free of externally imposed masters while I fail to admit my serfdom to the most imperious master of all: me.

Each of us is born with a set of sealed orders, said Kierkegaard. Finding ourselves here doesn't explain why we are here. Making life is a long process of figuring out what we're for, what life's worth living for, and what's to be done with the breath we're given. We need help unsealing and then making sense of our orders.

Trouble is, since Kierkegaard, we are consumed with the project of self-definition. To ask for help in figuring out life is to admit our vaunted self-sufficiency is a lie. Modernity forces us to write the story that defines who we are, who I am, heroically to choose from a variety of possible plots. My friend Stanley Hauerwas loves to point out the irony that the story that I have no story other than the story I have personally chosen is itself a story I didn't choose. De Tocqueville defined America as where one is free to think whatever one wants, but where all want to think the same thing. Jesus famously said that his yoke is easy, and his burden is light. We have exchanged the burden of God's externally imposed vocation for the far more burdensome assignment of never-ending self-fabrication (Charles Taylor).

Sunday between June 5 and June 11 inclusive

(if after Trinity Sunday) [Proper 5, Ordinary/Lectionary 10]

1 Samuel 8:4-11, (12-15), 16-20

Psalm 138

2 Corinthians 4:13–5:1

Mark 3:20-35

Out of His Mind

Selected reading

Mark 3:20-35

Theme

When many people heard Jesus preach, they did not say, "Here are the words of God!" Rather some said, "He is crazy!" Jesus applies an odd sort of rationality to our thinking about God, the world, and ourselves. He is not crazy; he just sometimes sounds crazy when we listen to him from the standpoint of what the world teaches us to regard as rational. To be a disciple, a follower of Jesus, is to be given the grace to think about God, the world, and ourselves in a different way—the way of Christ.

Introduction to the readings

1 Samuel 8:4-11, (12-15), 16-20

The people tell the prophet Samuel, "Give us a king," despite being warned of the oppressive servitude that will follow.

2 Corinthians 4:13–5:1
"So we aren't depressed," Saint Paul proclaims to the church at Corinth, because we have "a building from God . . . eternal and located in heaven."

Mark 3:20-35
Jesus goes home and is surrounded by a crowd. Some, having heard Jesus speak, deride him saying, "He's out of his mind!"

Prayer
Lord Jesus, help us not to be put off by you. You talk in ways that often make us uncomfortable. You intrude into areas that we would prefer to keep off limits. You make demands upon us that we don't think we can meet. Sometimes you confuse us and push the boundaries of our comprehension.

Give us the grace, Lord Jesus, to hear you when you speak and, upon hearing you, to receive you, and in receiving you, faithfully to follow you as you are, rather than as we would like you to be. Amen.

Encountering the text
Mark's Gospel is full of conflict in which Jesus deals with uncomprehending disciples and constant critics. In today's pericope from Mark 3:20-35, Jesus has difficulty with his family. His family charges, "He's out of his mind!" Jesus responds with talk of Beelzebul, probably because he was associated with demonic possession and insanity. An insane person is someone who is out of touch with reality, a person who, in his or her mind, is living in another world.

Clearly, Jesus has come proclaiming and enacting a very different sort of reality, another world that is counter to our expectations for reality. That reality is named "kingdom of God," a place, a system of values, a set of assumptions and expectations that is counter to the way we think the world works. Thus, Jesus is dismissed as "out of his mind." He's not out of his mind; he's in another frame of reference, another consciousness—that is, the kingdom of God.

What are the implications of this for contemporary followers of Jesus?

Proclaiming the text

Believe it or not, I got fairly good grades when I was in school. A major turning point in my life as a student came when a high school teacher whom I greatly respected said to me, "Son, you have a very good mind. Now why don't you use it!"

Fellow students who sat next to me in chemistry or world history didn't like to read. They had lots of trouble getting the key concepts of the class and spitting them back to the teacher on the exam. Me? I had the sort of mind that could rather easily catch on to most of what the teacher was saying and thereby win a good grade in the class.

A seminary professor once said to me, "You have an excellent mind." That made me feel good. But then he added, "Unfortunately you also have an undisciplined, rather disorderly mind."

I can see those of you who have been subjected to my sermons over the years nodding your heads in agreement with my professor!

Now here's a curious thing: nobody ever said of Jesus, as once or twice they have said of me, "That was a wonderfully rational lecture you gave." I looked it up in the concordance. Nobody ever said, "Jesus, you have one of the best furnished minds in all of Galilee."

What they said of Jesus was, "He's gone *existemi*!" "He's raving *existemi*!" Did you hear that in this morning's Gospel lesson? In Mark 3:21 the people said, "He has gone *existemi*! Out of his mind." Jesus is back home, and his family wants to be proud of the young rabbi that they have produced. Unfortunately, his family was hugely embarrassed because everybody, upon hearing Jesus teach and watching him work, said, "He's *existemi*! He's out of his mind."

By the way, there is much the same reaction to Jesus in John 10:11. Jesus says, in essence, "I'm so good a shepherd, I'm willing to die for a bunch of stupid sheep." And the class responded with one voice on the class evaluation form, "He's out of his ever-loving *existemi*!" Die for a stupid, $9.95 plus postage sheep? That's crazy!

Now I know what you're thinking. Unlike me, Jesus didn't have the benefit of a seminary education. I know that Jesus never published a book or major monograph. I know that he lived with his parents until he was past thirty years old, never held a job, never owned a home, never dated, and went around to lots of parties with twelve unattached men, but still I ask you, does that make Jesus guilty of raving *existemi*?

"Jesus, say something rational to us, give us something on which we can hone our sharp minds."

"Alright. Try this. You only grow up by turning and becoming as a little child. You can't get into the kingdom of God unless you revert and turn and become as a child. Want to win? You do so by losing. You get by giving. You live by dying."

Wow. That sure doesn't sound rational to us. Sounds like you're out of your mind!

"Jesus, say something thoughtful, but make it something that's practical so we can use it in our daily lives in the world."

"Alright. Try this. Blessed are you, the poor. Happy are you, the hungry. Oh, how fortunate are you who are divorced or unemployed. Congratulations to those of you who are spiritually poor, those of you who don't have much spirit."

What? Blessed? Fortunate? Happy? Are you *existemi*? Are you out of your ever-loving mind? Where I come from, when you are unemployed, people treat you like you have some sort of disease. They don't want to catch what you've got. In our world, those who are poor, divorced, or bereft are thought to be failures. Because we're here at church, we don't like thinking of ourselves as spiritually inept. We're sitting here this Sunday because we're spiritually rich!

And Jesus replies, "Oh, I'm not talking about the way that nine out of ten people think. I'm trying to teach you to have a different sort of mind."

Once there was a rich investment officer who was very, very successful. He built so many houses, he could hardly remember how many he had. We would call him a success and a model for our young to emulate.

"Soul, take ease, you've got so many houses you can't count them," he said to himself. That night the angel of God tapped him on the shoulder and said, "Hello, fool."

Now, the man who told that story is clearly *existemi*, out of his right mind.

Do you remember when Paul said to us, "Let the same mind be in you that was in Christ Jesus" (Phil 2:5 NRSV)? It doesn't say, "Try to have a right mind," or, "You should have a generally well-informed and disciplined mind." Paul says, "Have Jesus's mind."

In assessing the soundness of Jesus's mind, I remind you that sometimes, whether Jesus's way, the way of the cross, is seen as reasonable or crazy depends on what counts for reasonable.

Do you think it reasonable that more people are in jail in America (now over two million) than in any nation in the world? This is the "freedom" we so graciously brought to Iraq? Now if you think that sounds perfectly "reasonable," then there's a good chance that I'll never be a good enough preacher to keep you from thinking that the sometime-prisoner Jesus is certifiably "out of his mind." If you think that's reasonable, you may tend to hear Jesus and respond, "He's gone completely *existemi*!"

I got to know her at the university. She suffered from depression. She had difficulty fitting in to the life of a university student. Then she signed up for a course, "Feminist Cultural Criticism." I saw her after just two weeks of that class and she looked better than I had seen her in months.

"Best class I ever took here," she said.

"Why?"

"I thought I was crazy, but this class has helped me see the possibility that this university, and my whole culture, is crazy. I've been given a new way of thinking."

There are people gathering in congregations this morning who had the same thing happen to them after their baptism.

One of the world's oldest defenses against Jesus was, "He's *existemi*!" It wasn't so much Jesus was "out of his mind"; it was that he had a very different mind.

And I think that some of you will back me up when I say that it's tough to be held accountable, in our discipleship, to God's Son who happens to be not only Jewish, Galilean, crucified, and, since Easter, on the loose, but also, in the eyes of much of the world, a bit *existemi*.

And you know, *existemi* seems to be contagious, at least in this congregation. If you think about it in a certain way, one of the great joys of the Christian faith is that it's great fun to have your minds messed up by Jesus.

By the way, what is the episode that immediately precedes the people's charge of *existemi* against Jesus? What crazy, ridiculous thing did Jesus do right before they said, "He's gone out of his ever-loving mind?" I'll tell you. The charge that Jesus Christ is *existemi* was evoked by this ridiculous, crazy act by Jesus:

And Jesus then appointed twelve apostles to be with him. And he sent them out to preach his message, to have authority to cast out demons: Simon (whom he liked to call Peter), James son of Zebedee, and John the brother of James.

They didn't mind Jesus preaching because he made some awfully interesting points that made a lot of sense. They didn't mind him casting out demons or raising the dead, which was a very nice thing for him to do. But when he insanely gave everything he had and all that he hoped to do into the hands of twelve uneducated, imbalanced yokels, well, the world with one voice said, looking at his idea of disciples, "He's out of his mind."

They were troubled when they met Jesus, but when they met his assistants—that is, us—they said, he's *existemi*!

Relating the text

I wonder if one of the reasons why Jesus seems strange to us is because we have a too-limited notion of the "facts of life":

"We must reconcile ourselves to what George MacDonald called 'The Factitude of Things,' for the world is what it is, and not something else. When someone told Thomas Carlyle that Margaret Fuller, the New England transcendentalist, had said, 'I accept the universe,' he replied, 'By God, she'd better!'"

—R. Maurice Boyd, *Why Doesn't God Do Things Perfectly?* (Nashville: Abingdon Press, 1999)

A woman was telling me about the little church she serves in North Alabama. "We've got one of the ugliest church buildings you ever saw," she told me. "I fear that some Sunday when there's a big wind, it'll fall in on us."

"That's terrible," I said.

"Well, not all bad," she replied. "You know there are some folk who won't come to a church if it looks too good. We got a church where nobody, no matter how low they are, will be uncomfortable. There's something to be said for a church that's ugly in a world where lots of folk feel ugly."

And there's lots to be said for a church that sounds a bit crazy in a world in which lots of folk feel a bit crazy.

"In medieval times, as you approached the city, your eye was taken by the cathedral. Today, it's the towers of commerce. It's business, business, business."

—Joseph Campbell (1904–1987)

German theologian and pastor Dietrich Bonhoeffer warned his students who were to become pastors of the danger of theology used as a device to arm the preacher with authority. When theology becomes a kind of weapon to be used by the pastor to make the claims of Christ too rational and comprehensible, then theology becomes dangerous:

"The greatest difficulty for the pastor stems from his theology. He knows all there is to be known about sin and forgiveness. . . . The peak of theological craftiness is to conceal necessary and wholesome unrest under such self-justification. . . . The conscience has been put to sleep. Theology becomes a science by which one learns to excuse everything and justify everything. . . . The theologian knows that he cannot be shot out of the saddle by other theologians. Everything his theology admits is justified. This is the curse of theology."

—Dietrich Bonhoeffer, *Spiritual Care* (Minneapolis: Fortress Press, 1985)

St. Paul, in that beautiful passage in his letter to the Philippians, a passage that we read back on Palm Sunday of this year, says, "Let the same mind be in you that was in Christ Jesus."

Paul implies that Christians are those who have minds that have been made up by Christ. We're to strive to think about things in the same manner that Jesus thinks about things.

I looked up the English word *mind* in a biblical concordance. Frankly, I found that *mind* is not a big Bible word, just as I expected.

In numerous places we're told to love God with our *dianoia*, a Greek word that is often rendered in scripture as "mind." Having taught at a seminary and university for more than twenty years, and still do, I've made a big deal of loving God with a whole *dianoia*. I'm a preacher in a church that arose out of Pietism. Alas, when Pietism, which once had a lively intellectual tradition, goes limp, the heirs of Pietism have sometimes reduced discipleship into just a warm feeling. So you can imagine how much I used to hammer those pietistic Methodists on using their minds when dealing with God. First Peter 1:13 says, "Therefore prepare your *dianoia* with action; discipline yourselves."

I don't give a rip about what you *feel* about Jesus; I want you to *think* about Jesus. For God's sake, use your *dianoia*!

So I attempted to burrow that text from 1 Peter into the brains of my seminarians. I would tell them repeatedly, "Christian ministry is so difficult, so very demanding that you had better prepare your minds for action, discipline."

The mind is the coherent, intelligent, rational, wise way we are to serve Jesus. To that end I've given much of my ministry. I've recently gone all over Alabama, teaching and leading discussions with dozens of pastors and laity about the United States' Near Eastern wars. I began each session with, "We are here tonight, here in the church, to do some dianoia about an important subject. Tonight we are going to *dianoia* about the Iraq War like Christians."

When somebody would challenge my opinion on the war, or start yelling incoherently, I would say, "Hey, you idiot" (I would say this in love) "where's your *dianoia*?" And that would settle them down.

Church is where we come to use our *dianoia* in the service of God, rather than in service to some of the little "godlets" that so consume our minds elsewhere.

Hebrews promises a day when God will write the commands of God "in their *dianoia*." One day, in a fragmented world, everybody will just *dianoia* quite naturally because God's thinking will be written upon our brains.

And yet here's my main point: nobody ever accused Jesus of having a well-furnished *dianoia*.

Sunday between June 12 and June 18 inclusive

(if after Trinity Sunday) [Proper 6, Ordinary/Lectionary 11]

1 Samuel 15:34–16:13 or Ezekiel 17:22-24
Psalm 20 or Psalm 92:1-4, 12-15
2 Corinthians 5:6-10, (11-13), 14-17
Mark 4:26-34

The Mystery of God's Growth

Selected reading

Mark 4:26-34

Theme

Our relationship to Christ is due to the work of Christ. We are Christians because somehow, some way, God has reached out to us in Christ, our name has been called, and we have been summoned forth to follow the way of the good news. In countless ways God reaches out to us, calls our name, and summons us, scattering among us a word of vocational grace.

Introduction to the readings

1 Samuel 15:34–16:13

After the death of Saul, Samuel seeks out a new king for Israel, anointing David, the young son of Jesse.

2 Corinthians 5:6-10, (11-13), 14-17

"From this point on we won't recognize people by human standards," Paul writes to the church at Corinth, telling them of the transformation that Christ has worked in his life.

Mark 4:26-34

Jesus tells his followers a parable about a sower sowing seed, thus revealing something to them of the miraculous growth of the kingdom of God.

Prayer

Lord Jesus, we are here this morning because somehow, in some way, you secretly planted a seed in our hearts and minds. When we were sleeping—just focusing on ourselves, just dozing through the sermon, just daydreaming about nothing—you somehow got through to us, spoke to us, and enabled us to hear your voice. We are here this morning because you spoke to us.

So speak to us this morning, Lord. We will do our best to be wide open and awake. We will try to tune our ears to your word for us. We will try not to listen to our own fears and reservations and instead listen for you to call each of our names.

Lord Jesus, giver of the seed, giver of the growth, bring your word to harvest in us. Amen.

Encountering the text

Where should we focus our attention on this text? On the sower? The seed? The harvest? Who is the sower? We assume that it must be God, for scripture tends always and everywhere to speak first of God and only secondarily about us. That reading is justified by the allusion in verse 29 to Joel 3:13 in which the harvest metaphor is used for God's coming judgment. But how is it that God is unaware of how the seed sprouts and grows?

Maybe the sower is the Christian who goes about witnessing and evangelizing, thus scattering seed. The seed is sown, but the evangelist doesn't know how it grows; and, as we have noted elsewhere, the disciples sure don't know much in the Gospel of Mark! We doubt, though, that the disciples would be used in such a positive way in this parable. This is, after all, the Gospel of Mark.

So is the sower Jesus? Jesus certainly "scattered" a great many words as if they were "seeds." Perhaps, then, if the present response to his preaching is disappointing, there will still be growth and harvest.

Or perhaps the parable is about the seed and its surprising, uncontrollable growth. Human action is not the point but rather the mystery of God's grace. This interpretation seems linked to the parable of the mustard seed (4:30-32). As is said in Mark 4:1-2, 33-34, these parables are rarely simple or self-evident.

Let's cut through the possibilities and say that this parable is a story about God. God is the agent of the growth of God's reign. The growth of the reign of God is in God's hands, not ours. We do our work, but growth is finally up to God. Imagine telling this parable to hard-working farmers who had back-breaking duties. It's a reminder then that finally, when all is said and done, God's reign is up to God to grow. God is busy, even when God's work is not always visible to our unenlightened eyes. God's growth tends to be imperceptible. We will therefore want to interpret this parable as one of good news.

Proclaiming the text

I've been preaching now for over three decades. That's a lot of sermons! And the longer I preach, there is a sense in which I know less about preaching. When I was a young preacher, just starting out, I knew a great deal about preaching. I knew the best form for sermons—that is, the form that leads most directly to congregational assent. First say this, then that, and the congregation responds, "You nailed it, preacher! We got it!"

But now, more than a thousand sermons later, I know less about preaching than I once knew. Why do some of my "best" sermons—on which I have expended much effort—fall flat, roll over, die, and get greeted by a collective congregational yawn?

And maybe even more mysterious, why do some of my worst sermons (slapped together on a Saturday night, held together with tape and twine) succeed? I mumble something, wandering around in scripture, throwing out this or that undeveloped idea, and you come out at the end of the service, grasp my hand, and say, "Thank you, thank you. God really spoke to me today, preacher."

Here's what I think. Maybe I know less and less about preaching because I know more and more that preaching is not really something that I do. Preaching is what God does. It's not a sermon until God's speaking makes it a sermon.

Thus, Jesus told a parable about a gardener (surely the lousiest gardener there ever was) who began slinging seed with abandon. Most of the seed was wasted, victim of bad soil and terrible conditions. But wonder of wonders, some of the seed germinated, took root, and produced a fine harvest.

Jesus says that God's reign is just like that. Like what?

A couple of months ago I went through that spring ritual that is so dear to us. Forgetting the lousy results of last year's attempt at gardening, I went out and bought five or six little packets of seed. I followed carefully the directions on the back of the seed packets, unlike last year. I carefully prepared the soil. And I stand before you today happy to report to you that the seeds germinated, the sprouts came up, the plants are standing tall, and I think I can look forward to a good harvest. Of course, that depends on many factors beyond my control—weather, for instance, and whether I'll be around enough this summer to look after things properly.

To be honest, all sowing and harvesting is dependent on "many factors beyond my control." And I'll admit that I like to be in control. For me, the challenge of gardening is not being in control.

And as a preacher, the challenge of preaching is to invest myself in a craft in which I, the preacher, am not in control. It's not God's word until God speaks and makes it God's word. God's word is a gift that only God can give.

I have a friend who is a Baptist preacher who took off a few months, traveled around the country as a sort of sabbatical study, attended church in dozens of places, and listened to scores of sermons. I saw him the week he returned home and asked him, "What did you learn about preaching during your sabbatical?"

He replied laconically, "I learned that, when it comes to preaching, if anybody hears anything in a sermon, it's a miracle."

It's like seed that's thrown at random on the ground. Some seed sprouts; most of the seed does not. But that which sprouts is nothing less than miraculous.

You know this. You sit there in your seat on a Sunday. You could have just as easily been seated elsewhere. Your mind wanders, thinking of all the things you have to do once church is over. You're not in the best of moods, spiritually speaking.

And yet, miracle of miracles, wonder of wonders, you hear something. Something in the scripture, a word or two in the sermon, a tune by the choir, took root in your soul. You heard your name called. You rise, you soar, you have had a meeting with God, and you have been encountered. It's a miracle.

Jesus says it's like that with God's word. Sometimes it takes root in your heart. Sometimes it's all wasted. Sometimes God uses all this to reach out and seize your life, and sometimes God passes you by until maybe next week. It's a gift. It's a miracle.

Every sermon is therefore an act of faith. You listen, but if you hear your name called, that comes as gift. And wonder of wonders, enough of you receive the gift, often enough, to keep you coming back, Sunday after Sunday.

As a preacher, I love to watch God's word take root in each of your lives. I can see those gifted moments sometimes in your eyes, as I look out on the congregation. I also see it in your lives, as you live into your faith in new and challenging ways, ways that make me know that God has called your name, has used my poor sermon to speak to you.

These words, such small things—tiny seeds cast to the wind. But God takes them, uses them, and blesses them, and they become God's word for you. They become the bread of life broken and given to you, your bread, your life, your sustenance, your miraculous gift from God.

Relating the text

After that I will pour out my spirit upon everyone;
> your sons and your daughters will prophesy,
> your old men will dream dreams,
> and your young men will see visions. (Joel 2:28)

John Wesley, the father of Methodism, ignited a revival that swept across the world. A major aspect of that revival was Wesley's preaching. He preached sometimes in open fields, sometimes in little Wesleyan chapels where the common folk of eighteenth-century England heard him gladly. Early on in his movement he published a book of his sermons that were transcribed by faithful followers and edited for publication. He insisted that his lay preachers read, inculcate, and imitate his sermons before they attempted to preach on their own. In fact, Wesley's sermons comprise an essential part of Methodist doctrine to this day.

And yet for most of us, reading Wesley's sermons is an unedifying activity. (I have had the same disappointing experience in reading the sermons of Luther or Calvin.) The language sounds stilted and dry. The sermons are overly formal and devoid of illustrations, connections with everyday life, or any of those characteristics that we think are essential for sermons today. Of course they are not Wesley's sermons as they were actually preached. These are transcriptions for publication. Something was no doubt lost in the move from oral to written form. Still, one is baffled that thousands heard Wesley with such gratitude and to so strong effect.

Perhaps Wesley the preacher possessed an impressive presence in the pulpit. A stirring voice and imposing stature command the respect of an audience. Wesley must have been a strong figure when he preached.

Well, forget it. Wesley had a tiny physique, even for his day. He stood about five feet two and had delicate features. His voice, while said to be pleasing, was rather frail. What was there about the man that made his sermons rend the hearts of his hearers? A Swedish visitor came all the way to England to hear him preach in 1769 and, after hearing him preach, declared, "He has no great oratorical gifts, no outward appearance" (quoted by Richard P. Heitzenrater, "Wesley, John," in *Concise Encyclopedia of Preaching* [Louisville: Westminster John Knox Press, 1995], 500).

What did Wesley have that made his sermons so powerful? The answer is nothing. It was not the man who made the message move people with such power, nor even the message itself, though Wesley's sermons are well crafted and theologically substantive. Wesley's sermons "worked"; they taught, they moved, and they delighted (three characteristics that Augustine demanded of good sermons) because of God's speaking rather than Wesley.

The reasons for any sermon speaking to the hearts, minds, and souls of the hearers are always more theological than anthropological, due more to the nature of God than to the nature of the preacher or the hearers. *Theology* means literally "God words" (*theos* = God; *logoi* = words). But theology does not just mean words about God or our talk about the meaning of God. *Theology* also means God's talk about the meaning of God to us. Christianity is a "revealed religion," which means that it is based upon the conviction and the experience of a loquacious God. Preaching is not only what we say, even what John Wesley said, or what we hear, even the most astute of us listeners. Preaching is also what God says.

Wesley's sermons spoke to people because the God of Israel and the church deemed it right to speak to people through Wesley's sermons. We preach because God speaks, and a primary way for this God to speak is through preaching.

We preachers are subservient to the power of God to scatter the seed of the word and to give growth. As Paul put it in 1 Corinthians 3:7: "Neither the one who plants nor the one who waters is anything, but the only one who is anything is God who makes it grow." We preachers do not work alone.

When Paul's preaching authority was challenged by some in Galatia, Paul mounted no other defense for himself than God's action in his ministry: "I want you to know that the gospel I preached isn't human in origin. I didn't receive it or learn it from a human. It came through a revelation from Jesus Christ" (Gal 1:11-12).

In a sermon on 1 Samuel, John Calvin dared to speak of contemporary pastors as prophets, like Samuel, who are "the very mouth of God." As Heinrich Bullinger asserts in the Second Helvetic Confession: "The preaching of the word of God is the Word of God." This is an astounding claim to make for the speaking of mere mortals like us preachers and for the hearing of mere mortals like our congregations. Yet it is no more an astounding claim than that made by Jesus: "Whoever listens to you listens to me" (Luke 10:16). It is a claim that rests upon faith in a gracious God who condescends to us mere mortals through the scattered seed that is preaching. It is faith that is born of the story that begins with, "And God said . . ."

Several years ago, a Baptist campus minister from Mississippi brought a group of students through town and asked me to meet with them. They were college students on their way to do some good Baptist work in Appalachia.

During our conversation a kid with a baseball cap turned the wrong way on his head asked, "What do you do, as a Christian, when people really get mad at you and want to hurt you because you're a Christian?"

I said that I wasn't exactly sure to what he was alluding. "Being a Methodist, we have managed to rework the gospel in such a way that nobody could ever draw ire or get hurt being a Christian! I'm always so nice about Jesus that nobody has ever tried to crucify me; what exactly do you mean?"

He said, "Well, for instance, the other night we were talking about the war with Iraq after our fraternity meeting. Most everybody thought the president knew what he was doing, that the war was a good thing, that a preemptive strike was justified. All I said was that I thought the war was a very bad idea. I'm a Christian. That's not how we think the world is set up. That's not how we handle evil. Besides, I'm a Baptist and we tend to always be suspicious of the government, no matter who's in charge.

"That was when they started yelling at me. Told me if I didn't like living in America I ought to go someplace else. Called me names, even."

Now there's a kid who's got a strange notion of who's in charge, who sits on the throne. Where did he get the notion that the president may not have the last word on the world? There is no way, I submit, that he could have gotten this news about a new world except through the preaching of sermons in his little Baptist church in Mississippi. Somehow God took those sermons and miraculously managed to get them to take root in that young man's life.

Sunday between June 19
and June 25 inclusive
(if after Trinity Sunday)[Proper 7, Ordinary/Lectionary 12]

1 Samuel 17:(1a, 4-11, 19-23), 32-49 or 1 Samuel 17:57–18:5, 10-16

Psalm 9:9-20 or Psalm 133

2 Corinthians 6:1-13

Mark 4:35-41

Salvation, Now!

Selected reading

2 Corinthians 6:1-13 (with reference to Mark 4:35-41)

Theme

In Jesus Christ, God has opened wide the heart of God to us all. We are those who have experienced God's open heart and therefore we are those who, having been loved by God, open wide our hearts to others. We still have difficulty, to be sure, but we live with confidence in hope, buoyed by the good news that in Jesus Christ the salvation of the world has been and will be accomplished.

Introduction to the readings

1 Samuel 17:(1a, 4-11, 19-23), 32-49

A giant named Goliath threatens the tribes of Israel until a young man named David steps forward to challenge him.

2 Corinthians 6:1-13
Paul defends his apostleship to the Corinthians, urging them to accept the grace of God. He says, "Look, now is the day of salvation!"

Mark 4:35-41
One evening, while Jesus and his disciples were crossing the sea together, there was a great storm and the disciples were afraid. "Teacher, don't you care that we're drowning?" they asked. Jesus stilled the storm, then asked, "Why are you frightened? Don't you have faith yet?"

Prayer

Lord, give us eyes to see the outbreak of your kingdom among us. Help us acknowledge your salvation, working in us and in our world. And then give us the grace to live our lives in light of the good news, that knowing your sovereignty over our future, we might live in the present in the light of your salvation. Amen.

Encountering the text

Paul has an announcement—a message that has been entrusted to him— "Look, now is the right time! Look, now is the day of salvation!" In Christ, salvation is accomplished. Salvation, making our lives aligned with the life of God, has happened. Everything has been done that needed to be done in order to justify us sinners to God. In Christ, salvation is yet being accomplished as sinners (like the Corinthians) are hearing the grand announcement and responding to the news. Salvation for Paul is both a fact in the past and a fact with continuing significance.

In Christ, the world has shifted on its axis. We are living in a whole new world. We have exchanged citizenship. That means that we are enabled to live with and rise above a whole host of sadness—"problems, disasters, and stressful situations . . . beatings, imprisonments, and riot . . . hard work, sleepless nights, and hunger. Having nothing . . . yet owning everything."

Paul is thus honest about the Christian life. It is far from a painless, untroubled ride: "Corinthians, we have spoken openly to you." He has told the hard, cold, sobering truth about what happens to those who sign on with Jesus.

And yet at the same time, "our hearts are wide open." We live as those who "work together with him" (6:1). We work not to get somewhere with God; we work with God because—by the grace of God and the work of God in the cross and resurrection of Christ—we have arrived. Now is the time of our salvation. Now is the time to sign on with the Jesus movement. Now.

At the end of the letter to the Ephesians, Paul tells early Christians to put on various sorts of armament to withstand the wiles of the devil—the sword of the Spirit, the shield of faith, the breastplate of righteousness. He finally urges them to "take on the helmet of salvation and the sword of the Spirit" (Eph 6:17). Salvation is here depicted as a sort of defensive headgear, a helmet that protects Christians from losing consciousness, from being bopped on the head and forgetting who they are. Think of today's proclamation as part of that salvific defensive endeavor.

Proclaiming the text

How does it stand between us and God? In scripture, the question is never, "Is there a God?" but rather, "Does the God who is there care about us?"

With time we adjust to cosmic indifference. A favorite means of coping with the absence of a savior is to deny that we need saving. One of my cherished viewpoints of the National Cathedral in Washington, D.C. is the sculptured tympanum over the front door. Medieval interpreters spoke of the tympanum as component of the "doorway of heaven" and the "gateway to God" because it was here that one entered the cathedral and also the glories of the Christian faith.

In almost every medieval cathedral, that space is occupied by a depiction of the last judgment. One thinks of Notre Dame de Paris, in which a judging angel holds scales, weighing the merits of the good and the bad. Over Notre

Dame's scene of judgment, blessedness, and damnation presides the enthroned Christ, surrounded by his faithful apostles. In some churches Mary, mother of Jesus, is there, and sometimes Christ is on the cross.

At the US National Cathedral, contemporary sculptor Frederick Hart has rendered a peculiarly twentieth-century biblical subject: the creation of humanity. It's a Rodin-like sensuous Adam and Eve emerging from the hand of a creative God. Gone is any sense of the judging, saving God. God's greatest work is no longer the cross or our redemption; the greatest divine work is our creation. Neither atonement nor reconciliation but rather creation of humanity has become the message that the church celebrates before the world.

This suggests to me a humanity overly impressed with itself, getting along just fine, thank you. Our great desire is to be successful in achieving the human project, as we define it, immune from the judgments of God, rather than to be redeemed through the judgments of God. To paraphrase dear Flannery O'Connor, anybody with reasonable success in being successful, or even a good car, "don't need redemption."

No enthroned or even crucified cosmic Christ can be seen because, well, if you are as knowledgeable, as grand, and as glorious as contemporary upwardly mobiles, there is not much left for God to do for us. God gave us a grand start in fashioning us from the dirt at creation; then God retired, leaving us to fend for our gifted selves.

While celebration of humanity is the dominant story, it is not the story to which Christians are accountable. It is the conventional, popular cultural story that, at every turn, is counter to the gospel.

Paul, in his words to the Corinthians this Sunday, is bidding them to live into, and to live out of, a very different story of salvation. God has decisively moved to save. The fallen world, a place of suffering and difficulty, has become by the work of Christ the great stage of God's saving work. Now, Paul doesn't preach a future hope, a pious expectation that God will one day, some day, save. He preaches a present reality, a world shifted on its axis.

"The salvation of this human world lies nowhere else than in the human heart, in the human power to reflect, in human meekness and human responsibility," declared Vaclav Havel. Considering how Havel suffered at the hands of the Communists, it is touching for him still to think so highly of human prospects. Yet Havel's is a most conventional, limitedly modern thought; salvation is what we do by ourselves to save ourselves. This is the story that still has the world captive.

In scripture, salvation is what God does. In Genesis, God does not really create the world "out of nothing"—*ex nihilo*—but rather God works on the "earth [that] was without shape or form." Creation is that good that would not be there if God were not the sort of God who God is. God addresses the chaotic, formless stuff of darkness with, "Let there be light." God speaks to the chaos and in that address there is evocation of a world that God calls "good."

Creation is depicted by Genesis as a series of divine addresses. There is something about this God that speaks something out of nothing by commanding, summoning, addressing, calling, and preaching. Salvation, seen from this perspective, is a primary product of divine love, the grand result after a creative God goes to work with words.

The Bible says that God's world-making, world-changing creative work didn't end on the sixth day of creation. With Pharaoh's chariots pursuing them, the children of Israel falter on the bank of the Red Sea. Moses encourages them with, "Don't be afraid. Stand your ground, and watch the Lord rescue you today" (Exod 14:13). Upon arriving on the opposite shore, safe from the Egyptians, Moses leads Israel in a hymn, singing, "The Lord is my strength and my power; he has become my salvation" (Exod 15:2).

Theologian Karl Barth taught that salvation was the whole point of creation. God creates humanity a world so that God might have a grand stage on which to enact the drama of redemption. Paul tells the Corinthians that they are now actors in this drama.

When the God who brought forth the world comes so very near to us in Jesus Christ, salvation is the name for that decisive encounter. John 1 implies that incarnation is salvation, an intensification of what God has been doing since Genesis 1: "The Word became flesh and made his home among us" (John 1:14). When God goes to work, makes a move, and comes close (incarnation), that work (God in action) is "salvation" (God triumphant).

We tend to stress that we live in a culture of freedom of choice. But I think Paul would want me to add that all of our lives are lived in the light of a prior choice—not our choice, but God's. Early on, even before we got here, God chose never to be God except as God with us, God for us in Christ Jesus.

And that's the good news. Paul tells the Corinthians sure, we have our sufferings, our persecutions, and difficulty. God's kingdom is here, but it is not here in its fullness. And yet the present time is also the time of God's salvation. We have been, are being, and will be saved through God's loving work among us.

Now, let's go out and live in the light of that story. Amen.

Relating the text

In my first days as chaplain at Duke University, a delegation of campus ministers asked my support for "Declaration of Religious Rights and Freedoms on Campus." Their pronouncement assured Duke students that they would be "safe from unwanted evangelization." I reassured the group that it was unnecessary for me to sign such a declaration for they had nothing to fear from me: I was a Methodist. It had been so long since we had evangelized anybody on campus, wanted or not, that we had forgotten how.

When they resisted my self-characterization, I said, "Name one Jew [the campus rabbi was part of the group] who has been evangelized by some Christian on our campus." They could not. As I saw it, interfaith marriage was the rabbi's big challenge, not interfaith "unwanted evangelization."

"Sadly," I said, "you are losing Jews to the same 'faith' to which many Christians succumb—unbridled, consumptive capitalism that renders a university education into training to be more savvy consumers. Jews, Catholics, Protestants—anyone for whom 'success' is more than a big house and a big car—should be forewarned that when you send your kid to a first-rate, selective university like ours, she will come out less faithful than she went in."

It isn't that Christians are keen on "salvation" while others are not. It isn't that most people are too modern, too enlightened, and too sophisticated and secular to worry about something outmoded like "salvation." It is rather that we live in a conflicted supermarket of "salvations" that are based on very different ideas of what or who saves. About the time that Jesus was born, an inscription was placed throughout the Roman colonies proclaiming the *euangelion* (gospel) to the captive peoples that "Augustus has been sent to us as savior." So while we say what salvation in Jesus Christ is, we will also need to say what it is not. And in the church family of which I am a part, that takes some courage. Our now-dominant belief is that though there are different faiths, they are all fairly much the same. This is the sort of thing that people say when they are unwilling to admit that different faiths (and their different "salvations") may actually be different.

To say that Christian salvation is a peculiar, distinctive, even odd way of life and death is to threaten the dominant status quo that believes that differences in belief are dangerous, a threat to national unity. Religious differences must therefore be suppressed or trivialized in order to keep us religious fanatics from killing each other. Christian preaching of salvation takes another way in its unabashed, even joyful celebration of the Christian difference that is salvation in Jesus Christ. As Paul said of the plurality of salvations in his day, "Jews ask for signs, and Greeks look for wisdom" (1 Cor 1:22).

Jesus Christ is a name and a definition for the word *salvation*.

There are few more challenging words to be said by the church than *salvation*. Salvation implies that there is something from which we need to be saved, that we are not doing as well as we presume, that we do not have the whole world in our hands, and that the hope for us is not of our devising.

Most Christians think of salvation as related exclusively to the afterlife. Salvation is when we die and "get to go to heaven." To be sure, scripture is concerned with our eternal fate. What has been obscured in today's epistle on salvation as invitation is Paul's stress on sharing in a particular God's life here and now, so that we might do so forever. Salvation isn't just a destination; it is our vocation. Now. Salvation isn't just a question of who is saved and who is damned, who will get to heaven and how, but also how we are swept up into participation in the mystery of God who is Jesus Christ.

Check the references to heaven in a biblical concordance and you will find that almost none of them are related to death. Heaven is when or where one is fully with God—salvation. Now.

Look up *salvation* in the concordance and you will find a wide array of images. Luke–Acts uses the word *salvation* rather frequently; Matthew and Mark almost never use it, though we ought not to make too much of that. All of the Gospels may be fairly read as stories about the rich, peculiar nature of salvation in Jesus Christ. Salvation is a claim about God. God's self-assigned task is making "salvation happen in the heart of the earth" (Ps 74:12). God is addressed as "God of our salvation" (Ps 65:5). For some, salvation is rescue, deliverance, and victory. For others, it is healing, wholeness, completion, and rest. Isaiah speaks of salvation as a great economic reversal in which God gives a free banquet for the poor (Isa 55). Whatever *salvation* means, its meaning must be too rich for any single definition.

Because most of what we know for sure about God is based upon what God does, it is possible to say that salvation is not only what God does but also who God is. Whoever would make a world for the sheer delight of relationship and conversation and whoever would work a miracle like raising crucified Jesus Christ from the dead is properly known as "the God who saves":

"God is indeed my salvation; I will trust and won't be afraid. Yah, the LORD, is my strength and my shield; he has become my salvation" (Isa 12:2).

We would never know who God is if it were not for our having seen, touched, and tasted God's salvation in Jesus Christ (1 John 1:1). Though we could not come to God, God came to us in a stunning and peculiar act of salvation, and God thereby showed us as much of God as we need to know.

The Hebrew verb root *ya sha*—"save"—is found 354 times in the Hebrew scriptures, usually with God as subject. Proper names derived from this root—Elisha, Joshua, and Hosea—all indicate "God saves." Later, Matthew will underscore the theological significance of Jesus's name (Heb. "Joshua") with a commentary by the angel: "He will save his people from their sins" (Matt 1:21). When Jesus is welcomed into Jerusalem, people will shout "Hosanna" (Mark 11:9)—"Save us, we pray," from the Hebrew *hosi anna*.

I find it remarkable that *salvation* appears most frequently in Psalms and in Isaiah. In Israel's most dismal days, Isaiah dared to speak of God's promised deliverance. When the sky is dark, Israel discovered the God who saves.

Old Zechariah is filled with Holy Spirit when he sees the baby John, cousin of baby Jesus, and sings the "Benedictus." There will be "a mighty savior for us" arising in Israel, a new king, "a mighty savior for us in this servant David's house . . . who will tell his people how to be saved through the forgiveness of their sins" (Luke 1:69, 77). Something decisive has happened to us that comes to us from outside our efforts. Now.

Sunday between June 26 and July 2 inclusive

[Proper 8, Ordinary/Lectionary 13]

2 Samuel 1:1, 17-27

Psalm 130

2 Corinthians 8:7-15

Mark 5:21-43

The Spirit of Generosity

Selected reading

2 Corinthians 8:7-15

Theme

Our material possessions are, in reality, gifts of God, best used for God's work. In our society that teaches us to regard our possessions as our achievements, showing Christian stewardship and the generosity that we are enjoined to practice in the church is an act of resistance against the evil that would teach us that what we have is ours rather than a gift of God.

Introduction to the readings

2 Samuel 1:1, 17-27

David laments the deaths of Saul and his son, Jonathan.

2 Corinthians 8:7-15

Paul urges the Corinthians to excel in generosity, balancing their abundance with the needs of the less fortunate.

Mark 5:21-43

Jesus demonstrates his great compassion through powerful healing acts.

Prayer

Lord, teach us to be givers. Give us the wisdom to see our material possessions, not as our achievements, but rather as your undeserved, surprising gifts. Help us see the needs of others as our responsibility. We confess that we are guilty of thinking of what we have as "ours" rather than "yours." Our love of money is the root of much of our evil.

One more thing, Lord: forgive us for our resistance to sermons about money! Amen.

Encountering the text

Paul uses his persuasive skill to urge the Corinthians to be generous in their gifts for their less-fortunate brothers and sisters in Christ. Many times we pastors find ourselves in similar rhetorical situations.

Our congregations sometimes complain that we preachers talk too much about money. Truth be told, we probably do not talk as much about money as the Bible itself talks about this subject! We may find it easier to get a hearing on the subject of stewardship if we speak from one of the assigned lections for this Sunday.

Note that Paul, in 2 Corinthians 8:7-15, begins by praising the Christians at Corinth. He says that he is not commanding them to do anything. Rather, he cites Christ who "became poor for our sakes," saying that he is only offering them "advice." He then reminds them that, a year ago, they were in want. Now that they have abundance and others are in want, he wants them to strike a fair balance between their present abundance and others' need.

In other words, Paul pulls out all the stops, drawing upon a number of sources of motivation, in order to preach to the Corinthians on the issue of money: specifically, the issue of the stewardship of our abundance in the service of others' needs. Let us do the same.

Proclaiming the text

In today's epistle, Paul is preaching about a subject we would just as soon avoid: money. Paul tells the Corinthians to send some money to their fellow Christians who are in need. He says that he is not commanding them to do this, only suggesting that they send a gift to their less-fortunate sisters and brothers in Christ.

What gives Paul the right to tell the Christians at Corinth to give money to his pet cause?

In preaching to them about money, Paul provokes a head-on collision with some of this society's most widely held and deeply cherished values. He is speaking of life, and all that we have, as gift. You and I are not conditioned to think like that. We live in a society, ruled by something called the Constitution, in which our lives are seen as entitlements rather than as gifts. We live in a society of rights. We claim that people are born with certain "inalienable rights." People come to this world as a bundle of rights. Their lives consist of a lifetime of exercising these rights. The function of government is to give me the maximum room to exercise my inalienable rights.

In this sort of society, there is not much room for gift. Furthermore, there is no place for gratitude. If you give me my rights, you really haven't given me anything. My rights are my entitlement. I don't feel gratitude because you have only given me what I already deserve.

Nobody I know thanks the government when he or she receives his or her social security check.

"I earned it," we will say. "This is my just desert."

Thus, for Paul to invoke the gift of Jesus, for him to remind the Corinthians of the giftedness of all that they have, sounds strange. Furthermore, every gift entails a giver and entails certain responsibilities and obligations. When we have no sense of our lives as gifts, we have no sense of obligation. To those who have been given nothing, nothing is required.

I was in a dinnertime conversation with a group of people who were talking about the then-current debate over affirmative action. Most of the people at that table could be fairly described as "self-made men." Each of them had achieved much in life through hard work and earnest effort. I therefore expected them to have a uniformly negative view of affirmative action, the notion that the government ought to take measures that would enable some people to have a hand up, a first chance.

You can imagine my surprise therefore when one of the older men in the group looked around and said, "Every person seated at this table has been the beneficiary of 'affirmative action.' We didn't call it that. What we called it was asking for help from someone who knew your father or calling up someone who owed your mother a favor. When I graduated from the University of North Carolina during the Depression, my daddy called me and told me not to bother coming home because there was no work. He advised me to go to Raleigh. He told me to go to Raleigh and to go to the office of a man whom he had once befriended and ask the man if he would hire me. I did so, and the man was good enough to give me a job out of respect for my father. That's affirmative action the old way. We didn't call it affirmative action; we called it looking for a favor from somebody who owed your father, or we called it the buddy system or networking, but it is still affirmative action."

The person who said that had been a United States senator, the governor of our state, and the president of our university. I thought it rather amazing, and even wonderful, that even in our society of allegedly self-made men and women, he could still see his own life as a gift, a hand up offered to him by others.

The poet Maya Angelou, speaking to our first-year students on the first day they arrive on campus, said to them, "You have been the beneficiaries of the best that this society has to offer. We have given you the best education we know how to give. We have told you all that we know. Now, you owe us something."

And then Ms. Angelou quoted Jesus, "To the one to whom much is given, will much be required."

In our society, programs like affirmative action have been challenged by those who cite "equality." We are not supposed to treat people in this society in any special way. Everyone is supposed to be equal. We are all working on a "level playing field."

But this isn't true. The idea of equality often denies history. We did not all arrive at this place in the same way. Each of us has a different past. For some of us, that past includes discrimination, deprivation, and a host of other particular historical factors that mock the notion of equality.

Paul challenges the notion of equality by noting that the Corinthians have been given more than others. And the ones who are given the most, have the most required.

Now I make these comments against a background of the plea of Jesus.

Early in my ministry, I remember hearing an older pastor brag, "I have been at that church now for six years and never mentioned money."

The implication was that people at that church knew their responsibilities and met them, with no prodding from the pastor. The pastor didn't nag or scold; rather, the money just spontaneously flowed into the mission of the church.

Curiously, few of us pastors mention money as often as the Bible mentions it. Jesus makes repeated and stinging statements about finances.

"Where your money is, your heart is," he said. That is a strong statement. If you want to look into the quality of a person's soul, look at that person's checkbook stubs. Where our money is, our heart is.

I have sometimes preached sermons on the theme, "It's not the money that's the sin; it's the way we use the money. Money is not evil; rather, the evil is not keeping money in its proper place."

And yet I can think of a number of stories Jesus told, and a number of his sayings, that imply that money is not neutral. In the teachings of Jesus, the poor are not the problem. The rich have a very big problem, and the poor are, regardless of why they are poor, the blessing of God.

And so St. Ambrose spoke to the rich in his congregation, telling them that they were guilty of "usurpation" in their riches. And St. Jerome said in a sermon that a rich person is automatically the recipient of ill-gotten gain—ill begotten either by him or his father.

I don't know that I would be able to make such sweeping claims, but at a minimum we could say that, from the perspective of Jesus, money is a big issue.

In my last congregation, if you were to ask me the number one pastoral care problem with families, I would say that it was money. This might have been a surprising thing to say since we were a blue-collar, inner-city congregation. Almost no one in that congregation was "rich" by our standards of judgment. However, most of us were the first in our families to have a surplus of funds. This meant that we were among the first in our family to have to make definite choices about how we would spend our money. We had made little money, but enough to get us beyond providing the basic necessities.

My single-parent, schoolteacher mother did not have to agonize over whether or not to buy me a car when I earned my license to drive. It was not even in the realm of possibility. However, by the time that I had children, I could afford to buy a car for my children, if I decided that was important. I had to make a conscious decision about these matters.

I learned, in my last congregation, that it does not take a huge amount of money to ruin a child.

Most of our churches could do a better job of helping us make better choices about money. Many of us are showing that we do not have the skills or values to make wise decisions about money. We act as if the acquisition of things, as if participation in the treadmill of materialism, is a neutral affair. And yet, the Bible would say that our souls are at stake in these transactions.

In my last congregation, a Sunday school class of young couples decided to spend six weeks studying some curriculum that was current in our denomination, entitled "TV and Christian Values."

I thought it was a rather silly enterprise to spend valuable Christian time looking at TV, analyzing television, and asking about the hidden ideological messages.

This shows how much I knew. The size of that class doubled. These young couples knew: it is not the "idiot box," but rather TV is the "ideology box." TV is busy indoctrinating our children into a whole scheme of values, values that are not Christian. The problem is not just the sexual content of the programs or the amount of violence. The problem is in the commercials. Those commercials are busy forming us into certain human beings who respond to the world in certain ways, ways that are not Christian.

The good news is that there are lots of people within this very congregation who are making certain conscious choices not to get on the materialistic treadmill.

We can make conscious decisions about these matters.

Now in this service of worship, among all the acts of worship we do, there is a certain stance, a disposition, an inclination. A friend of mine defines Christian worship as "bending the life toward God."

In just a moment we are coming to what may be the most radical, counter-cultural act of worship. We are going to pass the offering plate. When that plate is passed, much will be revealed about us and where we live. As Jesus says, where our money is, there is our heart also. Will we treat our lives as our possessions, our achievements, or will we come to view our lives as God's gifts? Will what we have be seen as an obligation to accumulate, to insulate, and to keep up things for ourselves? Or will our possessions be seen as a wonderful opportunity to exuberantly reach out to others?

Maybe it is time, in my family and yours, within each of our lives, to take a stand. Let us offer ourselves and our gifts to God!

Relating the text

"The American public voices concern about the reign of materialism in our society while wandering the corridors of the mall. Somehow we have been able to convince ourselves that materialism is bad for our collective health, but we proceed in our individual lives as if nothing mattered more than a fat wallet, especially one made of expensive leather."

—Robert Wuthnow, *God and Mammon in America* (New York: The Free Press, 1994), 5

In "The Revised Catechism," written in 1871, Mark Twain described the grip of greed. It was a bitter twist on the Westminster Catechism:

What is the chief end of man?—to get rich.
In what way?—dishonestly if we can; honestly if we must.
Who is God, the one and only true?
Money is God, Gold and Greenbacks and Stock—father, son, and
	ghosts of same, three persons in one;
These are the true and only God, mighty and supreme.

—Mark Twain, "The Revised Catechism," *New York Tribune,*
September 27, 1871, quoted in Justin Kaplan, *Mr. Clemens and Mark
Twain: A Biography* (New York: Simon and Schuster, 1966), 124–25

John Wesley confronted the complications that attend Christians' work in the world:

"I do not see how it is possible in the nature of things for any revival of true religion to continue long. For religion must necessarily produce both industry and frugality, and these cannot but produce riches.

"But as riches increase, so will pride, anger, and love of the world in all its branches. . . . So although the form of religion remains, the spirit is swiftly vanishing away. Is there no way to prevent this continued decay of true religion? We ought not prevent people from being diligent and frugal; we must exhort all Christians to gain all they can, that is, in effect, to grow rich. . . . If those who gain all they can and save all they can will also give all they can, then the more they gain the more they will grow in grace and the more treasure they will lay up in heaven."

—*The Works of the Reverend John Wesley, A.M.*, Vol. VII (New York: J. Collord, 1831), 317

Sunday between July 3 and July 9 inclusive

[Proper 9, Ordinary/Lectionary 14]

2 Samuel 5:1-5, 9-10

Psalm 48

2 Corinthians 12:2-10

Mark 6:1-13

Power in Weakness

Selected reading

2 Corinthians 12:2-10

Theme

Christians are not preserved from tragedy and heartache. In fact, discipleship sometimes thrusts us into painful situations. While Jesus Christ does not guarantee us no pain or difficulty, he does offer us a way through pain. The cross of Christ has relevance for our times of pain as God's demonstration of power in weakness. The cross continues, in every age, to be a challenging image of who God is.

Introduction to the readings

2 Samuel 5:1-5, 9-10

David becomes king of Israel and Judah and makes Jerusalem his capital.

2 Corinthians 12:2-10
Paul speaks of his painful "thorn in my body" from which he has prayed to God for deliverance but has not yet been healed.

Mark 6:1-13
Jesus calls disciples to assist him in his work, gives them instructions for their journey, and sends them out two by two.

Prayer

Lord Jesus, for our sakes you went willingly to the cross. Help us walk this way with you. You promised us that there would be a cross for each of us to bear. Strengthen us now that we might go into the world in your name without faltering.

Gracious God, who in the cross embraced us with a peculiarly powerful love, teach us your power that is manifested in cruciform weakness, that we might show the world some of the light of your love. In your name we pray. Amen.

Encountering the text

In much of 2 Corinthians, Paul argues on behalf of his authority to lead this troubled young church. He is an apostle authorized by the risen Christ. And yet, here in chapter 12, he speaks of a disability that he has. It is a weakness that, in spite of his earnest prayer, has not been lifted off his back. He does not specify just what his "thorn in my body" is. Remarkably, Paul, a person of prayer and intimacy with God, says that he has prayed for deliverance on many occasions and yet received no for an answer. It is here that Paul's theology of the cross becomes relevant to Paul's personal circumstances. Jesus Christ was not delivered from the thorn in his body. He embraced the cross, went willingly to an unjust and horribly painful death, and thereby revealed the truth about God. God is not pure power, as many think God to be. God is power in weakness, strength in suffering. God is suffering love as exemplified on the cross.

Proclaiming the text

Imagine standing before a grand gathering of the good and the wise and being asked to make a speech about goodness, beauty, the meaning of life, the point of history, and the nature of Almighty God—and having no material at your disposal but an account of a humiliating, bloody execution at a garbage dump outside a rebellious city in the Middle East. It is your task to argue that this story is the key to everything in life and to all that we know about God. This was precisely the position of Paul in Corinth. Before the populace of this cosmopolitan, sophisticated city of the Empire, Paul had to proclaim that this whipped, bloodied, scorned, and derided Jew from Nazareth was God with us.

As Paul said, he had his work cut out for him because preaching about the cross "is foolishness those who are being destroyed," foolishness and stupidity. A cross is no way for a messianic reign to end. Yet what else can this preacher say because, whether it makes sense to us or not, "God was pleased to save those who believe through the foolishness of preaching" (1 Cor 1:18, 21).

Tailoring his manner of speech to his subject matter, Paul says that he chose a foolish sort of preaching that was congruent with his theological message: "When I came to you, brothers and sisters, I didn't come preaching God's secrets to you like I was an expert in speech or wisdom. I had made up my mind not to think about anything while I was with you except Jesus Christ, and to preach him as crucified. I stood in front of you with weakness, fear, and a lot of shaking. My message and my preaching weren't presented with convincing wise words but with a demonstration of the Spirit and of power. I did this so that your faith might not depend on the wisdom of people but on the power of God" (1 Cor 2:1-5).

Paul says that he talks the way he talks and lives the way he lives because of what he has discovered about God. God has come as a crucified Messiah.

A crucified Messiah? It is an oxymoron, a violation of Israel's high expectations for a messianic liberator, a violation of our notions of how God must act to be a real God. In order to bring such a scandal to speech, Paul eschewed "lofty words or wisdom," the stock-in-trade of the classical orator. Rather than avoiding the scandal of the cross or attempting to sugarcoat its absurdity in order to make it more palatable, Paul limited his subject matter so that he knew "nothing among you except Jesus Christ and him crucified." His manner of presentation was through "weakness, fear, and a lot of shaking," a rather peculiar demeanor for a public speaker. Why? So that nothing might move his hearers, nothing might convince them but "the power of God." Paul talked the way he talked, and walked the way he walked, in light of the cross of Christ.

For God the Father to allow God the Son to be crucified, dead, and buried, is for God to be pushed out beyond the limits of human expectation or human help. The cross is the ultimate dead end of any attempt at human self-fulfillment, human betterment, or progress. While hanging from the cross in humiliation and utter defeat, there is nothing to vindicate the work of Jesus or to make the story come out right except the power of God.

Rather than base his proclamation on human reason, common sense, or artful arguments, Paul spoke to the Corinthians haltingly, hesitantly, in fear and trembling, so that if they were to hear and to understand, to assent and to respond, it would have to be solely through the power of God.

Paul says to the Corinthians that the cross is *moria*, moronic foolishness: "The message of the cross is foolishness to those who are being destroyed. But it is the power of God for those of us who are being saved" (1 Cor 1:18).

And then Paul mentions the "thorn in my body," that unspecified physical disability under which he labored, a disability that Paul prayed to be delivered from. And yet he wasn't. He was forced to bear his burden without relief, even as Jesus bore his cross without relief.

The story of Paul's unrelieved "thorn in my body" challenges many contemporary presentations of the Christian faith. Too often we present the Christian faith as a great unburdening, as empowerment by Jesus that enables us to rise above the pain of life in this world, as a prosperity technique whereby fairly successful people are empowered to be even more successful.

But today's testimony from Paul bears a cruciform truth that the church has to keep telling itself again and again: Jesus Christ sometimes delivers us from our sufferings and sometimes Jesus Christ thrusts us into suffering. Jesus Christ sometimes preserves us from pain but (more often, I think) gives us a way through pain. Salvation in Jesus Christ sometimes means deliverance from our difficulties, and sometimes it brings difficulties that we wouldn't have if we had not been met by Jesus!

Paul, man of unceasing prayer, says he prayed three times to be delivered of his "thorn in the flesh" and was not delivered (2 Cor 12:8). And through it all he has learned a great truth that even in pain and disappointment God says to us, "My grace is enough for you, because power is made perfect in weakness" (12:9).

A crucified God is known not only for what God does but also for what God does not do. A crucified God is one who doesn't always deliver us from our times of pain but stands with us in the pain. No matter how severe your thorn, a crucified God has been there before and meets you there even now so that we are able to say not that we have been delivered, unburdened, but rather that we have discovered the truth of the divine promise: "My grace is enough for you, because power is made perfect in weakness."

Relating the text

Note that Paul, in writing to the Corinthians about the folly of his preaching, rejects all classical means of persuasion. Perhaps he does this because there is no way for a speaker to get us from our expectations for God to God on a cross by conventional means of persuasion. When asked, "What is your evidence for your claim?" Paul simply responds, "Cross." What else can he say? The cross so violates our frames of reference, our means of sorting out the claims of truth, that there is no way to get there except by "demonstration of the Spirit" and by "the power of God." The only way for preaching about the cross to "work" is as a miracle, a gift of God.

To underscore the miraculous quality of cruciform Christian proclamation Paul said that he spoke in weakness and in much fear and trembling, hardly what we would expect to hear from an adept speaker. Yet Paul says he preached thus to show that nothing—neither the eloquence of the speaker nor the reasoning powers of the hearers—could produce faith in a crucified savior except the "power of God."

Martin Luther was fond of contrasting a "theology of glory," in which the cross was seen as optional equipment for Christians, a mere ladder by which we might climb up to God, with a "theology of the cross" that, according to Luther, calls things by their proper names and is unimpressed with most that impresses the world. A theology of glory preaches the cross as just another technique for getting what we want, whereas a theology of the cross proclaims the cross as the supreme sign of how God gets what God wants. The cross is a statement that our salvation is in God's hands, not ours, that our relationship to God is based upon something that God suffers and does rather than upon something that we do. To bear the cross of Christ is to bear its continuous rebuke of the false gods to which we are tempted to give our lives.

When self-salvation is preached—reducing the gospel to a means for saving ourselves by our good works or our good feelings or our good thinking—then worldly wisdom and common sense are substituted for cruciform gospel foolishness, and blasphemy is the result. It seems to me that the contemporary affluent church too often presents the Christian faith as a technique for getting what we want when the cross says that Jesus Christ is God getting what God wants!

All of our attempts to climb up to God are our pitiful efforts at self-salvation. God descends to our level by climbing on a cross, opening up his arms, and dying for us, because of us, with us.

Christian theology has always affirmed that the cross is not only a window through which we see the true nature of God as the embodiment of suffering love, but also the truthful mirror in which we see ourselves. Cruciform faith can't help but speak of our sin. Jesus was nailed to the wood on the basis of a whole host of otherwise noble human ideals and aspirations like law and order, biblical fidelity, and national security. The cross offers a good dose of honesty about the human condition. After Calvary we could no longer argue that we are, down deep, basically good people who are making progress by getting ourselves organized and enlightened.

Christians not only live like Jesus but also sometimes suffer and die like Jesus. Jesus was up-front in saying that the cross is not optional equipment for discipleship: "All who want to come after me must say no to themselves, take up their cross, and follow me. All who want to save their lives will lose them. But all who lose their lives because of me and because of the good news will save them" (Mark 8:34-35). When this episode is reported by Luke (9:18-26), Jesus goes on to relate cross-bearing to not being ashamed of "me and my words" (v. 26). The cross is not some chronic illness, not some annoying person. The cross is that which is laid upon us because we are following a crucified savior. For Paul, not only is the cross something that God does to and for the world, unmasking the world's gods, exposing our sin, forgiving our sin through suffering love; but also the cross is the pattern for Christian life. He could say, "I died to the Law through the Law, so that I could live or God. I have been crucified with Christ and I no longer live, but Christ lives in me. And the lie that I now live in my body, I live by faith, indeed, by the faithfulness of God's Son, who loved me and gave himself for me" (Gal 2:19-20). And yet, the good news is that Jesus's yoke is easy and his burden is light, which is to say as burdensome and difficult as Jesus and his words can be, they are less burdensome and more fun than most of the other burdens the world tries to lay on our backs.

As Christians we get to expend our lives in work more significant than that described by the lies by which most of the world lives. Working with a crucified God is a great adventure, a risky, perilous, wonderful undertaking, and so much more interesting than mere servility to the wisdom of the world. Every time someone is confronted by the cross of Christ and hears, believes, responds, every time someone is liberated from enslavement to the world's false promises, then we can take great satisfaction that the promises of God are indeed true, that God graciously continues, through our teaching and our sermons, to choose and to use "what the world considers foolish (*moria*) to shame the wise" (1 Cor 1:27).

Sunday between July 10 and July 16 inclusive
[Proper 10, Ordinary/Lectionary 15]

2 Samuel 6:1-5, 12b-19 or Amos 7:7-15

Psalm 24 or Psalm 85:8-13

Ephesians 1:3-14

Mark 6:14-29

The Perils of Power

Selected reading
Mark 6:14-29

Theme
Power can be a dangerous thing. And yet, power can also be a means of doing good. There is worldly power—the power of armies and nations, the power of force and coercion. And then there is the power that is unleashed in the world through the presence of Jesus Christ. In the world's eyes, Jesus was not a powerful person. But in the eyes of faith, we are led to see that there is impotency in the world's brand of power and that there is great strength in the peculiar power of Christ.

Introduction to the readings
2 Samuel 6:1-5, 12b-19

David brings the chest containing the covenant to Jerusalem, making that city the center of worship for Israel. Steeped in liturgical language, these words focus on the power and presence of the holy.

Ephesians 1:3-14

From prison, Paul gives the scattered churches in Asia Minor a vision that will unite all things into Christ. Nothing is left out, for the cosmic vision of Ephesians encompasses heaven and earth.

Mark 6:14-29

Herod, hearing of the deeds of power done by Jesus and his disciples, wonders if John, whom he beheaded, has been raised from the dead. The disturbing story of John's martyrdom is recounted as a reminder to all of the dangers that lie ahead for those who are faithful.

Prayer

Dear Jesus, give us the strength not only to love you but also to follow you, to walk behind you wherever you lead us. And if it be your will that we should walk with you into the valley of death, through a time of suffering, to find ourselves rebuked and scorned by the world, then stand by us and fill us with your peaceful power, that we may be the brave disciples that you deserve. Amen.

Encountering the text

What effect did it have upon Jesus when he heard that his fellow kinsman John had been savagely murdered at the order of Herod? Was it for Jesus a foreshadowing of his own fate on the cross?

Today's Gospel is a time to remind the congregation of the cost of discipleship. Those who follow Jesus are sometimes treated like Jesus. The powerful of the world like Herod do not sit idly by when their power is challenged. And in countless ways, Jesus is a challenge to the world's power.

We tell the story of the death of John the Baptist in July on a Sunday after Easter. Perhaps there is a point to this. Easter doesn't stop the suffering and the violence, and yet any suffering that is encountered by disciples is set in the context of Easter. Easter continues. That means that not even the absolute power of the King Herods of the world will be able to defeat the love of God in Jesus Christ. In a weird way, our story today from the Gospel of Mark and our proclamation of it in July is an Easter story, a story that not only speaks of the cost of discipleship but also hints at the ultimate triumph of God in Jesus Christ.

Proclaiming the text

Lord Acton famously said, "Power corrupts, and absolute power absolutely corrupts." I know that he said this because one time in a sermon I quoted Lord Acton as saying, "Power corrupts." A parishioner corrected me in a letter the next week, saying that Lord Acton said no such thing. Lord Acton's stress was on the word absolute.

One would have expected Lord Acton to stress the bad effects of absolute power in government. He wrote brilliantly throughout his life in defense of democracy and against governmental tyranny over the individual.

And yet, the longer I live, the more I wonder if perhaps I was right. Power, whether it is absolute or not, can be corrupting. What is there about power that corrupts?

From a Christian point of view, we might say that power gives us a taste of what it might be like to be like God. After all, don't we like to define God in terms of omnipotence—absolute power? To be God is to be able to do anything that you want. How typical of us to define divinity on the basis of power or the ability to do anything we want.

Power is something that separates us from God. God is all-powerful, and we have numerous ways of being reminded daily that we are not all-powerful.

Perhaps we are separated from God in another way in this matter of power, in that, in the wisdom of God we human beings are not given absolute power. There are definite limits on what we can do. For instance, the Bible says that we cannot, just by our own power, add an inch to our stature. Paul famously complained, "I don't do the good that I want to do" (Rom 7:19). Paul said that he could certainly will to do what is right, but then sin made him powerless to do what is right.

When the Bible says, "Revenge belongs to me; I will pay it back, says the Lord" (Rom 12:19), I wonder if in this matter of power that's what's under consideration here. God gives us power over some things, but not over all things, including vengeance. "Revenge belongs to me." The Lord is unwilling to entrust us with vengeance. When I try to give someone just retribution for some injustice they have committed, I cannot be trusted with vengeance. I might be tempted to say, "I am doing this for your own good," or "I am doing this to you because you deserve it," when in reality what I mean is, "I am doing this punishment to you because it makes me feel good." And how do we know? We do not always know our innermost thoughts, and we have notorious difficulty being honest about our innermost thoughts, and so God says, "Revenge? Let me handle that. You do not have the power to work revenge, no matter how justified, on anybody."

And from what I can observe, in life, the trouble is that some of us are in situations in which we have been given a good bit of power over most matters in life, so maybe we are deluded into thinking that we have power over just about everything. For instance, I have been given the power to earn enough money to be sure that my family is well housed and well fed. My mother was a schoolteacher, and hers was the only salary that came into our house. And I remember my mother sitting at the dining room table in the evening, going over her meager bank balance one more time, saying, "The man at the garage says I've got to have two new tires. Where on earth am I going to get enough money to buy two new tires?"

In that moment my mother must have felt very powerless. She was a strong person by nature, but she did not have the economic power to buy two new tires for the car.

With my life it's been different. Since college, I've never had to agonize over buying tires for the car. In fact, when it comes down to it, I don't agonize over much of anything. I have the economic power to get my heart's desire. And I am saying there is a spiritual danger lurking there. The danger is that since I have the power to accomplish so much in my life, I get deluded into thinking that I have the power to do anything I want. With a little more effort I can be almost like God. Such is the sin that is always lurking in power—absolute power or any kind of power.

Aggravating this is the fact that we are modern people. And the birth of the modern world was accomplished, in great part, as an act of power. Through science, technology, mass production, and progressive enlightenment we could have incredible power over the world and over our lives. Potency is the great promise of the modern world. The promise of the serpent to Adam and Eve back in the garden is thus fulfilled among us in the modern world: they would be like God.

I have all this on my mind because today's Gospel (Mark 6:14-29) tells of a tragic event that happened early in Jesus's ministry. All of the Gospels begin with John the Baptist—the forerunner of Jesus, the prophetic figure who preaches in the wilderness, preparing the way for the advent of the Messiah. John baptized Jesus, and thus Jesus's ministry was inaugurated. John and Jesus must have been very close.

And yet, early on, Jesus hears the news of the brutal capital punishment of John the Baptist.

John's was a powerful voice. From the wilderness he preached strong, fierce sermons proclaiming the coming judgment of God. And now that voice is silenced by a more politically powerful voice. The voice of Herod is more powerful than the voice of John the Baptist. In fact, it wasn't even the voice of Herod that led to John's execution; it was the whim of a dancing girl and her mother.

By the way, we ought not to confuse this Herod with other notorious Herods in scripture. This was Herod Antipas. He was a relative of Herod the Great who massacred the little children of Bethlehem, and a relative of Herod Agrippa I who executed John's brother James. But when it comes down to it, who cares that this was Herod Antipas? When you've met one Herod, you've met them all; they are all powerful governmental figures, and they are all killers. One of the perils of being in politics in any age is that you must wield power, and the power you must wield inevitably is the power of violence. Just about no countries are nonviolent, particularly when their sovereignty (the word *sovereignty* was once applied only to God, and now it is applied to nations) is threatened.

Herod Antipas had an affair with his brother's wife, and John the Baptist called him to account. It took a lot of guts for a little preacher to stand up and call this adulterous politician to account. How much fortitude it took we are learning here: it cost John the Baptist his head.

John the Baptist, a man driven by the power of the word of God, is silenced by Herod Antipas, a man who wields the power of the sovereign Roman state.

So once again, governmental violence has triumphed. The king has silenced the preacher. Once again, a good person has been annihilated by the evil power of the state. You don't have to come to church and listen to the Bible to hear a story like that. When it comes to power, the person with the largest guns or the biggest bomb or the sharpest stick wins.

That is a rather conventional observation and you don't need the Bible to tell it to you. You can read about the perils of governmental power in the news. You certainly don't need me to prove that to you in a sermon. And yet, if we read a bit deeper, we may discover a more interesting message. The message may not be simply that the powerless suffer because of the powerful; but the message also might be that there are different forms of power.

Gandhi taught India that the power of truth was stronger than the power of falsehood. The British Empire was telling a lie when it said that India was better off under British rule than if it were free and independent and democratic. Gandhi sought to tell the truth like John the Baptist. But Gandhi was able to do more. He also enacted the truth because he believed that nonviolent power was stronger than the power of violence. Thus Gandhi called his autobiography *Gandhi an Autobiography: The Story of My Experiments with Truth*. The liberation of India from the British Empire was a painful, violent process in which truth and nonviolence prevailed.

Not only did Gandhi talk about the injustice of British rule, but also, through the nonviolence of thousands of his followers, he exposed the evil behind the often-benevolent face of the empire through his experiment with the truth. The British had claimed they were in India for benevolent reasons, but as the world watched British soldiers massacre unarmed Indian civilians, the world came to a different verdict, and so did the British people.

Herod Antipas is powerful enough to simply speak and a prophet's head is served up on a platter. That's power! But in suffering and dying, John the Baptist reveals the weakness that lurks in Herod's brand of power. Here is a king who not only has besmirched his sovereignty by having an affair with his brother's wife, but also has stooped to killing the prophet John the Baptist, on the word of a young girl who has pleased him in her dance for him. This is power?

There is a great irony behind this violent story of the abuses of power. Herod executed John the Baptist in order to shut him up. But here we are today, still talking about John the Baptist, still remembering his prophetic words, still admiring his courage. We wouldn't be talking about Herod Antipas (who among you have ever heard of him until I mentioned him in this sermon!) except he plays a bit part in the drama of our salvation in Jesus Christ. He couldn't shut up the gospel just by executing some of its preachers. The word goes on. This story is being told. New contemporary disciples are being instructed and encouraged by this story. It's enough to make you ask, "Who has real power? Where does true power come from, power that doesn't end when a ruler goes out of office, but power that continues to subvert the old world and bring forth a new world?"

A concluding note: the story of John the Baptist closes, not with what Herod has done or what the executioner has enacted, but with an account of John's disciples, the students who had followed him throughout his life. In Jewish tradition, the sons of the father were expected to give an honorable burial to their father. John must have left no family because his disciples stepped up and provided a burial tomb for him. Can you imagine what courage that act of devotion required? It took courage to ask for the body of someone who had been publicly executed by the government. The government officials did not look kindly on people who came to collect the body of an enemy of the state.

I remind you that when Jesus was crucified, his disciples did not gather and demand his body to be given an honorable burial after a dishonorable execution. There was nobody to give Jesus a decent burial but a member of the Sanhedrin.

So if you thought courage died with John the Baptist, think again. John's disciples show John's courage in their stepping up to give John the Baptist a respectful entombment. See what Mark is doing? The seemingly small detail is revelatory. The courage continues. Herod thought that he had once and for all put an end to the nuisance of this troublesome, outspoken prophet. But Herod is powerless to shut John up. The preaching continues. The gospel continues. The courage continues.

Right here in this congregation, the courage continues. Looking out on you this morning, I don't see many people that the world would regard as important, powerful people, and yet, it is a promise of the gospel that Jesus is busy subverting the old world and creating a new world through you. Every time you speak up for love in the face of hate, every time you tell the truth about injustice and reach out and attempt to subvert the injustice, you are showing power, true power, the power of God in Jesus Christ. The grand promise that gathers us, in these weeks after Easter, is that nothing, and no power on earth, will be able to defeat you!

Relating the text

The great Russian novelist and Christian, Tolstoy, lamented that in Constantine it was as if the power of Caesar triumphed over the power of Christ. No one told the emperor that imperial power is quite different than gospel power:

"No one said to [Constantine]: 'The kings exercise authority among the nations, but among you it shall not be so. Do not murder, do not commit adultery, do not lay up riches, judge not, condemn not, resist not him that is evil.'

"But they said to him: 'You wish to be called a Christian and to continue to be the chieftain of the robbers—to kill, burn, fight, lust, execute, and live in luxury? That can all be arranged.'

"And they arranged a Christianity for him, and arranged it very smoothly, better even than could have been expected. They foresaw that, reading the Gospels, it might occur to him that all this [true discipleship] is demanded. . . . This they foresaw, and they carefully devised such a Christianity for him as would let him continue to live his old heathen life unembarrassed. On the one hand Christ, God's Son, only came to bring salvation to him and to everybody. Christ having died, Constantine can live as he likes. More even than that—one may repent and swallow a little bit of bread and some wine, and that will bring salvation, and all will be forgiven.

"But more even than that: they sanctify his robber-chieftainship, and say that it proceeds from God, and they anoint him with holy oil. And he, on his side, arranges for them the congress of priests that they wish for, and order them to say what each man's relation to God should be, and orders everyone to repeat what they say.

"And as soon as one of the anointed robber-chiefs wishes his own and another folk to begin slaying each other, the priest[s] immediately prepare some holy water, sprinkle a cross (which Christ bore and on which he died because he repudiated such robbers), take the cross and bless the robber-chief in his work of slaughtering, hanging, and destroying.

—Leo Tolstoy, "Church and State," trans. Aylmer Maude,
The Arena, vol. 22 (1899), 458

Sunday between July 17 and July 23 inclusive
[Proper 11, Ordinary/Lectionary 16]

2 Samuel 7:1-14a or Jeremiah 23:1-6
Psalm 89:20-37 or Psalm 23
Ephesians 2:11-22
Mark 6:30-34, 53-56

The New Household

Selected reading
Ephesians 2:11-22

Theme
The church is a new family, formed, called, and built by God out of formerly feuding and fractured humanity. From those who were divided, Jews and Gentiles, a new household has been formed, a new people called the church. To be in the church is to be a member of an alternative community, a new people with values, views, and virtues different from the world in order that the world, through Christ, might be saved from itself.

Introduction to the readings
2 Samuel 7:1-14a
David proposes to build a great house for God. But God tells the king that God will establish the House of David forever.

Ephesians 2:11-22
The writer to the Ephesians speaks of Christ having established a new family, a new house in which Christ is "the cornerstone."

Mark 6:30-34, 53-56
The sick and the hurting come to Jesus for healing and help.

Prayer

Lord, once we were no people, diverse, separated, walled off from one another. Now, by the great mercy of Jesus Christ, we have been brought together in the church. Old boundaries, old walls have been overcome, bridged. We who were once strangers have become family.

Help us, O Lord, in our life together, to demonstrate to a fractured and hurting world that Jesus really makes possible the existence of a people who are able to live by their convictions, who are able to live as sisters and brothers in all that we do and say. To the glory of your name, Amen.

Encountering the text

We do not know much about the originating circumstances of the letter to the Ephesians. Reading between the lines, we know that we are reading an epistle addressed to a church, or churches, struggling with the stunning fact that even Gentiles have been included in the promises of God to Israel.

From two once alienated, hostile groups, Jews and Gentiles, God has made "one new person out of the two groups, making peace." Those who were once distant from the promises of God—namely, the Gentiles—have been brought close to God by the amazing grace of God in Jesus Christ.

We pastors, who struggle constantly with problems of unity within the congregation, with barriers between people, with the never-ending project to unify people within the church, ought to hear in this Sunday's epistle a word with which we can identify.

The text raises issues such as the following: How did we all get here? On the basis of our intelligence, our spiritual perception, or on the basis of God's call? What hope is there for the historical boundaries between people ever being bridged? What is the basis and ultimate hope for the church? Is our hope in Christ or in ourselves?

We will read the epistle as a strong affirmation of the work of God in forming and preserving the church. In a day when our images of God tend toward the deistic, detached, interested but not too active God, we will hear this text as assertion that God creates, establishes, calls, evokes, and preserves the new humanity called the church. Thus, we will intend for our sermon to be a strong, affirmative word of hope to the contemporary congregation. We are here today, in the church, because God has intended us to be here, because God sustains that which God calls, because we are God's way of reclaiming a lost world.

Today we are troubled by the divisions that cut across our society. Is there any hope that the walls between us can be bridged? Our faith asserts that the hope is Christ, the one who brings together those who are "far off" and makes us sisters and brothers. Christ's major means of healing our divisions, of making those who were strangers into beloved siblings, is the church.

He is our cornerstone, the basis of any unity we hope to achieve. On him, the promises of God have their origin and their basis.

No doubt some interpreters of today's epistle might stress, in this text, that this is probably addressed to a bitterly divided church; no preacher keeps telling her congregation to act like Christians and get along with each other if they are already doing that. Yet I have chosen to stress that here we have clearly a new reality being formed, a household, a place with boundaries between itself in the world, a people who do not come naturally, for I think that's where we are today.

Proclaiming the text

They can't find the cornerstone for the United States Capitol. There was a great dedication ceremony and laying of the cornerstone in the early nineteenth century when construction of the Capitol began. But over the years, it sank, covered by gathering debris of the ages. Now, it can't be located. There is a commission charged with digging here and there in order to find it. The cornerstone represents the history and dedication of the building, a sign and symbol of its purpose. We must not lose sight of our cornerstone, because it helps us to know why we are here. Take that as a parable on our text for this morning:

> So now you are no longer strangers and aliens. Rather, you are fellow citizens with God's people, and you belong to God's household. As God's household, you are built on the foundation of the apostles and prophets with Christ Jesus himself as the cornerstone. The whole building is joined together in him, and it grows up into a temple that is dedicated to the Lord. Christ is building you into a place where God lives through the Spirit. (Eph 2:19-22)

You can imagine what these words meant to those who first heard them, these Gentiles who had no part in the promises of God to Israel.

In our church youth group, when I was growing up, I remember the question was often, "Will the Jews be saved?" That question is not really a biblical, New Testament question. Romans 7–8 is clear: the promises of God are irrevocable. God has made a promise to preserve and to love Israel, and God keeps God's promises.

No, the big New Testament question is, "Will the Gentiles be saved?" What about those who do not have the scriptures, who know nothing of the words of the prophets, the promises of God to Israel? What about them? What about us?

Yes, says Ephesians, by an amazing act of God in Christ, the promises of God to Israel are brought even to the Gentiles. Thus, the writer to the Ephesians says in 1:5 that we outsiders, we Gentiles, have been destined by God "to be his adopted children" through grace, "which he poured over us" (1:8). What a great phrase; we have been brought close to God through Christ.

We can only be in God's family through adoption. No one comes in here naturally; Christians are made, not born (said early church leader Tertullian).

We, who weren't in the family, have "received an inheritance" (1:11). We weren't in the will, Gentiles as we are. Now, we're heirs to a fortune. By the seal of the Holy Spirit (1:13) we are marked as "God's own people" (1:14).

"At that time you were without Christ. You were aliens rather than citizens of Israel, and strangers to the covenants of God's promise. In this world you had no hope and no God" (2:12). You were (in a great phrase) "far away" (2:13). Now we're close; the wall is down (2:14).

Which brings us to the scripture that is our word for this Sunday.

The writer uses an architectural metaphor. Note that the verbs are passive. He doesn't say, "You decided to join the church." The writer says, you are "built," you are "joined together," "Christ is building you into a place where God lives through the Spirit" (2:22); your relationship to this new family is not something you do. It's something done to you: grace.

Note that the passage begins with political talk—talk of aliens, citizens. These people have exchanged their citizenship in one country for that of a new country. If you thought that being a Christian is something that comes naturally, the natural, normal American thing to do, think again. Nobody comes in here by natural generation—that is, by birth. You have to be adopted, transferred into, built into this household.

I think that right there this text seems most strange to us.

My parents never worried about whether or not I would grow up Christian. It was the natural, normal American thing to be Christian. I woke up a few years ago and realized that, whether or not my parents were justified in believing that, no one believes that today. The world in which Christianity was normal, natural, and American has ended. I find among us a new aware-ness that if our children are to grow up in this faith, we will have to make them grow up that way.

Being Christian is no longer the normal, natural, American thing to do. Our children watch an average of fifteen hours of television every week. They are in church a maximum of a couple of hours per week. When watching televi-sion, they are being bombarded with images of success, of the good life, of the goal of humanity that may be at great variance with how the Christian faith defines these matters. Suddenly the church and its teaching, witness, worship, and work become important ways of instilling in us and our young a way counter to the world's ways.

Years ago a Catholic theologian spoke of "anonymous Christians," or, people who were good and sincere, but who did not formally embrace the Chris-tian faith. They were sort of Christians at large, anonymous Christians, even though they did not know that was who they were.

No, they may have been good people, but they were not Christians. To be a Christian is to be someone who self-consciously follows, or is attempting to follow, the way of Christ, someone who is attempting to let the story of Christ form and guide his or her life.

A church without boundaries, with no borders, without distinctive marks, is hardly a church. Thus, today's scripture from Ephesians speaks of the church as a building, a house, a place. Perhaps there was a time when it was enough, in our culture, to be merely sincere, to have a warm feeling in your heart at the mention of the word *religion*, to try to do the best that you could in life, in a wholesome sort of way.

Now, things have changed. We are beginning to feel, as North American Christians, like aliens, like missionaries in the very society that we thought we had created.

In such a time, a text like today's from Ephesians begins to make sense again. The church is an identifiable new family. It is bigger than that which we normally call "family," for it is made up of all those diverse people whom Jesus has called to follow him. Think of being a Christian as if you are taken out of your human family and made a member of the family of God, the "household of faith," as the writers calls us. It's a house with Christ as its cornerstone, that stone upon which the whole house is built, that foundation upon which everything else rests.

I hope that you take comfort in this. Too often around here we are guilty of presenting the Christian faith as something that we do or decide. Listen to us when we talk of, "When I gave my life to Christ" and, "When I asked Jesus to come into my heart." It's all about me, my, myself.

But note that today's passage from Ephesians speaks of us in the passive tense and of God in the active voice. It is God who has called us here. God made a decision for us. God builds us as parts of this new household. God has broken down the dividing walls between women and men, between the races and the ages and social classes. If you are here in church today, following Jesus, it is because you have been put there by God in Christ.

I say this is a comfort because it reminds me that, when all is said and done, my relationship to Christ is (thank goodness!) not just a matter of what I feel or do or say, but what God in Christ, through the church, has done. I don't always feel, act, or speak like a Christian, but that's not the point. The point is that I have been called forth to be part of this strange, wonderful new divine experiment in human family called "church."

Haven't you found this true yourself? How many Sundays have you come here empty, not really believing anything for sure? Then, through the music, the reading of scripture, the singing of hymns, or maybe even the sermon, you have felt faith growing strong in you?

I was once asked, "Do you think it is okay to say the words of the creed, even when you have trouble with some of the things that it says?"

It is not your creed; it is the faith of the church. Sometimes, when we say the creed, you are anything but sure of your faith. But the great thing is that it isn't your creed. On those Sundays, the church is saying it with you, for you, until that time when you are able to say it for yourself.

Sometimes we pray a prayer of confession here. You may not feel like confessing your sin. Fine. We'll do it for you. We'll confess and perhaps you will sense our confession as your confession, and you will join us in Christian honesty about sin. This is what was meant by the church in saying, long ago, that the church was a "means of grace." By that we meant that the church was a human means through which God gets to us and does for us that which we could not do on our own.

In such moments, you give thanks to God that you were fortunate enough to have been invited, called, built, joined into this household. You have not been left on your own, so far as your faith is concerned. You're part of the family, the family of God called church.

People, we are up against something! And you are right to expect the church to give you the skills and the insights you need to resist the world and its lures.

So today's epistle declares, "now you are no longer strangers and aliens" from God. But some of you are learning today that by being close to God, you are aliens from this society, at odds with some of this culture's dominant values. You have been joined to a new family, a new household.

With Christ as our cornerstone, we are a new people, a visible "building" for all the world to see that Jesus makes possible a viable, visible alternative to the way the world gathers people, a new people by water and the word. Amen.

Relating the text

When my daughter was sixteen years old, she entered a high school classroom. Odd, there were nozzles sticking up out of the desks. Someone was playing with the nozzle while the teacher called the roll. The teacher shouted, "Don't touch that! You want to blow us all up?"

Harriet had never heard of a classroom where one could be hurt.

Then the teacher began to teach "safety rules." The whole week was spent on learning safety rules. If she thought she knew how to pour liquid from one beaker to the next, she was wrong. There was only one right way to do it.

During the first week, someone behind Harriet asked the teacher, "What is that chart up on the wall? What do those strange numbers and words mean?"

"You're not ready for that," said the teacher. "Those are the sacred signs and symbols of our faith. You must wait for that."

At the end of the week there was an exam on the safety rules. Each student who passed the exam received a white robe—the liturgical garment of the faith—and goggles. "Now," said the teacher with a sense of expectancy, "now you are ready to enter the world of chemistry."

Later in the semester, the day came when the teacher pointed to the chart and said, "Now you are at last ready to learn the secrets. I am going to teach you how to do things with these symbols that you have never done before. I am going to take you places you would never have gone had you not had the good sense to take chemistry."

And the chemistry textbook was not just full of facts, figures, and formulae; it had short biographies and pictures of heroes who braved ignorance and injustice and taught us how to pasteurize milk. Saints!

Around the first of December, Harriet came in with a bag of groceries. I watched as she reached in the bag and retrieved a package. "Heat-activated deodorant," I heard Harriet read aloud. She instinctively flipped the box over, saying to herself, "I wonder what this has in it? Something that reacts at about 98 degrees, I guess." And she read the list of chemicals in the deodorant.

As someone who is supposed to be in the conversion business, in inculcating the practices of an alien faith, I stood in awe of that moment. Here was a miraculous transformation in the life of my daughter, which had been worked in less than four months. Now, when Harriet looks out the window in the morning, she no longer sees the same world she saw four months ago. She has been adopted into a household called chemistry.

Sunday between July 24 and July 30 inclusive
[Proper 12, Ordinary/Lectionary 17]

2 Samuel 11:1-15 or 2 Kings 4:42-44
Psalm 14 or Psalm 145:10-18
Ephesians 3:14-21
John 6:1-21

What Are You Looking For?

Selected reading
John 6:1-21

Theme

We live in a society that encourages us to put ourselves at the center of our world. Yet, church is where we gather to put Jesus at the center. The risen Christ comes among us, not simply to meet our needs, but to rearrange them in order to reveal himself to us. In church, sometimes we get more than what we were looking for. We get the Christ, the one who is looking for us that he might call us, change us, transform us.

Introduction to the readings

2 Samuel 11:1-15

King David schemes to have Uriah killed so that he can take Uriah's wife as his own.

Ephesians 3:14-21

The writer to the Ephesians prays that these new Christians might "have the power to grasp . . . [the] width and length, height and depth" of the love of Christ.

John 6:1-21

A large crowd follows Jesus, attracted by his powerful signs.

Prayer

Lord, we come here this Sunday with so many needs. Some among us are sick and in pain or we love someone who is sick and in pain. We have tough decisions to make and come seeking help with those decisions. Our families are not what they ought to be, and we need help. We have so many needs.

Yet amid all of our questions, our pains, and our tribulations, we have one great need: to be near you, to know your will for our lives, to love you as we ought.

Come near to us, Lord. Speak to us, even when what you have to say to us is different from what we expected. Be with us. That is our greatest desire. Amen.

Encountering the text

John's account of the miraculous feeding is curious, when compared to the Synoptic Gospels, for a number of reasons. John links the feeding to the story of Jesus's walking on water and to Peter's confession of faith. Probably, John means thereby to make a strong point regarding the identity of Jesus as the exalted Christ.

Moreover, we should take note that this feeding is set by John in the context of Passover. In John's Gospel, Jesus cleanses the temple at Passover and uses the occasion to speak of his impending death (John 2). Later, in John 13,

Jesus will speak again of his death in the context of a Passover meal with his disciples.

Unlike Luke's account of the miraculous feeding, as well as Mark's, this meal is not presented by John as a sign of Jesus's compassion for the hungry multitudes. Rather, this feeding is used by Jesus as an opportunity to perform a sign that will be considerably greater than the crowds expected. This is a typical Johannine moment. In John's Gospel, they come to Jesus asking for water, and he offers "living water." They come hankering for bread, and he gives them "bread from heaven." So again, in today's passage from John, we are alerted that bread means considerably more than what we mean when we say bread.

We come to Jesus with our bodily, carnal, immediate needs only to be surprised that Jesus seems to be about more than the meeting of our needs. Nothing so satisfies us as a good meal. After their miraculous meal, the crowd immediately thinks of monarchy. Moses gave bread, manna, in the wilderness of the exodus. They hail Jesus as the new king.

John offers us an exalted Christology. Jesus will not be controlled or utilized by the crowd for our purposes. He will not be jerked around in fulfillment of our wants.

Proclaiming the text

"Jesus understood that they were about to come and force him to be their king, so he took refuge again, alone on a mountain" (John 6:15).

Believe it or not, we spend a fair amount of effort selecting the hymns that we sing on Sunday morning. We try to key the hymns to the assigned scripture lessons for the day, the season of the church year. But we also, believe it or not, take into account what you like in your hymns. We ask ourselves, "Do they want to sing this hymn?" It makes a big difference what sort of music you like. I must say, that is probably the main reason why one hymn is selected for singing on Sunday: Does the congregation like this hymn?

While that's a fair question, isn't it interesting that we rarely ask an even more basic question: Does God like this hymn?

Of course, that's a frightening question, frightening not only because there are bound to be many answers, many of them conflicting, but also because it is such a basic question. Frightening because the scriptures note that Jesus drove away about as many people as he attracted. Jesus obviously based his ministry on more substantial questions than, "Do the people like what I have to say?"

This brings me to today's scripture from John. It's a story about Jesus, but first it is a story about a crowd. "A large crowd followed him," says John. Can there be a surer sign of success than this? Who can argue with numbers? Look at the bottom line—a large crowd. Jesus has become popular.

Then John tells us why they were following Jesus, "because they had seen the miraculous signs he had done among the sick" (v. 2). Jesus has healed the hurting multitudes. He has brought to people that to which we give the largest portion of our national product—health care. If there is one indisputable, uncontested good that we have, it is health. Great crowds are following Jesus because they see his signs. He heals them. He meets their needs.

Curiously, Jesus does not continue to meet their needs. Next verse: "Jesus went up a mountain and sat there with his disciples." Even a dedicated do-gooder like Jesus needs a break, a temporary respite from meeting people's needs.

Jesus looks up from his mountain retreat and "saw a large crowd coming toward him." Having a bit of fun with Philip, Jesus asks, "Philip, how much money do you think it would take to cater a meal for such a crowd?"

Philip replies that six months' wages might provide a snack for them, but not much. A kid is found who has a few loaves and a couple of fish. Jesus commands the people to sit. He takes the lad's food and gives thanks, and they all eat their fill. Jesus is the compassionate one who feeds the hungry, hurting multitudes.

Please note, however, that this story does not end with Jesus's feeding of the multitudes. The people are naturally impressed. "This Jesus must be quite a prophet of God who has come into the world!" they exclaim.

Surely Jesus is gratified by their exclamation. At last, they appear to have gotten the point. After so much rejection, at last the people see who Jesus is and proclaim him Lord. At last, the Jesus movement is getting somewhere.

No. Jesus rejects their acclamation. Next verse: "Jesus understood that they were about to come and force him to be their king, so he took refuge again, alone on a mountain."

That's curious. Right at the point when people have at last accepted Jesus, have acclaimed him Lord, he nervously withdraws, departs the crowd to be alone.

Why? Why did he withdraw precisely at the point when his coronation was being arranged?

The people need bread. Jesus has given them bread. They acclaim him as king. What else could Jesus want?

Do you remember, at the beginning of Jesus's ministry, how he was tempted in the wilderness? Satan met Jesus and offered him this world and heaven too. "Make stones into bread," said Satan. Jesus refused.

Isn't bread good? Isn't feeding the hungry self-evidently good? Why did Jesus refuse, and why, when he did feed people, was he so put off by their calling him king?

Something in Jesus recognized that he could not meet the needs of so many people who were clamoring after him without at the same time denying who he was called by God to be. In the wilderness, Satan tried to transform Jesus into a wonder-worker. Jesus refused. Now, Jesus has given bread, and when the grateful crowds attempt to crown him king, Jesus withdraws. When the crowds find him the next day, Jesus rebukes them for caring only about their bellies (6:26). They ask for a sign from Jesus, perhaps hoping for another free meal. But Jesus refuses and launches instead into his famous "bread of life" discourse, in which he identifies himself with what they truly need. Many of his disciples say, "This message is harsh," and many of them no longer follow Jesus after he stops giving them bread but now says that he is their "bread that came down from heaven" (6:60, 66).

Jesus refused to do for the crowds what they wanted, as if to do so would be a forsaking of his vocation. "Jesus, what will you do for us?" must be subsequent to the prior question, "Jesus, who are you and what is your mission?"

I confess that I think most of us show up at church to get help making it through the week, to obtain a sense of inner peace, to receive guidance in making difficult decisions that are before us.

Yet note that this story, which at first seems to be about us, before it is done is a story about Jesus. We come to church thinking mostly about ourselves, but then the scripture talks mostly about God.

That's why I think this story is told to us. When will we ever learn? Christianity, following Jesus, is not merely another helpful means of helping us get what we want. Rather, following Jesus is the means whereby God gets what God wants. Jesus cannot be enlisted as another helpful therapeutic device to enable us to get what we want before we meet Jesus. The gospel implies that we do not know what we want, what we need before we meet Jesus.

How well this was understood by the atheist, Nietzsche: "Christianity is a system, a whole view of things, thought out together. By breaking one main concept out of it, the faith in God, one breaks the whole: Nothing necessarily remains in one's hands. Christianity presupposes that man does not know, cannot know what is good for him, what evil; he believes in God, who alone knows it" (quoted by Philip D. Kenneson and James L. Street, *Selling Out the Church: The Dangers of Church Marketing* [Nashville: Abingdon Press, 1997], 82).

I heard William Sloane Coffin say that he did not know how you attracted people to the gospel by appealing to their essentially selfish needs and then end up offering them the unselfish gospel of Jesus.

John says that Jesus performed a great miracle, feeding hungry people, but not so much a miracle as a sign, something that points beyond itself to something greater and more important than the sign. The bread blessed and given for the people was a sign that God was among them, not among them as fulfillment of all their hearts' desires, but present as Jesus.

This God was even greater than their hunger. This God was there to be worshipped, to be obeyed, to be followed, even when the following did not appear to meet their needs.

Let us listen and learn.

Relating the text

The great theologian Karl Barth said people come to church asking, "It is true?" But today, most people in the pew are simply asking themselves, "Will it work for me?"

I spend a great deal of my summers roaming about the country, speaking to preachers about how to improve our preaching. (This surprises some of you that I should be so employed!) There are many reasons why we don't communicate as preachers. We don't communicate because we are not good as preachers, because we don't prepare, because we don't know enough about the gospel, because we misunderstand the human condition.

But today's scripture suggests to me that there are excellent reasons for not communicating, for being rejected. People bring many things with them in their listening to a sermon. They have been preconditioned; their ears are not in tune with the message; their understanding is blocked by metaphors that they have received from the culture, which makes it very difficult for them to hear the gospel.

Some of my communicative failures are due, not to me, but to Jesus.

Several years ago, a woman came to my class who was a practitioner of something she called "destructivist art." Destructivist art involves, at least in her case, throwing hydrochloric acid on a canvas, while viewers watch the canvas rot. This was alleged to be some sort of statement about George Bush.

After she showed the class some of her art, a few members of the class said, "This is the most wonderful thing we have ever seen." However, the majority of the class felt totally excluded by her communication. Many of them were even angry. "This isn't art!" they blurted out. "This is the dumbest thing we've ever seen."

She responded to their questions with grace and good humor. By the end of the class, most of the students were still unconvinced, uncomprehending of her work.

"There are good reasons for not understanding this art. Don't be so hard on yourself," she reassured them. "This art is very demanding. If this art is really making a critique of the present structure of society, then if one is caught in those structures, or benefiting from those structures, there are good reasons why one should not be able to understand. In a way, your inability to comprehend this art is, in itself, a validation of what I am claiming to be the aims of this art."

The thing that impressed me as a preacher was her willingness to have her hearers not understand her. I was struck by how she seemed utterly unperturbed by our failure to receive, to comprehend what she was trying to say.

I think she was about something larger than our acceptance, the meeting of our needs. I think she was trying to do something to us. I think she wasn't trying to speak to us where we were; I think she was trying to take us someplace else.

Modern people want to be entertained. At school, at work, at home, we want to be amused, captivated, entertained. We would rather watch sports than do sports. This entertainment mentality severely undercuts our ability to grow morally or intellectually, maybe even spiritually. Neil Postman says that in order to compete with television, teaching—which once was thought of as formation or inculcation—has been reduced to popular entertainment:

"Drawing an audience—rather than teaching—becomes the focus of education, and that is what television does. School is the one institution in the culture that should present a different worldview; a different way of knowing, of evaluating, of assessing. What worries me is that if school becomes so overwhelmed by entertainment's metaphors and metaphysics, then it becomes not content-centered but attention-centered, like television, chasing 'ratings' or class attendance. If school becomes that way, then the game may be lost, because school is using the same approach, epistemologically, as television. Instead of being something different from television, it is reduced to being just another kind of television."

—William Kilpatrick, *Why Johnny Can't Tell Right from Wrong:*
Moral Illiteracy and the Case for Character Education (New York:
Simon & Schuster, 1992)

Is there a message here for the church?

Sunday between July 31 and August 6 inclusive

[Proper 13, Ordinary/Lectionary 18]

2 Samuel 11:26–12:13a or Exodus 16:2-4, 9-15

Psalm 51:1-12 or Psalm 78:23-29

Ephesians 4:1-16

John 6:24-35

Making Sense of Jesus

Selected reading

John 6:24-35

Theme

To be a Christian means to be someone who is related, in a vital, life-changing way, to the person of Jesus Christ. Christianity is not so much a philosophy of life as it is a relationship with a life-giving person. This is a different way of thinking about faith, a different way of making sense of ourselves and the world, a way of making sense of the gift of relationship to the risen Christ.

Introduction to the readings

2 Samuel 11:26–12:13a

After orchestrating the death of Uriah, David marries Bathsheba, Uriah's wife. The prophet Nathan tells a parable that moves King David to repentance.

Ephesians 4:1-16
Paul tells the Ephesians to forbear each other in love in order that Christ's body, the church, might be edified.

John 6:24-35
The crowds seek bread from Jesus. Jesus tells them that the true bread they ought to seek is the bread that brings eternal life.

Prayer

Lord, before we speak, before we think, we pray. We pray because the knowledge we seek and the thoughts we need are not self-derived. We need that insight, that notion that comes to us from outside the limits of ourselves and our ways of making sense of the world. We badly need you to reach down to us, to offer heaven to our vision, to give us a glimpse of your glory. Empty us of our presumption, our presuppositions, in order to fill us with your powerful presence.

So, empty-handed, without prior claim, we hold our open hands out to you, confident that you will not pass us by without miraculous gift. Amen.

Encountering the text

This portion of John's Gospel can be a great challenge to the biblical interpreter and the preacher.

What am I saying? The entire Gospel of John is a great challenge to interpreters and preachers!

The Fourth Gospel is rich in similes, metaphors, symbols, and poetic images. Sometimes it seems almost too rich. You and I, being modern, Western-type people, have lost much of our skills for interpreting such vivid, evocative literature. We are, in our post-Enlightenment, rationalistic prejudices—how should we say it—supernaturally challenged.

Jesus requires of us not necessarily primitive, nonrational thinking but rather thinking of a different order. We come to a text like today's Gospel so full of metaphor, so resistant to simple, straightforward interpretation, and we are perplexed.

Let us not be overly perplexed. Let us trim our preaching to the peculiar subject matter that is presented to us in this chapter of the Fourth Gospel; the risen Christ in all of us is elusive, yet at the same time engaging presence and miraculousness.

Proclaiming the text

The young rabbi was new in town. A couple of months after his arrival I went by the synagogue to welcome him to our community. During the course of the conversation, I asked him, "Now that you have graduated from theological school and are on your own, do you miss school?"

The young rabbi replied, "As a Jew, you're never really 'on your own.' And I don't really miss much about school except when I'm reading scripture. As you probably know, it takes at least two Jews to read Torah—one to read, the other to help interpret."

I didn't know that. When it comes to faithful reading and interpretation of scripture, no Jew is alone in that undertaking, left to his or her own devices. It takes at least two Jews to read scripture.

Perhaps that's why theologian Stanley Hauerwas says (in his book *Unleashing the Scriptures*) that the biggest mistake the church made was to allow us Christians to take the Bible home with us in an attempt to read the Bible by ourselves. Scripture is a group, corporate, communal product, and the interpretation of scripture is a group, corporate, communal product.

Most of you have had the experience of reading some passage of scripture, home alone, only to have the same passage discussed at your Bible study group and have your interpretation challenged, corrected, and enlarged through discussion with others.

And yet, when it comes to scripture as God's-word-to-us revelation, it's more than a simple matter of "two heads are better than one." Scripture is what the church has produced; revelation is what the living, risen Christ speaks to us. What we need, as readers and hearers of scripture, is someone else to open our eyes, interpret the word. We require a power beyond our meager powers. We need another to speak scripture to us or we'll never get it.

Well, once again, we are on the Gospel of John as today's Gospel and, once again, the crowds are clueless. They don't get it. You know the Gospel of John. That's the Gospel where nobody ever gets it. Jesus in John's Gospel talks and talks and his words just sail right over the heads of his hearers. He says "living water" and they think H2O. He says "bread" and we think a loaf of bread. We just don't get it.

What is an essential, pervasive quality of a follower of Jesus in the Gospel of John? Ignorance—pervasive, unmitigated, unrelenting ignorance. In John's Gospel, we find it almost impossible to think about Jesus. Is that so surprising, when you think about it? This Gospel opens with the declaration, "In the beginning was the Word, and the Word was God."

"The Word" is how John's Gospel first names Jesus. God Almighty speaks a word to the world and the Word was made flesh and moved in among us. This "Word" was God. Jesus is the eternal Word.

And yet, he was no self-evident, easily understandable word to us. A word, who was God, stood among us and addressed us, but we couldn't readily hear. As John says, we loved "darkness rather than light." He spoke to us wonderful words, and we remained in the dark.

And why not? After all, the Christ, God's Son, was "from God"; he "was God." He is eternal; we are temporary. He is the one "came down from heaven" (as John puts it); and we are fixed here on earth.

Most of us think about things on the basis of our past experience and our previous concepts. We see something strange, something new, out of the ordinary, and what do we do? We immediately attempt to put this strange thing in the context of what is not strange, the unknown explained by what is known. This is how we make sense of the world. We "make sense" by making things fit within the pattern of what is already known.

And for most of life's experiences this works. I am encountered by a strange phenomenon and I exclaim, "What in the world is that?"

And you say, "Why, that's a hippopotamus."

And I persist, "What is that?"

And you explain, "That's an animal."

And I say, "I see."

Notice that I asked, "What in the world is that?" I'm determined to fit each new, strange experience into my world, making sense of the unknown on the basis of what is previously known.

Which is a long way around to a defense of the ignorance of the disciples and the crowd when it comes to making sense of Jesus, the eternal Word, God's Son, Light of the World.

If Jesus is truly God's Son, with God, as God, then we will have the utmost difficulty in making sense of Jesus. Our accustomed ways of thinking will fail, and we will be frustrated in our attempts to conceptualize who Jesus is and what he means.

Just before today's Gospel Jesus states that the writings of Moses (that is, much of what we call the Old Testament) "bear witness to me." Trouble is, we've had the witness of Moses and all the writings of the Hebrew scriptures, but that's not much help.

Nobody there that day said, "Oh, Jesus has just miraculously fed a whole multitude. That's got to be related to 2 Kings 4:42-44, in which Elisha miraculously fed hungry people. I get it! You're the new Elisha."

Jesus confounds them with talk of food from heaven and water that eternally quenches thirst. He refers them to the miraculous food that Moses fed the Israelites within the wilderness. None of that helps their incomprehension.

Please note that Jesus reminds them that the manna that enabled the Israelites to survive was "from God," not from Moses but "from heaven."

And though they don't understand, Jesus's comment is an interpretive clue. Jesus has fed the hungry multitude (last Sunday's Gospel) and we want to crown him as a king. Jesus has compared the bread that he gave the multitude to manna, the bread in the wilderness. And we still don't get it.

And maybe we can't get it except "from heaven" as a gift—a gift from God. Maybe what we need doesn't arise out of the biblical text but is something that is added to our reading and hearing of the biblical text, a gift "from heaven." Maybe the one who so befuddles and confuses (the eternal Word) is also the one who interprets and explains. Amid all the confusion and misunderstanding there is one who stands with us, who patiently keeps teaching us, who doesn't stop loving us despite our incomprehension.

Maybe comprehension, understanding, is not the point. The point is to allow Jesus (the One who has "come down from heaven") to keep working with us, to keep surprising us. And thus, you are here this morning.

So what if you don't fully understand Jesus this morning? So what if you don't fully understand this sermon this morning? The point is that you are in the presence of the One "come down from heaven." The point may be more than understanding. The point, if you must have a point, is presence.

And by the way, if you understand, it's a miracle! That is, it's a gift, a gift from heaven. Gift. Grace.

Relating the text

I've been married to a woman now for more than forty years. I have, therefore, had the opportunity to listen to her, to be with her, to know her as well as anyone in the world.

Yet despite all that, even after all those years, she is still able to surprise me. She is still a mystery to me in so many ways, for she is not an extension of me or merged with me. She exists, in her difference and individuality. Sometimes she is against me, in order that she is really with me.

Is this a parable that is applicable to today's Gospel?

_____

Do you know what a challenge John's Gospel—particularly today's pericope—is to my self-understanding as a preacher? I assume that my job as a preacher is to make Jesus accessible to the people in the pews, to explain Jesus, to put Jesus down on the bottom shelf where everyone can get it. So I take some mysterious, odd text, such as today's Gospel, then I rework it, boil it down into three accessible ideas, four basic principles, two points that should be written down on a notepad by everyone in the congregation.

I thus make Jesus accessible to the congregation.

But let us attend to the first chapter of John. The Word became flesh and moved in with us (John 1). The Word has come close to us, spoken to us, revealed himself to us.

Revelation, explication, elucidation is God's business, not mine. Only God can speak accurately and truthfully of God.

All my pitiful, anxious attempts to make Jesus readily available to my hearers may be a sinful attempt to contain and to tame Jesus.

Therefore, a more theologically appropriate assignment for me as a preacher—an assignment that is more in line with the peculiar subject matter of the gospel—is to let Jesus speak himself, to let him encounter us, as he encountered his first hearers, as he is, as he will be, not as we might like him to be.

The Gospel of John is a Gospel that begins with explicit praise of the incarnation, God in the flesh, God with us. The Trinity is that dynamic, dialectic interaction that is at the heart of the incarnation. The Trinity is that interaction between the self and the other, just as the Trinity embodies both the particularity of God and the communion of the three as one. As Martin Luther puts the practical, continuing consequences of the incarnation: "It is the honor and glory of our God . . . that, giving himself for our sake in deepest condescension, he passes into the flesh, the bread, our hearts, mouths, entrails, and suffers also for our sake that he be dishonorably handled, on the altar as on the cross."

Every time we utter the name of God in discourse, every time we make Eucharist, we continue to proclaim the glory of a dynamic and communion-craving God who is willing to be dishonorably handled by us so that we might be honorably handled by God.

All trinitarian conversation must begin with the incarnation; here the reality of God as Trinity stands or falls in terms of divine self-disclosure.

How do we make sense of the world? How do we conceive of our earth home? In Mercator projection maps of the world, in which the globe is split apart and spread across the page like so many pieces of an orange peel, we can clearly see the world, but there are great gaps in our knowledge, vast spaces between the parts, separation, a lack of unity. This is one of the problems of modern knowledge. We see the parts but not their sum. We focus on the pieces, sometimes with great accuracy and insight, but there's no "big picture," no overall, sweeping, panoramic view.

We tend to see the trees but not the forest.

When most of our congregation's exposure to the Bible is through short lectionary readings each Sunday, in which we jump from text to text, reading out of context, is not this in danger of becoming something like a Mercator projection of scripture? Perhaps we preachers ought to strive, while being attentive to the individual texts, at the same time to see the big picture of scripture.

In two large rooms in the Pompidou Center, in the Museum of Modern Art in Paris, there is an installation by the artist Joseph Beuys (1921–1986). A large black grand piano occupies the center of one of the rooms. The top of the piano is nailed shut. The two rooms are covered, walls and ceiling, with about a foot of thick, sound-absorbent padding. The piece is entitled Plight (1958/1985). Here is our plight as preachers, as communicators, as workers in words and sound. There is an instrument for making music, but contextual factors within modern life smother and suppress the sound.

When I was in seminary learning to preach, I got the impression that my greatest challenge as a communicator of the gospel was the skeptical, critical, analytical "modern world." My plight, as a preacher, was to stand in the premodern, prescientific world of the Bible and yet speak to the modern world. The preacher, so I assumed, artfully bridges the two-thousand-year gap between the Bible and the modern world. When the preacher is bridging that gap with a text like today's Gospel, then we really have our work cut out for us!

Perhaps we preachers, struggling to make the old Bible comprehensible to the new, modern world, need to be reminded that the modern world is an intellectual construction dating back not much further than Descartes, a way of viewing reality but a view that need not necessarily be honored as the last word on "reality." Modernity has its own intellectual limitations. It is a limited way of looking at the world

In preaching, we are moving, little by little, toward new and otherwise un-available descriptions of reality. We are on our way, in the sermon, toward a new heaven and a new earth, a new world. Christian preaching is not merely the skillful description of the world as it is but a bold, visionary, and demand-ing call to be part of a world that is to be. Christian preachers are heralds who proclaim the true sovereignty of God in territory whose ownership is still under dispute.

Sunday between August 7 and August 13 inclusive

[Proper 14, Ordinary/Lectionary 19]

2 Samuel 18:5-9, 15, 31-33 or 1 Kings 19:4-8

Psalm 130 or Psalm 34:1-8

Ephesians 4:25–5:2

John 6:35, 41-51

Bread of Life

Selected reading

John 6:35, 41-51

Theme

Jesus says that he is the "bread of life." We have deep hungers, you and I, hungers that can only be fed by the bread that fills and satisfies. Jesus is that gracious bread. Come to him and be fed.

Introduction to the readings

2 Samuel 18:5-9, 15, 31-33

Solomon takes over the rule of Israel from his father, David, and begins a long and wise reign.

Ephesians 4:25–5:2

The letter to the Ephesians gives instruction to new Christians on how they ought to live.

John 6:35, 41-51

Jesus compares himself to "bread that came down from heaven."

Prayer

Lord, we come before you this day as those who are empty. Some of us have tried to assuage our hungers in the wrong places. Some of us have attempted to act as if we were self-sufficient unto ourselves, in need of no nurturance outside ourselves.

Bread of heaven, feed us until we want no more. Fill us with your Spirit. Feed us in your love. Nourish us with that food that forever satisfies. Amen.

Encountering the text

In the Gospel of John one never knows. Water is not really water. Wind is more than wind. Bread is not only bread. Jesus loves to speak in double-talk in this Gospel, talk that means much more than it first means. Today's Gospel is a great example of Johannine speech that points beyond itself to something more than itself.

Why not speak clearly, with concision and simplicity, because here is speech in service to the risen Christ? In John's Gospel, Jesus is the exalted, reigning Lord from chapter 1 onward. He moves serenely through the text, speaking, declaring, pronouncing words that are pregnant and full of power.

Bread, the most common, essential, and mundane of foods, is spoken of in today's Gospel. In the hands of Jesus, bread is more than bread. Bread is life.

A metaphor, when it is right, subsumes something from our daily experience and changes it, sheds new light on it. In fact, the very word *metaphor* is made from the Greek words meaning "to change" or "to transform" and "to shed light upon." When an appropriate metaphor is used, our understanding is transformed, moved, changed. We are enlightened; we see things in a new light. When Jesus calls himself bread, we are seeing Jesus in a new way and bread in a new way. Something from ordinary life is being used to shed light on something extraordinary, namely, the risen Christ.

Jesus saves us, yes. But he also feeds us. He becomes from us the very stuff of life.

This Sunday our concerns are more for nurture than for conversion. Not only does the risen Christ raise us from death to life, dramatically transforming us and our world. But the risen Christ also stays with us, nourishes us, cares for us, feeds us, giving us what we need to keep at discipleship.

All of the Johannine metaphors are in service of the aim that we might have "life in his name" (John 20:31). John has transformed some traditional stories about Jesus (which we find in Mark 6:30-54; 8:11-21) into a wonderful meal (John 6:1-15), into teaching about bread (6:25-59).

John loves to begin with our misunderstanding and form a dialogue with Jesus out of our misunderstanding. This enables him to interpret what's going on with Jesus, enabling Jesus to respond with high theological interpretation. Jesus picks up on this historic experience of manna in the wilderness, that "bread that came down from heaven," to show how he is this wondrous bread.

We also see another Johannine convention: the "I am" statements. When Jesus pronounces "I am" in this Gospel, it is a lofty, serene, exalted statement about Christ. He is bread filled with life. I am the manna-bread from above (vv. 41 and 51).

John's Gospel has no story of the Last Supper, no mention of "this is my body" as in the Synoptic Gospels. Verse 51 of today's text is John's substitute for those words. In this Gospel, it's all miraculous, wondrous offering of Jesus to us; it's all Eucharist, from start to finish. He is bread in the wilderness.

When all is said and done, John 6 is a passage not to be analyzed, dissected, and argued. It is to be received like bread, savored, received as a gift, digested, ingested for life, life eternal.

Proclaiming the text

I never met a bread I didn't like. Flat, chewy Near Eastern bread. Hearty, hard-crusted Greek bread. Dark, heavy German bread. French croissants. My mother's biscuits. I love about every bread I've met.

Bread is basic, we sometimes say. In eating bread, we are back in touch with the basic stuff of life, the "staff of life," as bread is sometimes called. Food can get fancy, elaborate, but it never gets much better, and certainly not more basic, than bread.

In today's Gospel, Jesus says that he is bread "that came down from heaven" and the "bread of life."

Part of me has always resisted the Gospel of John. I like better the earthy, more mundane accounts of Jesus in Mark or Luke. In those Gospels, we are on the road with Jesus and you can almost taste the dust in your mouth. We visit in people's homes. We sit and listen to sermons. We overhear the conversation at a table. Jesus talks much like most people talk with stories about farmers and conflict in families and seeds and flowers.

But in John's Gospel from the first, Jesus seems oddly detached, exalted, serene, floating above the fray. He is with his disciples, but he is also above them, talking in ways that sound strange, in ways they hardly ever understand. Today's Gospel, when Jesus stands before them and pronounces, "I am the bread that came down from heaven," what are we supposed to do with that? It sounds weird.

Or perhaps, when you think about it, it's the time when Jesus—who has been "the Word," Spirit, a strange and exalted figure in this Gospel—comes down to earth and finally enters our world and gets to us.

We may not know much about Spirit, truth, or "the Word," which occupies much of John's Gospel, but we do know about hunger. We know that gnawing feeling in the pit of the stomach when we go without food. We also know that gnawing pain in the heart of the soul. I know lots of people today who are hungry, but not just for bread. Jesus seems to be talking about that kind of hunger here.

When we are hungry, it's a reminder that we are creatures who need nourishment or we die. But there is another kind of death among us. It is the death of the soul, that wasting away that comes when we lose our lust for life, when our eyes seem dull to the world, and when we don't know if we can go on. Death is known to us. Not dramatic, momentary death, but death that comes day by day, drop by drop.

Maybe you came to church today because you are hungry.

I've heard people say that before. "We are not really being fed at this church." They didn't mean that the church was not providing enough covered dish suppers. They meant that their souls were being malnourished. There was not enough substance in the preaching, or the music, or the worship to sustain them through the week and the daily demands of discipleship.

Jesus promises that he is bread. He is the bread come down from heaven, just like the Israelites had manna in the wilderness to sustain them on the exodus from Egypt. Jesus says he is like that bread, come down from heaven to sustain us.

What is your image of Jesus? For some of us, Jesus is the bleeding body hanging on a cross. He just hangs there. For others of us, he is the one who sits up on high, God enthroned in heaven.

Today I want you to think of Jesus in the way he urges here—as bread. He is that bread that satisfies you when nothing else can. You chew on him, bit by bit, take your time, and savor each morsel. It is not dramatic. Just life giving. Take time to enjoy him, to let him become part of your life and thereby give you life.

Sometimes we speak of the dramatic incursions of God among us, those striking, life-changing moments when it is as if God has invaded your world, swept over you, and grasped you with intensity.

But today, on his summer Sunday, Jesus bids us to think of him as bread, as a meal, as that daily, life-giving, sustaining presence that keeps us going.

When I ask people why they are here in church, Sunday after Sunday, this is one of the main reasons they give: "I am here to get nourished to make it through the week." In this church, there is rarely anything too dramatic, too striking. Mostly, when we are at our best, it's just the weekly, ordinary reading of scripture, praying of prayers, singing of hymns, preaching, and listening to sermons. Perhaps this is why the table, the Lord's table, rather than the pulpit ought to be the true visual center of a church.

For you, it is that which enables you to keep on keeping on as a disciple. It nourishes you. It is your bread. It is your life. Jesus bids us to feed upon him, to ingest him, bit by bit, to take his being into our lives, to let him nourish us unto life.

Furthermore, note that Jesus's stress here is on bread given, more than on bread eaten. He is the bread that comes down from heaven, as a gift. All bread, when you think about it, comes down from heaven. All bread is a gift of God, of God's rain, sun, and soil. Our relationship to Christ is utterly dependent upon Christ. And, in today's Gospel, Christ promises to give us what we need to keep us going.

I was conducting a workshop in a little church on the meaning of the sacraments. We had discussed baptism and its meaning. Now we were working on the Lord's Supper. I had told them that a sacrament is some experience from everyday life that is lifted up, in the context of worship, and thereby sanctified, given sacred significance because of its use in worship. But that sounded too sanctimonious, too abstract. So I asked them, "What is the most memorable meal you ever ate?"

They told of memories of meals in fancy French restaurants in Toronto, of a great little bistro they discovered on a trip to San Francisco, of an elaborate ten-course extravaganza in an expensive hotel in New York.

Then one man said, "The best meal I ever had was in World War II, the morning after a night of terrible battle. I staggered up over a hill and saw a woman from the Red Cross in a little trailer in a muddy field. I staggered through the muck to her trailer. She was handing out stale doughnuts and cold coffee. When she handed me mine, she smiled. After the night I had suffered, in that place, at that time, I'd have to say that was about the best meal I ever had."

Jesus says, "I am bread. I am bread come down from heaven to nourish you forever." I believe in such bread. Come to him and be fed forever. Amen.

Relating the text

My first encounter with hunger—with real, pervasive, day-after-day malnutrition and slow starvation—was with a student mission team in Honduras, second poorest country in our hemisphere.

I remember the day I held in my arms a little boy of five, yet he looked only two or three. His little belly was bloated, just like I had seen in pictures of the starving. You could press in his tummy and feel the starvation.

That little boy became for me a kind of "sacrament," a concrete, physical embodiment of what hunger looks like, feels like. Before we rush too quickly in our interpretation of today's text from John, rushing from the physical to the spiritual meanings of hunger, let us pause to reflect upon the millions of our fellow human beings for whom hunger is not a metaphor, not a symbol of something else. It is their daily life. And death.

When Jesus spoke, "I am the bread of life," he spoke to those who knew hunger, real hunger. There may be a sense in which those of us who have never known hunger are at a distinct interpretive disadvantage when it comes to understanding today's Gospel.

Perhaps that is but one of the reasons why Jesus calls the poor "happy."

When we hold up a loaf of bread at the Eucharist and call it blessed, what do we mean?

The farmer plowed the earth and sowed the seed.

Rain watered the ground and the seed began to sprout.

The farmer plowed and weeded and nurtured and harvested in due time.

The grain was processed by the miller. The flour was transported by the trucker. The baker took the flour and worked it into dough in the early morning hours of a day before dawn. And then the risen dough was baked. The bread was packaged, shipped, unloaded, delivered, put on the shelves by the grocer, bought by someone with the money she had made at her job; it was taken home and served.

When we hold up a loaf of bread, we lift up all of human community, the world, life itself.

Say a prayer, when you eat bread.

"A good meal ought to begin with hunger."

—A French proverb

"A good meal makes a man feel more charitable toward the whole world than any sermon."

—Arthur Pendenys

When I conduct workshops on worship, exploring with laity the meaning of the sacraments, I will sometimes say to them, "The Lord's Supper or Eucharist means anything that *bread* means." Then I ask them, "What does *bread* mean?"

They use words like *nourishment, hunger, joy, community, family, memory,* and *life* to say the meaning of *bread*.

"Well," I say, "the Lord's Supper means all of that in the Bible and in our church. Think of the Eucharist as bread in the name of Jesus. Know that, and you understand all you need to know about the Lord's Supper."

"A hungry man is not a free man."

—Adlai Stevenson (1900–1965)

John Calvin asserted that Christ is present in the Lord's Supper. How is he present? Where is he present? Calvin was reluctant to define the real presence of Christ in the Eucharist. Instead, he said, "I would rather experience it than understand it."

So too, when Christ says, "I am the bread of life that came down from heaven," we should be reluctant to explain the precise meaning of that metaphoric, symbolic statement. Rather we should testify how, in our experience of the risen Christ, he is for us the bread of life.

Bethlehem, the place of Jesus's nativity, means literally "house of bread, city of bread." God, who provided bread in the wilderness and sent his Son as bread from heaven, made Jesus to be born in Bethlehem.

Sunday between August 14 and August 20 inclusive

[Proper 15, Ordinary/Lectionary 20]

1 Kings 2:10-12; 3:3-14 or Proverbs 9:1-6

Psalm 111 or Psalm 34:9-14

Ephesians 5:15-20

John 6:51-58

Projection

Selected reading

John 6:51-58

Theme

We project our images of God upon God, in our fumbling human attempt to think about God. Yet at the same time, God is also projecting God's great love for us upon us, in Christ. In Jesus Christ, God comes to us, reaches out to us in ways we can comprehend. Our God is a determinedly self-revealing God who speaks, acts, and reaches to us. This is what we mean by incarnation, God in the flesh among us.

Introduction to the readings

1 Kings 2:10-12; 3:3-14

Solomon asks God for a discerning mind.

Ephesians 5:15-20

The letter to the Ephesians exhorts early Christians to give thanks to God at all times, praising God in word and in deed.

John 6:51-58

Jesus speaks of himself as "the living bread that came down from heaven."

Prayer

Lord, before we come to you, you come to us. Before we think of you, you have conceived us. Before we decide to follow you, you decided in the cross of Christ to reach out to us. Before we felt gratitude for you, you showered blessing upon us.

We confess that we enjoy thinking of ourselves as masters of our fate, the sole actors in our world, the determiners of our destiny.

Today, in church, remind us that you come to us, before we come to you. Today, in the hymns, the gathered people, the prayer and the word, come to us again. Amen.

Encountering the text

Today's Gospel is toward the end of John 6, which is Jesus's "bread of life" discourse. Jesus continues to pile up images of the "living bread" in today's Gospel. We will not continue to reflect upon the metaphor of bread; rather, this Sunday we will focus on Christian thinking.

The Gospel of John can seem so abstract, so "spiritual" and strange, that it is difficult to connect with our world. One of our problems with John's Gospel is that John is pioneering with new ways of thinking about God. In John, "the Word became flesh and made his home among us" (John 1:14). That invasion of divine glory requires that John rethink everything.

This Sunday, we will think about how the modern world tends to miscon-strue Christian thinking. We will also defend what the world considers to be the strange ways that Christians speak and think.

We take our cue from the opening of today's Gospel. Jesus says, "I am the liv-ing bread that came down from heaven." I am putting the stress on the "came down from heaven" portion of that verse. Jesus comes to us, comes down to us. This is a very Johannine thought. Jesus comes to us from the outside, not only outside our world, but also outside our consciousness. He is the word, the word that formed the world, made flesh and dwelling among us. He is God Almighty in the flesh, standing before us.

Throughout John's Gospel, we see John reaching for a variety of metaphors in an attempt to describe what has happened among us in the incarnation. Here he speaks of Jesus as "bread that came down from heaven." Whoever Jesus is, he is one who has come to us from the outside, come from the outside to us. He is both outside us yet among us in ways we can comprehend. He is from heaven, but he is also bread.

We propose, in "Proclaiming the text," to do a teaching sermon that, while it arises out of the Gospel for today, is not a specific treatment of the text. The sermon is an extended meditation, a teaching sermon using the images of "projection" and "illusion" to speak about the way Christians think about God. In a way, the sermon is a defense of the faith, a defense of Christian believing as a sophisticated, discerning way of moving in the world. Don't be put off by the rather intellectual tenor of today's "Proclaiming the text." There are times when Christians are strengthened by thinking through the faith, gaining the intellectual insight that enables us to share our faith with others intelligently and to defend our faith in the face of its detractors.

Here, as the summer ends, the congregation gathers to reflect upon the way in which, in our thinking about God, we do not simply project our images of God out into the universe. Rather, God in Christ projects love and revela-tion toward us. This is the basis of our faith—not what we think or feel or imagine, but rather what God reveals.

Proclaiming the text

The student emerged from the Easter service saying, "I know what you Christians are up to. We studied all about this in philosophy. This is called 'projection.' Feuerbach said that you've got this desire to live forever, therefore you projected your infantile wish onto the universe and named that 'God.'"

I replied, in love, "That shows just how little you know. If we were going to project a God, we would certainly not have projected this one! We've demonstrated, time and again through the centuries, that we are capable of producing many more accessible and likable Gods than this one!"

His thinking is quite typical of the modern world. The modern view of God as infantile wish-projection probably had its birth in March of 1907 when Freud read the paper "Obsessive Actions and Religious Practices." (I get this story from Robert Coles, "Freud and God," in *The New Religious Humanist*, ed. Gregory Wolf [New York: Free Press, 1997], 104–20.) In that paper, Freud claimed, on the basis of his work with neurotic patients, that the "petty ceremonials" of religion are basically a sort of personality sickness. God is only a symptom of deep inner insecurities. "One might venture to regard obsessional neurosis as a pathological formation of a religion, and to describe that neurosis as an individual religiosity and religion as a universal obsessional neurosis." Only sick people could be religious.

It is the nature of modernity to reduce most human phenomena to something that can be said to be "only" something else. There is no reality in modernity outside the self. Therefore, what we call "God" is only a projection of something within ourselves. What we call "music" is only a series of sound waves bouncing about the atmosphere. What we call "art" is only a series of marks upon a canvas that stimulate the neurochemical processes of the brain. Reductionism is a hallmark of modernity.

Freud continued this line of thinking in his infamous *The Future of an Illusion* (1927). There he dismisses "the fairy-tales of religion" as only an illusion "derived from human wishes": "The effect of religious thinking may be likened to that of a narcotic." This, as you can imagine, was something like what Marx said when he charged that religion was "the opiate of the common people." Religion is a cheap drug.

Ana-Maria Rizzuto charged, in her 1979 book *Birth of the Living God: A Psychoanalytic Study*, that contemporary psychoanalysis had never been able to break free of Freud's prejudiced, reductionistic, vehemently negative account of religion.

She notes that the human being is an inherently imagining and projecting creature. In order to live in the world, we are constantly projecting images on our mental screens, images that are variously accurate or inaccurate representations of the world. For instance, the toddler has a fixation with a baby blanket. Whenever the child feels insecure, it grabs the blanket and feels better. Why? Surely the blanket is a reminder of the comforting presence of the parent. When he or she is holding the blanket, the toddler feels close to the parent. This feeling of closeness is a projection.

But it is not a lie. Rather, the child is busy projecting the comforting presence of the parent, through the object of the blanket. There really is a parent somewhere. There really is a connection between the child's projection of the parent and the parent, the child's feeling of security when holding the trusted blanket and a parent who makes the child secure.

Rizzuto notes how such a projection is absolutely essential to our self-definition. We are busy painting mental pictures of the world in order to live in the world. These mental pictures, although sometimes inadequate and often limited by our imagination and our experiences, are nevertheless connected to the world.

As creatures, we are desperate to place ourselves in the world, to figure out where we have come from and where we are going. *Reality* and *illusion* are not contradictory terms. Freud, in naming a whole host of psychological realities as "ego," "superego," "libido," and so on, was busy forming "illusions" that proved to be very serviceable in mapping the human psyche. We can argue about whether or not his projections and illusions were helpful, but why should we call them "sick" in the way that Freud dismisses religion? We cannot be human without illusions. We are busy living by various illusions—science, fairytales, religion, whatever. As children, we play with toys and games. Later as college students, we learn to play with ideas and words and images, sounds and notions. All of this is our attempt to do business with the world, to find our way amid the sometimes-confusing cacophony of stimuli.

One of the reasons science works for us is that it is such a successful illusion and projection. Science makes theories about the way the world is. It has ways of testing and confirming its theories. But even when its theories are not completely confirmed, they are helpful ways of construing the world. And even when the theories of science are confirmed, they are still theories, images of what is going on in the world.

Illusions are not false, not lies; rather, they are projections from the richness of human experience into our consciousness by which we organize and make sense out of experience. Those who make theories of the world are busy assembling information about the world in such a way as to enable the rest of us to live in the world with a little less anguish and confusion. This is not some kind of naive, sick endeavor, but our natural human attempt to live creatively in the world.

Maybe the reason Freud's thought is so abusive toward religion is that it sees perceptively that religion is a major competitor for the question of, "Who gets to name the world?"

Being religious, seen from this point of view, is a way of thinking about the world. German sociologist Max Weber said that the sacrifice of the intellect is the first thing that religion asks. But he was wrong. Being religious is being intellectual.

Faith is not a way of killing all thought, but it is a way of thinking that is more creative than what most of the world thinks when it is thinking.

Think of our tendency to project images upon the world, not as arising from childish wishes, but from the natural human tendency to think about the world. Our imaginations therefore might be compared to a movie screen on which images are projected. When I say the world is a "rat race," that is an image. When I say that life is "a bowl of cherries," that is a projection. I am not being crazy to engage in such projection. My projection must be set next to experience and critiqued, but it ought not be too easily dismissed.

We are individuals who live in a precarious relationship with the world. As users of language, we are busy building up in our mind intellectual constructs that enable us to move in the world.

But what if the world I live in is not only my projection, but also God's? Think about that. Christians claim that the God of Israel and the church, the God of Abraham, Isaac, Jacob, and Mary, is more than a helpful metaphor. This God is a reality. It is typical of modern humanity to think that we are the only actors, the only speakers.

But what if the Bible is right in its claim that God is busy acting and speaking to us? What if my images of God are not simply my projections out of my own ego needs, but gifts, gifts from a ceaselessly revealing God who is determined to be known? I have admitted that, when I think, I am busy projecting certain images upon the screen. But what if God is also busy projecting images upon the screen? What if when I say "God," I am not just throwing my projections and wishes out into the universe, but I am also being bombarded by images of the good shepherd, the waiting parent, the crucified savior, the patient teacher, the (last Sunday's sermon) bread from heaven? These are images that have been projected upon me by the Christian faith.

What if I myself am God's projection, a construct in the mind of God, something that God is working on as a project?

Surely you have sat in some classroom in school and had some stunning insight, that "Aha!" experience. Normally, we think of these experiences as self-derived. We say things like, "In that moment it all came together for me. It all came to me. I figured it out."

But what if those moments are literally times when "it came to me"? What if this Sunday, your faith is not something that you summoned forth within yourself, but rather it was something that was given to us from the outside, placed upon us?

In today's Gospel Jesus says, "I am the living bread that came down from heaven." He comes to us. Comes to us from outside our consciousness, bringing something to us we could not have had on our own, showing us something about God we could not have merely projected on our own. He comes to us before we come to him.

Think about it.

Relating the text

Today's "Proclaiming the text" notes how so much of modern life is conceived of something that we think, we do, we say. How different is the action in the world rendered in the Bible!

The prophet Jeremiah speaks of Israel as a glob of clay in the hands of God. The potter at the turning wheel pushes down the clay and forms it into a pot. The clay is passive. The potter—who is God—is active. That clay pot bears the imprint of the creator. So what if my thoughts are not exclusively my thoughts but rather are ideas not merely self-derived, given to me by the great consciousness of God?

Plato taught that all of our thoughts are implanted within us, groping sketches of the ideal world that exists in the mind of God. What if I never really "think for myself" but instead I think those thoughts implanted in me by my creator?

Think about it.

"A rock pile ceases to be a rock pile the moment a single man contemplates it, bearing within him the image of the cathedral."

—Antoine de Saint-Exupéry (1900–1944)

C. S. Lewis kept arguing for the objective reality of the God whom Christians worship. It was the sheer otherness of God that impressed Lewis and won his undying fascination. Lewis, like many believers, was impressed by how the God of the Bible is a God who is so much larger and more interesting than anything we could have thought up on our own. Sometimes the otherness of God is abrasive, difficult for us.

Lewis commented, "Nothing which is at all times and in every way agreeable to us can have objective reality. It is of the very nature of the real that it should have sharp corners and rough edges, that it should be resistant, should be itself. Dream-furniture is the only kind on which you never stub your toes or bang your knee."

"To see what is in front of one's nose needs a constant struggle."

—George Orwell (1903–1950)

"The last advance of reason is to recognize that it is surpassed by innumerable things; it is feeble if it cannot recognize that."

—Blaise Pascal (1623–1662)

Sunday between August 21
and August 27 inclusive

[Proper 16, Ordinary/Lectionary 21]

1 Kings 8:(1, 6, 10-11), 22-30, 41-43

Psalm 84

Ephesians 6:10-20

John 6:56-69

The Joy of Self-Forgetfulness in Christ

Selected reading

John 6:56-69

Theme

The key to our lives is not in us but in Jesus. Jesus is not only the full revelation of who God is but also the revelation of who we are and who we are meant to be. We cannot learn our true purpose and meaning by focusing on ourselves. Christians believe that one of the great gifts of the Christian faith is that we are rescued from our self-obsession and our self-preoccupation to turn toward Christ, the true destiny of our selves.

Introduction to the readings

1 Kings 8:(1, 6, 10-11), 22-30, 41-43

In a grand assembly, King Solomon prays to the God of Israel, dedicating the new temple to the God who keeps covenant and steadfast love.

Ephesians 6:10-20
Be strong in the Lord by putting on the whole armor of God.

John 6:56-69
Jesus commands his disciples to abide in him, speaking of a relationship with himself that is nothing less than their food and drink.

Prayer

Lord Jesus, in this time of worship, draw us out of our cares and concerns, our aches and pains, and into the sphere of your love. Raise us above petty preoccupation with all the things that we think we must say to you and give us the grace to listen to all that you would say to us. In this hour, save us from ourselves that we might be redeemed to live more fully for you and to love more faithfully. Amen.

Encountering the text

A rather strange text confronts us in this week's Gospel. Jesus says things here that cause friction in the minds of his disciples. What on earth can he mean by this strange talk of eating his flesh? His disciples justifiably ask, "This message is harsh. Who can hear it?"

No wonder John says, "Many of his disciples turned away and no longer accompanied him."

When Jesus turns to his remaining disciples after this difficult teaching and asks, "Do you also want to leave?" they reply, "Lord, where would we go? You have the words of eternal life . . . you are God's holy one."

Many have noted that John's Gospel displays a "high Christology." Jesus in this Gospel is the Lord. The disciples play a role, but everything in this Gospel is subordinated to the claim that Jesus Christ is Lord. We know little about the disciples in this Gospel or in any other. John does not give us a list of the disciples who stayed and the ones who left. In fact, before this Sunday's pericope ends, Jesus sadly notes that one of his inner-circle disciples will betray him.

This isn't a story about the disciples, that is, about us; it is a story about Jesus Christ, the light shining in the darkness, the bread from heaven.

In a cultural milieu in which many people think that they come to church to hear advice for their personal problems, to get ethical instruction on how to live better lives, or to feel something or think something religious, this Sunday's Gospel is a reminder that the purpose of church, the source of the gospel, the reason why we're here is Jesus.

Many have noted that the Gospel of John doesn't have much in the way of ethics. Unlike Matthew, there are no long lists of ethical admonitions and injunctions. One might be hard-pressed to answer the question, "How are Christians supposed to live our lives?" in the light of the Fourth Gospel.

Why is that? It's because this is not good news primarily about us. It's about Jesus Christ, the bread from heaven, the one who speaks "words of eternal life."

Proclaiming the text

Poet Laureate Billy Collins opened one of his poetry lectures by first bantering a bit with his audience, telling them how wonderful it was to see them there, how great it was to see how many people were interested in poetry. Then he said, "Now, enough of that. Let's get this off you and focused back on me."

He was kidding, but Collins's audience laughed because they knew the sentiment to be true of themselves. We live in a culture in which there is constant pressure to focus upon, become preoccupied with, and to cultivate ourselves.

We all embody the aphorism of Oscar Wilde, who is reported to have said to someone at a London party, "Come over here and sit next to me. I'm dying to tell you all about myself."

Poet Walt Whitman in *Leaves of Grass* asks, "Why should I pray, why should I venerate? . . . One world is aware and by far the largest to me, that is myself." It is hard to believe that there was ever a day when Whitman's "Song of Myself" was considered radical or even interesting. Today we are all singing that song. We have no world that interests us more than the world that is ourselves. We are the most interesting project we undertake. Through such self-absorption, the human landscape has not grown; it has shrunk. The value of everything is reduced to the question, "What's in it for me?"

Protestant Reformer Martin Luther defined sin as "the heart curved in on itself." Curved in on ourselves, focusing mostly upon our needs, our aches and pains, we wither and die. This is the sin that afflicts us today.

"I would die if I didn't get to play golf at least once a week," a man in my church once told me.

"Surely you exaggerate," I said. "Golf can't be that great."

"Oh, but it is," he replied. "There's nothing better than to be out on a nice day, focusing all my attention, all my thought and affection on that little white ball. All burdens are lifted from my back; all concerns are put on the shelf. All I want to do is to get that little ball into that little hole on the green. It's . . . wonderful!"

Recently I was asked to reflect on "the pause" that occurs in those last fleeting moments just before I stand up to preach a sermon. What do I think about? What runs through my head in those moments as I enter the pulpit and I begin to preach?

I pondered that question and I realized *not much*. Before that moment, when the congregation is singing the hymn before the sermon, I confess that I do sometimes wonder, *How do I look? Am I going to do well? Will they like what I have to say? Have I come here with the right sermon, at the right time, for the right congregation? Will they like me?*

But in that pause, in that moment just before I preach, I find that I am not thinking about anything except the sermon. My whole being is being caught up, focused on the demands of the sermon. I become what I am intending to preach.

It is a wonderful, all-too-rare (in this culture) moment of self-forgetfulness. It is close to what Charles Wesley meant in his hymn when he spoke of being "lost in wonder, love, and praise" when one is in love with Jesus. It is the self-forgetfulness of the artist who becomes obsessed with the art, preoccupied with the moment, wholly focused on the thing itself, giving the art absolutely everything that it deserves.

I think it is something close to what Jesus said in saying, "All who want to come after me must say no to themselves, take up their cross, and follow me." It's quite an achievement, in this culture, to say no to oneself when we are encouraged by so much around us to focus upon ourselves, to care and feed our adorable, all-important me.

Or maybe self-forgetfulness is not so much an achievement as a gift.

When you are in love (I hope I'm describing something that most of you have experienced!), part of the joy of being in love is that you find yourself "consumed" (as we sometimes say) by the object of your love. You find yourself thinking all the time about the beloved. Every waking moment—and sometimes much of our sleeping moments as well—is preoccupied with the one who is the object of our love. Eventually, if a relationship develops, we find ourselves no longer thinking in terms of "I" and "you," but rather in terms of "us" and "we." Much that was once "me" has now been expanded to include "we."

Well, something very much like that happens to the believer and Jesus Christ. We find ourselves being drawn out of ourselves and into Christ. We find that we are thinking less of ourselves and more about others. Our needs seem to grow smaller as we are given more responsibility for the needs of others.

The love for Jesus beckons us on one of the most important journeys we will ever undertake: the long, countercultural journey outside of ourselves toward the true center of our being who is also our creator and our savior. Christians sometimes say, "Jesus Christ saves us from our sins." True. But this Sunday I'm thinking that it's also true to say, "Jesus Christ saves us from ourselves!"

And when we are in love with someone, to continue my earlier analogy, we don't prattle on about our love; we focus on the one we love. We don't say, "You know, I am a great lover of someone. I am so perceptive and caring and have found a worthy object of my affection." No! We say, "My life has been commandeered by another. A wonderful person has come into my life and changed everything."

Furthermore, when we love someone we would never say, "I'm in love with someone because I get great things out of the relationship. Whatever I ask, she will do for me. I can use her to get anything I want." That's not love! Love that loves someone in order to get something out of that person isn't love by anyone's standards.

And yet, sad to say, that's how we are sometimes guilty of thinking about the Christian faith. Are you anxious? Are you in need of reassurance and comfort? Then come to Jesus; he'll fix that.

In today's Gospel we have a strange story, even for a strange Gospel like the Gospel of John. Jesus makes some wild assertions about eating his flesh and drinking his blood. He disciples are clearly baffled by his words. Some of his disciples even desert him after hearing these weird words. Jesus asks his remaining disciples, "Do you also want to leave?"

They respond, "Lord, where would we go? You have the words of eternal life."

Maybe the point is a lack of understanding. Maybe the point is not that we always hear what we want to hear. Maybe the point is Jesus.

Sometimes when we come to church on a Sunday we get new insights or fascinating ideas. Sometimes we come here anxious and perplexed and leave comforted and at peace. But our understanding and our peace and reassurance are not the point. The main thing we get is the presence of God in Jesus Christ, and that is point enough for being here.

It's not about us. It's about God in Jesus Christ coming to us as he is, rather than how we might like him to be, speaking to us words we need to hear rather than words we might want to hear.

Ah, what a gift, what a strange and wonderful gift, to be given by this faith—the ability to love someone other than ourselves, the wonder of having our life caught up in some grand project greater than ourselves—for a few glorious moments on a Sunday morning, standing outside ourselves.

Lord, you really do have the words of life. Amen.

Relating the text

The modern novel has devoted itself to the exploration and mapping of our consciousness. Most novels are a peek inside someone's brain.

Scripture, unlike the modern novel, is noted for its "lack of interiority." Numerous events are reported, but we're rarely told what's going on inside the participants' minds. For instance, take Jesus's call of his disciples in Mark: no interiority, no interest about what was going on inside of them or what quandaries they may have been facing. All of the interest in the story of the call of the disciples is in what is going on outside. There is nothing in the disciples as interesting as what is going on outside of the disciples. Nor do the Gospels ever give us a privileged peek inside the brain of Jesus. There is nothing as interesting in the inner life of Jesus as his movement in the world. The Gospels tell us what Jesus does; rarely do they describe what he's thinking or feeling.

But in the modern world it's all about us, all about our thoughts and feelings.

I might also note how the Jesus Seminar of a few years ago, in its attempt to recover and reconstruct the "historical Jesus," was preoccupied with Jesus's own self-awareness. Was Jesus aware that he was the Messiah or not?

This strikes me as a peculiarly modern infatuation. What difference does it make? Are you fully aware of who you are and the significance of what you are doing? Must you wait to do anything until you are completely aware of who you are and what you are doing?

Most of us learn to get over such purely internal questions and go ahead and live into the world.

William James can justly be called the Father of American Philosophy. His philosophy of Pragmatism is as American as apple pie. James famously said that it is rather futile to debate the truth or falsity of religious assertions. The main thing, in regard to the validity of a religious belief, is in its "cash value." That is, what is the work that a religious belief actually does in a believer's life?

Note what has happened here. James has skillfully moved us away from the question, "Is this actually true?" to the pragmatic, utilitarian question, "What good does this do me?"

Like I said, Jamesean Pragmatism is as American as apple pie.

Theologian Karl Barth often spoke about theology as a "scientific endeavor" in which everything is keyed and focused upon the object of scrutiny. Scientific thinking, said Barth, is that manner of thought that is exclusively focused upon the object of scrutiny. Everything is determined by the object. Our interpretation of scripture is "scientific" in that it is focused on and receives its form and modulation from its object. It's not about us; it's about the one who is the bread of life. It is a great gift to have one's life swept up in a meaning and a mission greater than oneself. It is a great gift to give us modern, Western people the means to have something more significant to think about, something more important to live for, than ourselves.

Sunday between August 28 and September 3 inclusive

[Proper 17, Ordinary/Lectionary 22]

Song of Songs 2:8-13

Psalm 45:1-2, 6-9

James 1:17-27

Mark 7:1-8, 14-15, 21-23

Work Righteousness

Selected reading

James 1:17-27

Theme

Christians are called to be "doers of the word." Active engagement, righteous work, and godly activity are all part of the Christian life. And yet, there is a difference between our vocation to be a disciple and the work that we do in order to make a living. Christians see work as a gift of God, a sharing in God's creativity. Yet we also know that it is sinful to make of our work an idol, to fail to keep work in its place in our lives.

Introduction to the readings

Song of Songs 2:8-13

"Rise up, my dearest, my fairest, and go," sings the love to her beloved in the Hebrew love poem, the Song of Songs.

James 1:17-27

"You must be doers of the word and not only hearers," says the letter of James, an early Christian exhortation to embody our faith with our lives, to not only believe in Christ, but also to work in his behalf.

Mark 7:1-8, 14-15, 21-23

The disciples of Jesus are criticized for not following the biblical laws of purity. Jesus defends his followers and warns his critics about confusing the commandments of God with mere human traditions.

Prayer

Creative God, who fashioned the world and all of its inhabitants, who flung the stars into the heavens and set the planets in their courses, we give you praise, that you have deemed to give us creative work to do in your world. We thank you, that you left enough work to be done that we can contribute to your creation with the work of our hands, hearts, and minds. Give us the strength to do the work that is set before us. Give us good work to do all the days of our lives. And help us, when our work is done, to be able to enjoy your promised rest, to lay down the tools of our labor and rest secure in your love rather than in our achievements. Amen.

Encountering the text

Our congregations have little exposure to the letter of James. Luther was put off by James's repeated insistence upon the need for good works done by Christians. He thought that James undercut what was for Luther the great doctrine of the faith—justification to God by faith in Jesus's work for us rather than in our good works for God.

James stresses that our faith in Jesus must issue forth in good works. He criticizes those who only hear the word but fail to do the word. Therefore, James has a great deal to say, including this Sunday's selection, James 1:17-27, about the need to be busy embodying our faith in the world.

We ought to note that this Sunday's selection opens with the assertion that "every good gift, every perfect gift, comes from above." Even our good works are gifts of God, signs of God's remarkable grace that enables even sinners like us to do good in the world.

This bifocal emphasis—God's gracious gifts and our responsive good work—will inform our proclamation for this Sunday. While James is an affirmation of the need, even the joy of our work, there is also a critique of our work within the Christian tradition. We are to respond to God's gracious work among us in Christ. We are not the sole workers in the world. There are limits to our work.

Work is a problem for us. There is much data to suggest that many of us have done a poor job of keeping our work in its proper place. We need to think about our work in light of the bifocal emphasis of the gospel. We will let the letter of James serve as a catalyst for reflection upon the significant role of work in our lives.

Proclaiming the text

A group of us pastors were discussing the plight of the American family. Most of us pastors expend most of our pastoral care time in care of people in marriage and family and their troubles. What were the causes of our current family life problems? Some mentioned the problem of affluence—some people have more money than they know what to do with. Some mentioned the sexual revolution, violence, and sex in the media. Then one of the pastors said, "I think the major problem in my congregation is that too many of my people are working too hard and too much. Mom and Dad virtually abandon the family in order to work for all the stuff that people think they need. Teenagers neglect their studies with after-school and weekend jobs. Overwork has become our biggest sin."

Do you agree with his assessment? There is an increasing body of research that indicates that many American workers are stretched to the breaking point. Things have changed in the workplace. Beginning in the late 1940s, Americans have worked increasing hours each decade. By the 1990s, the average American worked a month longer per year than in the 1970s. You are probably not surprised that employed parents with children at home have the highest hours—eighty-five to eighty-seven hours for mothers and sixty-six to seventy-fix for fathers. With all these increased working hours, no wonder that America has more than doubled productivity and consumption since the 1940s.

If we are all working longer, where did these additional hours come from? We have no means of increasing the number of hours in a day. If we are going to work more, we must find those extra hours somewhere. Saturdays are a first casualty. Americans have 40 percent less free time than in the 1970s. We are even robbing ourselves of sleep. Average Americans get sixty to ninety minutes less sleep per night than we ought.

Many worry that we are eating too much in calories, but we are afflicted with less time to enjoy our food. The average work lunch "hour" is now down to thirty-seven minutes. Many of us lament the sad state of our nation's marriages and families. I believe that we need not look far to find some of the reasons for our distress. The family dinner hour is no longer sacred. Twelve percent of working parents sit down for a meal with their children once a week or less. Working parents average just over three hours with their kids on workdays.

With globalization, jobs go to where labor is cheap. American businesses trim costs to compete by cutting wages and jobs. Competition is fierce for the jobs that we have. I know a man who works in an office in which half of the workers have been laid off in the last year. Do you think that he can afford to be the first to leave at five in the afternoon?

Many of the jobs that are being created in the "new economy" pay less than our old jobs, and many are part-time with no benefits.

Behind these statistics are real people—people in our community, people who sit next to you in the pews on Sunday. Sometimes the person who is being worked to death is you.

And I, as your pastor, may also be part of the troubling numbers. One study found that 70 percent of clergy worked more than sixty hours each week and 85 percent were at home two or fewer evenings each week.

But this is church, for most of us (except for me!), our day off from work. Let's think about our work from a Christian point of view. What does the Christian faith have to say to us in our worries with work?

At the beginning of the story, in Genesis, God works in creating the world. Then God gives humans the joy of creative work. God, seeing that "there was still no human being to farm the fertile land" (Gen 2:5), created Adam to "farm it and to take care of it" (Gen 2:15). In many places in the Bible, work is seen as a source of great happiness (Prov 28:19).

And yet the Bible also knows that work is a dubious gift. Adam and Eve are punished by having to work the earth when they disobey God in Eden. After the fall, God tells Adam, "cursed is the fertile land because of you; in pain you will eat from it every day of your life" (Gen 3:17).

The writer of Ecclesiastes says that "there's nothing better for human beings than to . . . experience pleasure in their hard work" (Eccl 2:24), yet later Ecclesiastes also admits that our ceaseless striving and labor is pointless.

Many Christians have been urged to speak of their work as their "calling." But in scripture, your call is primarily the call to be a disciple, a follower of Jesus. Work is what you have to do to eat, and money earned from work enables you to give to those who have nothing. But work is not glorified as our only purpose in life.

In other words, our faith has been ambivalent about work. Work is at once a gift of God, a sharing in divine creativity; and at the same time it can be a curse, a toilsome degradation.

Many people in our time have lost any sense of work being a gift of God—activity that is to be done in the service of and for the glorification of God—and think of work as merely the means whereby we obtain wealth and status for ourselves. Perhaps we are now seeing the sad results of our perversion of the gift of work, our making of work into an idol to be worked for and sacrificed for at the expense of health, family, and soul.

What's needed is a twofold focus on work. Our work is a good gift of God, God's gracious gift to us that enables us to contribute to the world, to have a share in making the world more like God intends it to be. God hasn't done everything in the world but graciously leaves something for us to do.

However, work can be drudgery. Many contemporary jobs are boring and meaningless. The main value of our work is not service of God but rather simply putting food on the table. Work must not be allowed to take over our lives. We are called by God not to be computer programmers, maids, janitors, and school teachers, but to be disciples. Our discipleship is our primary "vocation," our jobs are what we do to make a living, and our discipleship is what we do to make a life.

It's time for each of us to prayerfully examine how we spend our time and what our schedules say about our priorities. Some of us may need to make some major decisions; some of us may simply need to do a better job of getting our lives in better order in regard to our work.

All of us need to be reminded that our lives, our families, and our work are all gifts of God. We don't have to ceaselessly, relentlessly work. There is nothing we can do to earn a right relationship with God. Our lives are finally not the result of what we do or do not do, but rather the gracious result of what God has done for us in Jesus Christ. We don't have to earn God's love, because that love has already been graciously given to us. We do not have to work hard to make our lives count for something, because, in Jesus Christ, God has already given us eternal life in Christ. Amen.

Relating the text

As a pastor, I listen to those who work. I've noted some common themes:

1. Most of us spend most of our time interacting with other people at work. Therefore, the work environment is a large determinant of our emotional and spiritual well-being.

2. Many people love their work but rarely for the money. For many, work is a challenge to be met, a game to be played, a possibility to be fulfilled.

3. Because much of our own work requires much interaction with other people, people with few "people skills" have a miserable time at work.

4. Much work is repetitive, boring, and dull; therefore, for many, work is a mere means to an end. They work only to get away from work and engage in their hobby, leisure activities, or family life, where their real gifts are exercised.

"The return from your work must be the satisfaction that work brings you and the world's need of that work. With this, life is heaven, or as near heaven as you can get. Without this—with work which you despise, which bores you, and which the world does not need—this life is hell."

—W. E. B. DuBois (1868–1963)

"Real success in business is to be found in achievements comparable with those of the artist or the scientist, of the inventor or the statesman. And the joys sought in the profession of business must be like their joys and not the vulgar satisfaction which is experienced in the acquisition of money, in the exercise of power, or in the frivolous pleasure of mere winning."

—Justice Louis Brandeis (1856–1941)

"The major institutions now optimize the output of large tools for lifeless people. The inversion implies institutions that would foster the use of individually accessible tools to support the meaningful and responsible deeds of fully awake people. Turning basic institutions upside down and inside out is what the adoption of a convivial mode of production would require. Such an inversion of society is beyond the managers of present institutions."

—Ivan Illich, *Tools for Conviviality* (Berkeley: Heyday Books, 1973), 116

"With the collapse of the medieval structure, and the beginning of the modern mode of production, the meaning and function of work changed fundamentally, especially in the Protestant countries. Man, being afraid of his newly won freedom, was obsessed by the need to subdue his doubts and fears by developing a feverish activity. The outcome of this activity, success or failure, decided his salvation, indicating whether he was among the saved or the lost souls. Work, instead of being an activity satisfying in itself and pleasurable, became a duty and an obsession."

—Erich Fromm, *The Sane Society* (New York: Henry Holt, 1955), 179

"But work is also capable of creating the dark night—when, for example, our work contributes to the devastation of the planet, to the despair of the young, to hoarding when we ought to be sharing, to control and power games instead of celebrating, to putting people down instead of lifting them up, to injustice instead of justice."

—Matthew Fox, *The Reinvention of Work* (New York: HarperCollins Publishers, 1995)

Sunday between September 4 and September 10 inclusive
[Proper 18, Ordinary/Lectionary 23]

Proverbs 22:1-2, 8-9, 22-23

Psalm 125

James 2:1-10, (11-13), 14-17

Mark 7:24-37

Expect a Miracle

Selected reading

Mark 7:24-37

Theme

The good news of Jesus Christ is good news for the desperate. Jesus reached out to those living in desperation who were outsiders. He showed us God's compassionate love of those in need. We who are in the household of faith—the church—need to be reminded from time to time of the powerful, expansive, miraculous love of God in Christ.

Introduction to the readings

Proverbs 22:1-2, 8-9, 22-23

God is maker of both the rich and the poor. It is the duty of the powerful to share with the powerless.

James 2:1-10, (11-13), 14-17
Do not show partiality to the rich. And faith without works is dead.

Mark 7:24-37
Jesus heals the daughter of a Syrophoenician woman and then heals a deaf man with a speech impediment.

Prayer

Lord Jesus, give us the honesty to admit our need. Make us bold to reach out for help when we are down and desperate. And then instill in us a boldness to believe that your love is sufficient for our need and your grace reaches out to us in our desperation.

Help us also, in our times of comparative comfort and contentment, to notice and to embrace others whose needs may be greater and whose desperation may be deeper than ours. Preserve us from drawing boundaries and limits to your love. Stir up in us and in our church a willingness to reach out to those on the margins, the defeated and the desperate, showing them in word and in deed that your love is more than enough; your love is a miraculous sign of God with us. Amen.

Encountering the text

Our Gospel contains two stories, verses 24-30 and 31-37, both of which occur in Gentile territory. We are clearly beyond the confines of Israel, and here, out on the margins, Jesus is encountered by a woman and her sick daughter. The woman is a Gentile, of Syrophoenician origin.

We have here also an exorcism, a miracle story. Jesus simply announces a cure for the daughter and the daughter is cured. The response of the crowd is amazement—Jesus performed not only a healing wonder but also a miracle for a Gentile woman.

Though Jesus affirms the primacy of his mission to Israel, the woman in her persistence is a kind of model outsider, a person from the margins who pushes in and is blessed by Jesus for her persistence.

The story is probably meant as a justification for the early church's astounding mission to the Gentiles. The effort beyond the boundaries of Israel is based in the ministry of Jesus himself. As such, it reminds us to be attentive to these persistent people in pain who, in desperation, push in and are blessed by Jesus. That's the way we will interpret this Gospel story in our proclamation this Sunday.

Proclaiming the text

Years ago there was this television evangelist, a "faith healer," who had a popular television show. On the show there was music and then a short sermon, but the focus of the show was on his "expect a miracle time." During this point in the show, people would file down to the front, hobbling on crutches, dragging their oxygen tanks along behind them, or being pushed in wheelchairs. As the choir sang, the evangelist would reach out to each one of these people in turn, pressing on their forehead, shouting things like, "Come out of her, demon!" or "In the name of Christ I command you to be healed!"

On the whole, this seemed more entertainment than worship. It was manipulative and theologically questionable. Is this really the gospel? Demand that you be healed and you will be healed? I hated to see this show-biz faith healer playing on the ignorance of simple people.

A friend of mine started a new service on Saturday evenings at his church. He called it the "Seekers Service." They don't sing any hymns, and there is only a snippet of scripture read during the service, if any. He never preaches a "sermon" but rather has "thoughts for the day." I went to one of these services to see what he was about. It all seemed strange to me. And yet, to my surprise, there were a good many people at the service. I kept wondering, *Are the people here really seeking Jesus Christ? Is this just "Christianity-lite," in which Jesus is presented as the solution to every problem and the cure for every ache and pain?*

At the conclusion of the service, after the simple "thoughts for the day," I engaged a woman in conversation over a cup of coffee. When I asked her why she came to Seekers Service she said to me, "I think this church maybe saved my life. I had been turned off by the church earlier in my life. And then my life got so out of control. I was desperate. I was going down for the third time. I needed help in the worst possible way, so I came here."

I confess that I was somewhat ambivalent about what she told me. I am glad that she found the help that she needed at this service. It is wonderful to see the church reaching out to people's needs. But ought needy people define the content of our faith? She said that she was "desperate," that she was willing to try anything, even the church. That's okay, but should this woman, in her desperate, try-anything approach, set the tone for who we are as a church?

I remember some of the older members of my church who had served in World War II telling me that in war, "there are no atheists in foxholes." They meant to pay tribute to the vibrancy of faith in God during the tough time of war. When the chips are down and we are utterly desperate, when the bullets are flying, then nearly everybody believes in God. There are no atheists in foxholes!

Is this foxhole believing, as I called it, really a credit to God? After all, who wouldn't turn to God when the bullets are flying and you realize that you are terribly vulnerable? It seems to me a much greater compliment to belief in God to say that there are "no atheists by the pool at the country club" or "there are no atheists who are presidents of banks." That is, in times of prosperity and contentment, rather than in times of desperation and need, people find a way to love God.

And yet, there's today's Gospel. A person in deep despair reaches out to Jesus, asking for nothing less than a miracle. And Jesus responds with a healing wonder. Though I may have some misgivings about foxhole believing and desperation, try-anything-even-Jesus faith, today's Gospel indicates that there just seems to be something about Jesus that had a way of attracting desperate people. And Jesus had a way of loving desperate people.

Take this morning's Gospel. Most of the time, in the Gospels, Jesus has to go out to the people. He did not set up office hours, did not hunker down in a church and wait for people to come to him. No, he moved out on a journey, intruded, reached out to people where they were. Perhaps that's why we find him out here in Gentile, pagan territory.

But in today's Gospel we see a different dimension to Jesus's ministry: people actually come to Jesus. Here is this woman who comes to Jesus in desperation. She doesn't just show up at one of Jesus's sermons; she pushes in to Jesus. Jesus is exhausted from his work of ministry. Jesus is trying to get away for some badly needed rest and rejuvenation. But this pushy woman comes to him and demands healing for her desperately ill daughter.

Many times in his ministry, particularly in the Gospel of Mark, Jesus has difficulty getting people to listen to him, to follow him down his narrow way. But not here. This woman pushes into the house where Jesus is staying and demands to be part of what Jesus has.

Of course she is desperate. Her daughter is ill. As a pastor I have watched parents, when their children are ill, drop everything, stay home from work, sit up all night in prayer and anguish, camp out at the hospital and refuse to leave. This woman is like that. She is the very picture of desperation.

But is that any great compliment to Jesus? She has probably been to every doctor she can afford. She is introduced to us as a Syrophoenician, which is a Gentile, a pagan. If she is a pagan, perhaps she has bent the knee at a dozen different altars, beseeching all of the pagan gods for healing. Healing was a major function of nearly all the prominent pagan gods. All of that having failed, at last she comes to Jesus. Is that anything to celebrate?

This woman, being a pagan, probably knows very little of Jesus's teaching. She is ignorant of his mission and his program. Is it fair of her to ask so much of Jesus when she has not yet given anything to Jesus? Is it right of her to demand a wonder from a preacher whom she has probably never even heard preach?

I think today's Gospel says a great many people come to Jesus just that way. And that's okay.

At first, Jesus appears to brush this woman off. After all, he has a mission to redeem the "lost sheep of the house of Israel." He's got enough work to do among his own people. She is a Gentile. He has not come primarily to proclaim good news to her; he is preaching good news for Israel. It would take months of careful teaching just to bring her up to the level of the average Jewish child in Sabbath school in her knowledge of the faith of Israel. She's an outsider, utterly innocent of the faith of Israel. He is exhausted. How can he possibly summon up strength to deal with her?

And yet, before the story is over, he receives her. Though there are many good reasons for turning her away, he doesn't. Her need is desperate and so is the love of Jesus. This woman needs a miracle in the worst sort of way. And that is what she gets. Jesus miraculously reaches out beyond all the perfectly good reasons for why he need not reach out and heals her little girl. This woman in her desperation expected a miracle, and in love Jesus gave her a miracle.

There is something to be said for people who know that their situation is desperate, that their needs are not minor. When it comes to thinking about Jesus, there is something to be said for anybody who throws caution to the wind, who doesn't mind the possibility of rejection or failure, who pushes in and demands of God that God be all that God can be. Expect a miracle!

And there is even more to be said for a savior who is willing to save the desperate. I am not saying that this woman received a healing miracle because of what she believed or what she did; a miracle is by definition an unwarranted, gracious, undeserved gift of God. I'm saying that the God we meet in Jesus Christ had compassion for the desperate, even when their desperation was out beyond the boundaries of the faith community.

Most of you in the congregation this morning have been associated with the church for a long time. You have been a Christian ever since you can remember. Furthermore, you are reasonably well fed, well clothed, and well-off. You did not come here starving, thirsty, and desperate.

But there may be—even in this polite, dignified gathering of God's people— some of you here this morning who are desperate. Some of you here need a miracle in the worst sort of way. You are desperate. And that is a fine way to meet Jesus.

And your presence here reminds us that Jesus is perfectly capable of greeting those who are in extremis, people at the end of their rope. That can be a great place to encounter Jesus.

I'm sure that the good, Torah-believing, Jewish faithful grumbled as they watched Jesus, a fellow Jew, reach out in compassion to this Gentile pagan, this ignorant-of-the-faith outsider. I say that because I feel some grumbling in my heart whenever I see Jesus reach outside the bounds of my church and do some wonder for someone who isn't a member of our faith community.

But part of me is also bothered by a church that seems to do best with people who are not too troubled, not too needy, not too distressed, that is, people like most of us here this morning.

So here's a question: can we love Jesus enough to love it when he reaches out to those on the margins, desperate people who sometime makes us less-than-desperate people uncomfortable? From this story of the Gentile woman and her daughter, as well as from my own experience in the church, from what I've seen of the love of Jesus, I would say that part of the fun of being a Christian is to watch Jesus work even among those who are not Christian.

It is fun to watch Jesus reach out to the desperate with a divine, desperate love that challenges our boundaries and makes us glad that Jesus, in love, has reached out to each of us.

Relating the text

What will we pastors say to people who come to us for counseling when they feel let down by those they love? We often hear laments like this: "No matter what I do, my daughter [or mother or brother or friend] seems to let me down. Should I continue to let myself in for such pain?" What else can we say? Love does not count the wrongs. Loving others is always a risk. But, to be in relationship is to forgive.

We are living in a time in which there have been some major changes in the way we think about the church of Christ. Traditional thinking about the church in the past century tended to see the identity and function of the church primarily in terms of teaching, worship, pastoral care, and social engagement. The church in North America was here to help America be a better country, occasionally providing some assistance and some advice to those who ran the country. Some have characterized this view of the church as the idea that the church was a "chaplain" to a specific nation, community, or interest group.

Now and then you see a newspaper story about some church that is running a soup kitchen or a program for the elderly. The story sometimes seems to have as a subtext, "See? The church is relevant after all! Look what it's doing to help our community."

This chaplaincy view was gradually displaced by an understanding that emphasized the importance of outreach to the world, the church as mission. The church doesn't have a mission to reach out to the world occasionally; the church is a mission, God's mission to the world. It is noteworthy that this was stressed by theologians such as Stephen Neill (1900–1984) and Lesslie Newbigin (1909–1998), both of whom served as bishops in India. Faced with new realities in the world, the challenge for the church was to provide a witness in a non-Christian culture. Neill and Newbigin were concerned that the church recover the vital sense of being the means whereby God moves into the world to retake the world for God's kingdom.

The "chaplaincy" models of church have impoverished our understanding of the critical impact of mission on Christian theology and theology on Christian mission. Today's Gospel shows Christ reaching out, a sign of God's kingdom-building in a desperate, hurting world.

As a child, I loved cowboy movies. Cowboys were rough and tough characters who were willing to use a gun to set things right. But in many cowboy movies there came that touching scene when the cowboy's girlfriend got sick, or maybe she was shot by a bad guy, something bad like that.

And then the cowboy would walk out from town, stand alone on the hillside, take his big cowboy hat off, bow his head, and in the moonlight mutter something like, "Lord, this is Joe. I will admit I haven't lived the life I should have lived. I'll admit that I haven't done like I ought to have done, but now I have just this one thing to ask of you. Please, Lord, not for me, but for her, make her well. I'm begging, Lord. Sincerely, Joe."

It was very touching to see this strong, self-confident cowboy down on his knees, desperately pleading to God for something the cowboy didn't know how to fix. And yet is this the way one ought to come to God? Is it good for people to wait until they are at the end of their rope before they pray? Is it right for them to crawl before God in desperation, after having neglected God most of their lives, hoping for a last-minute reprieve?

I think today's Gospel from Mark indicates that sometimes people do just that.

I've got a friend, a pastor, who volunteers a day a week at a jail for youthful offenders, spending his day with young car thieves, drug dealers, and worse. When I asked him why he, a busy pastor, had found it necessary to expand his ministry into the jail, he said, "I do it for selfishness. I got so sick and tired of running errands for people who weren't desperate. The gospel wilts when it never applies to people who are desperate."

Sunday between September 11 and September 17 inclusive

[Proper 19, Ordinary/Lectionary 24]

Proverbs 1:20-33 or Isaiah 50:4-9a

Psalm 19 or Wisdom of Solomon 7:26–8:1 or Psalm 116:1-9

James 3:1-12

Mark 8:27-38

The Journey

Selected reading

Mark 8:27-38

Theme

As Christians, we are those who are called to be on a journey with Jesus, a journey called discipleship. We do not always know where the journey will lead, but we know who leads the way. We do not always know everything about Jesus when we begin the journey, but we know that who he is will be revealed along the way.

Introduction to the readings

Proverbs 1:20-33

This section of Proverbs praises the attributes of Lady Wisdom.

James 3:1-12

The epistle of James speaks of the destructive capacity of human speech and language.

Mark 8:27-38

Jesus journeys with his disciples, stopping just long enough to ask them, "Who do people say that I am?"

Prayer

Lord, you have called us to walk this way of faith with you. You spoke to us, reached out to us, and we followed.

Sometimes the journey is difficult. Sometimes our walk with you is great joy. Your journey led you to a cross. We wonder if our journey with you might lead to a cross as well.

Walk with us, Lord; stay with us as evening approaches. Be for us bread for the journey, water in the wilderness. Be patient with our weakness to walk as you would have us to walk. Do not walk so far ahead of us that we lose sight of you.

Walk with us, Lord. Amen.

Encountering the text

Mark created the Gospel form as a way of communicating the truth of Jesus. Isn't it interesting that Mark used the image of a journey as a way of organizing the story of Jesus? In Mark, and in the other Synoptic Gospels, when Jesus invites people to come and follow him, he invites them to a journey.

Today's Gospel is a moment along the way of the journey with Jesus. Jesus pauses to ask his disciples, "Who do people say that I am?"

It is a test. As usual in Mark's Gospel, the disciples flunk. Peter confesses that Jesus is the long-awaited Messiah, the anointed one of Israel. Strangely, when Peter protests Jesus's prediction of his suffering and death (strange because who would expect a Messiah to suffer?), Jesus rebukes Peter in the harshest of terms, calling him "Satan."

Let us interpret this episode as an example—and there are certainly many others in Mark's Gospel—of the way in which Jesus's identity gradually unfolds for the disciples. The disciples in Mark must learn, in their everyday experience of Jesus, by listening to his words and observing his actions, who Jesus is. Alas, in this Gospel, the disciples don't seem to learn much! They are forever giving the wrong answer, as Peter does here. They seem unbelievably thick-headed and hard-hearted.

We contemporary disciples might take heart from Mark's rather unflattering depiction of the first disciples. After all, we struggle to get the point of Jesus, and sometimes we don't. We are on a lifetime journey with Jesus, in which his meaning for us unfolds gradually as we journey.

There are those who think, when they "accepted Christ" or were "saved" or "decided to become a Christian," that that was the end of their journey with Jesus, the goal. No. That journey begins with our decision to walk with him, but that is *just* the beginning, not the end of the story of discipleship.

Faithfulness to Jesus requires a willingness to learn, an expectation that there will be twists and turns along the way, surprises. It was so for his first disciples. It will be so for us.

In preparing to preach on the theme of journeying with Jesus, it might be helpful for you to recall particularly demanding and difficult journeys you have experienced. Have you had journeys that were a surprise and a delight? What are some of the factors that keep us going when a journey gets tough?

The image of discipleship as a journey is rich and varied. Let us use that richness and variety to strengthen contemporary disciples on their walk with Christ.

Proclaiming the text

Have you noticed? The primary way of telling the story of Jesus is as a journey. You can see this in all of the Gospels, particularly Matthew, Mark, and Luke, but especially in Mark. Jesus is always on the way to somewhere else. Mark tells the story of Jesus with a breathless tempo. Mark says that Jesus did that and then immediately (*immediately* is one of Mark's favorite words) Jesus went on to somewhere else.

The image you get of Jesus's followers, his disciples, in a Gospel like Mark's is a group of people who are always breathlessly trying to catch up, who are always just one step behind Jesus as he moves on to somewhere else.

I love the way Mark begins his Gospel with the calling of Jesus's disciples. A couple of the disciples were at work one day, bent over their nets, working on them. (Tony Campolo says that the disciples seemed to be the worst fishermen in the world—they were always mending their nets!)

At any rate, while they were working, they saw this strange figure up on the road above them, calling to them, "'Come, follow me,' he said, 'and I'll show you how to fish for people'" (Mark 1:17).

Mark says they stopped everything they were doing, left their father, and went trudging right after Jesus. One would think they might have asked, "Well, who are you?" Or one would at least think they would say, "Fine. But where are you going?"

They asked none of that. They just stumbled after Jesus. Maybe that's exactly the way it happened. In fact, in Mark's Gospel, that is the image you get of discipleship. Discipleship is following Jesus on a journey without ever knowing exactly who he is or precisely where he is going.

I love another episode in Mark, when the disciples are not mending their nets but are in a boat on the sea. A storm comes in, the sea gets ugly, and it appears that the boat is going to be swamped and everyone will drown.

Lo and behold, who should they see out on the sea at that point but Jesus. Mark says that Jesus was out walking past the disciples. He isn't coming out there to pull them out of the boat; he's just out for a stroll. Walking past them!

Jesus is always on the move.

Then, when you get to the very end of Mark, Mark says that the women came to the tomb on Easter morning. But by the time they get there, they are greeted by a "young man in white" who tells them, "You're looking for Jesus? Sorry. Just missed him. By this time in the morning, he is already all the way out in Galilee! Go!"

Isn't that typical of Jesus? Just about the time we are about to get the point, almost ready to catch up with him, he is on the way somewhere else!

It is a journey that is an adventure. In fact, one of the things that makes a journey an adventure is when we don't know the destination. We have a word for it, coming from the name of a ship (*The Serendip*) in a story about a group of adventurers. The word is *serendipity*. It means making a surprising discovery while on a journey somewhere else. And if you have been journeying with Jesus very long, you know that it is quite typical to keep making surprising discoveries with Jesus, even when you are on the way somewhere else. I think that is the main reason why this Gospel ends the way it does. Mark ends his Gospel with the women at the tomb who are in shock that Jesus is not there. He is going before them to Galilee. That sums up the entire experience with Jesus. Just when they get there, he has already moved on to somewhere else.

Helpful later commentators added a number of verses to the ending of Mark, but they are not in the earliest copies of this Gospel. The thing just ends, with the women standing there stupefied and amazed and Jesus moved on to somewhere else.

I think this is Mark's way of saying that, because of Easter, this journey is not over; in fact, it is never over until God says that it is over. We certainly thought that Good Friday and the cross led to the end of the story, that death had had the final word. But no, we get to the cemetery and find out that Jesus is not there. He has moved on. The journey continues.

So if you are thinking about faithful discipleship, don't think about getting your head straight on a list of fundamental beliefs. Don't think about discipleship as memorizing a whole string of Bible verses. Think about discipleship as a journey, a journey with Jesus.

This is the story that each of us is finishing for ourselves. Each of us is busy tagging along behind Jesus, being surprised by Jesus, trying to figure out what he said at the last stop. Being amazed at the places that he leads us on this adventure.

I have a few specific things to say about the nature of the journey, as I have observed them:

1. The journey with Jesus is not only an adventure but also a relationship. You are not following a set of laws, not trudging along behind a set of beliefs. You are walking with Jesus. Christianity is not so much a set of intellectual propositions that you must affirm. Rather, it is a relationship with someone else.

And you don't always know what turns that relationship may take.

In fact, I think of the analogy of a marriage.

When I marry people as a pastor, I try to do premarital counseling. What do we do in premarital counseling? Some people think that the purpose is to sit down and to talk to the couple about "what they're getting into."

But how do I know what they are getting into?

Those of you who are married, when you got married, did you know what you were getting into? Of course not. Who can know where life will lead us and how people will change? The main thing is, we commit ourselves to being on a journey with another human being, no matter where that journey leads, even through things like "sickness or health, for better for worse," and so forth.

The church has you make these promises precisely because you do not know where the journey will lead. If you did know every step of the way, you wouldn't need the promise to stay with the journey, even through sickness, worse times, poverty, and all the other vicissitudes of life.

2. A journey implies movement from here to there. Therefore, in characterizing discipleship as a journey, we are saying that it is a long process. Get ready for growth. Get ready for surprise.

My theory for why the church tends to bolt down pews is that, when you come in here on Sunday morning at 11:00, you never know where you might be located by noon! We bolt down these pews to give the illusion that things are fixed, stable, complete. No, we are on the move for Jesus. He may accept us "just as I am," as we sometimes sing, but he will not leave us just as we are. We are on the move.

3. As with any journey, there are times when we wonder if the journey is working. We have setbacks, long stretches of boredom when the scenery is not that interesting.

If you have ever been on a long trip with a group of people, you know that during the course of the trip you will know those people at their best and at their worst. People get tired. They become difficult to deal with. Because the church is a journey, this means that you will not always enjoy being on a journey with the other people.

Don't feel guilty. On this journey, there will be peaks and there will be valleys. Keep walking.

4. (I hope you are writing this down. It will be on the exam.) The call to discipleship requires certain disciplines for keeping at it. As we have said, the journey, like any journey, is not always easy. Perhaps your journey with Jesus began with a flash of light and great enthusiasm. But eventually, over time, enthusiasm wanes. The exciting journey of faith becomes less exciting.

The church that we enjoyed going to during the first few months becomes dull and routine. However, it is important to keep at it; it is important to keep walking.

You need some disciplines for the journey. I have found that when I am going on any long trip, it is very important to eat right, to get enough sleep, and to structure my life so that I have the energy to keep going.

It is the same way with the journey of discipleship. What are some of the disciplines of the journey? I think of the importance of regular Bible study and the value of beginning each day with some meditation. These can be ways of keeping you focused, of developing the habits you need to keep going.

I think of Sunday worship as a discipline. Just getting out of bed, getting dressed, and coming to church—don't knock it; this is an important discipline.

Some modern people say that they feel God is far from them or absent from their lives. But they don't consider how often they have been absent from God. In just coming to Sunday worship, you are putting yourself in the right place to keep on the journey. Perhaps today, sitting in church, your journey is going well. But your journey will not always go well. There will be valleys and times when you wonder if you can make it. At those times, the resources that you gained here during Sunday morning worship can be invaluable, life-giving.

The book of Acts says that the first name given to Christians was "the Way." That's a good name. To be a disciple means to be someone who is following Jesus along the way.

Pray that God will give us the grace to walk that way well.

Relating the text

"The journey is the reward."

—Taoist saying

Several years ago, we had a representative from the organization Teach for America visit our campus. Teach for America tries to recruit this nation's most talented college graduates to go into some of the nation's worst public schools. This is Teach for America's method of transforming our schools into something better.

One woman stood up in front of a large group of Duke students—a larger group than I would have supposed would come out to this sort of thing—and said to them, "I can tell by looking at you that I have probably come to the wrong place. Somebody told me this was a BMW campus, and I can believe it looking at you. Just looking at you, I can tell that all of you are a success. Why would you all be on this campus if you were not successful, if you were not going on to successful careers on Madison Avenue or Wall Street?

"And yet here I stand, hoping to talk one of you into giving away your life in the toughest job you will ever have. I am looking for people to go into the hollows of West Virginia, into the ghettos of South Los Angeles, and teach in some of the most difficult schools in the world. Last year, two of our teachers were killed while on the job.

"And I can tell, just by looking at you, that none of you are interested in that. So go on to law school or whatever successful thing you are planning on doing. But if by chance, just some of you happen to be interested, I've got these brochures here for you to tell about Teach for America. Meeting's over."

With that, the whole group stood up, pushed into the aisles, pushed each other aside, ran down to the front, and fought over those brochures.

That evening I learned an important insight: People want something more out of life than even happiness. People want to be part of an adventure. People want to be part of a project greater than their lives.

I once heard an old pastor lament the presence of many "stillborn Christians." That is, there are people who have been "born again," as Christians sometimes say; they have taken the first steps of faith, but they never seem to get around to the next steps. They don't seem to grow past their birth.

When we are called to Christ, we are called not only for the gift of justification, that grace of God that makes us right with God, but also to receive the unfolding gift of sanctification, that grace of God that helps us to grow up into Christ.

– 165 –

Sunday between September 18 and September 24 inclusive

[Proper 20, Ordinary/Lectionary 25]

Proverbs 31:10-31 or Jeremiah 11:18-20
or Wisdom of Solomon 1:16–2:1, 12-22

Psalm 1 or Psalm 54

James 3:13–4:3, 7-8a

Mark 9:30-37

Does God Have a Plan for Your Life?

Selected reading
Mark 9:30-37 (related to James 3:13–4:3, 7-8a)

Theme
There are those who assert that "God has a plan for my life." Is that the way God works—devising plans for each of our lives and keeping us always following that plan? The providence of God may be considerably more supple, free, and resourceful than the statement "God has a plan for my life" allows. God is love, and in the loving purposes of God, there may be a sort of "plan" to love us now, so that God might love us for all eternity.

Introduction to the readings
Proverbs 31:10-31
Proverbs extols the valorous woman—the wife and mother who shows great wisdom in all her undertakings.

James 3:13–4:3, 7–8a

James says there are two paths that one can follow in life. One path is the way of worldly wisdom that ultimately leads to death. The other path, that of heavenly wisdom, is humble, merciful, and fruitful.

Mark 9:30-37

In this passage, Jesus instructs the Twelve that he is to be betrayed, killed, and then resurrected on the third day. Then Jesus teaches his ambitious followers about the shape of faithful discipleship by taking a little child in his arms and blessing the child.

Prayer

Lord, show us your way. Enable us to look beyond the challenges, difficulties, and dilemmas of the present moment and take the longer view. Lift our vision up to eternity, so that we might see your purposes being worked out among us.

And then, having seen your way, give us the courage to follow your way, moving in step with your grand purposes for the world. Amen.

Encountering the text

In today's Gospel, Jesus promises his disciples that he will suffer. This is not what his disciples have planned! They are planning on using Jesus as a technique to help each of them achieve greatness. In response, Jesus calls to him a little child and blesses the child.

Children tend not to make plans. Life is so fresh and frightening to them, every day is new and strange. Could this be part of what Jesus means when he says that we must "become as a little child"?

We will use today's Gospel, along with a brief mention of today's epistle from James, as an occasion for a teaching sermon on the notion of "God has a plan for my life." We will attempt to help the congregation think through the notion of a divine plan.

Proclaiming the text

From time to time I've heard people say, "I believe that God has a plan for my life." Perhaps they are talking to me about some difficult decision they have to make. And they want to make that decision against the background of their conviction that God has a plan that intends to work out in their lives. They would like to make their decision on the basis of that plan.

I've had prospective brides or grooms say to me, "I knew that God had a plan for the one I ought to marry. It just took me until I was thirty-eight years old to figure out what the plan was."

I confess that sometimes I wonder that as life in the contemporary world becomes more uncertain, even at times chaotic, as we lose our confidence that we can predict the future and know just what tomorrow will be, maybe people of faith talk more about God having a plan. Perhaps we assert all evidence to the contrary, but despite the seeming chaos, God really does have a plan. We often can't see that plan and can't say for sure, when looking at a given event, that God's plan is being worked out. We nevertheless believe in the plan because we really need to believe that there is a plan.

As somebody said, "If you want to make God laugh, just have a plan." This quip suggests that God is not so much the one who makes and follows plans, as the one who disrupts our plans! As today's reading from the letter of James says, we have our ways, our plans, and our strategies for getting what we want in the world, but those ways, plans, and strategies are quite different from God's.

There are biblical and theological reasons for questioning the widespread notion that "God has a plan for my life."

While I'm not so sure we ought to call it a "plan," I really think that scripture maintains the belief that God's purposes are being worked out among us, in our time and our history. And the Bible frequently shows how our efforts are sometimes improved by or resisted or brought to fruition because of the unseen hand of God moving behind the scenes of the story. Thus, Joseph could say to his brothers, who had tried to kill him and ruin his life, at the end of the story, "You planned something bad for me, but God produced something good from it" (Gen 50:20).

It is a great comfort to know that all of our mess-ups and misdeeds may not be the last word. God has a sort of plan, and ultimately, "we know that God works all things together for good for the ones who love God" (Rom 8:28).

God keeps working God's good plan, despite our human mistakes.

And yet there are moments when God appears not only to disrupt our plans but even to disrupt God's plans. For instance, Jonah is told by God that God is going to destroy the wicked city of Nineveh. That is just fine with Jonah because he hates Nineveh, too. But then, after Jonah preaches a one-sentence, dyspeptic sermon telling Nineveh what God plans to do, the whole city of Nineveh repents. And what does God do? God changes God's previously announced plan.

This sort of thing suggests to me that if we are going to apply the word *plan* to God, we must somehow leave room for God to be God. In stating that God has a plan for our lives or anything else, we have to allow for God's freedom and God's sovereignty. God appears to allow for our freedom and our sovereignty or at least for a degree of it. The people of Nineveh change. And God shows in this case that God is free to change. Furthermore, by the end of the book of Jonah, we find out that Jonah changes, though it takes a bit longer for Jonah to change than for the people of Nineveh to change.

God has somehow created the world, not just to follow a lockstep plan, but with great love, lovingly leaving some room for us to grow and develop and for us to learn from our mistakes, enabling us to change and actually do better than maybe we, or even God, thought we could do. If God has a plan, that plan plans to give us some degree of freedom in responding to God in our own lives.

This is what makes me troubled by some talk about God's plan. Sometimes it is put forward as a sort of deterministic scheme in which God has already predetermined (or, as we sometimes say, predestined) what people will do, so people are like robots who are hardwired to respond to God in certain ways.

First Timothy does not say that God has a plan to save all of us, but rather it says that God wants all of us to turn and fall into the arms of the loving God. The future that God wants for us is a bit more dynamic than is suggested by the word *plan*. God has this grand desire for us, not a point-by-point, step-by-step plan for us. God has created us so that we can from time to time thwart the desires of God. Whether we can forever—no matter what God does—thwart the desire of God is a question for another sermon! But for now let's just say that God is not known for being sternly and irrevocably committed to a plan, because God is known to be a living God who is fully active, seeking love. And the word *desire* seems so much more appropriate to describe God and God's great love for the world than the word *plan*.

"God so loved the world that he gave his only Son, so that everyone who believes in him won't perish but will have eternal life" (John 3:16). Note that John does not say that God has a plan that some may love him and some may not love him. John says that God gave—in a reckless act of love—his only Son, so that God's desire for the whole world might be accomplished.

I am also troubled by some people who think that "God has a plan for my life" in that sometimes it can make them terribly troubled and fearful. Some people seem to imply that, believing that God has a plan for their lives, they must therefore be very careful every step of their lives to be sure that they don't take a step forward until they are 100 percent sure they are taking the exact step that God has put into God's plan for their life.

What happens when they prayerfully consider some plan of action and take it only to wake up and find they have taken the wrong action? We do this all the time. And when we do, the important thing is not to think that we have defeated God's alleged plan but rather to cling to our belief in God's constant ability to redeem our deeds and our lives. As Luther said on one occasion, "God can ride a lame horse or shoot with a crooked bow." God is able to take our mess and constantly, creatively weave it into God's good purposes.

I am saying here that if God has a plan, it will be wonderfully adaptable and flexible according to the larger purposes of God. I remember a man in his mid-sixties, who had spent his life as an accountant, who told me that he was convinced, through events of his life, that God really wanted him to be a preacher, to go to seminary, and to go into the ministry. I immediately felt a great sense of sadness that here was a man who, toward the end of his career, felt that his life decisions had been contrary to God's plan for his life.

"Still" the man said, "as I look back over my life, I am amazed at how well God has used what I have been. If I had gone to seminary and become a preacher, as I think God might have liked for me, I would never have been able to be a lay leader of the church and to make the difference and the contribution that I have made."

I thought this was a beautiful statement of faith. It is not so important for us to love God's plan. The important thing is for us to love God. Loving this God means that we love a God who is alive, active, and infinitely resourceful ultimately in getting what God wants. God didn't give us a plan; God gave us Jesus Christ.

By the way, it seems to me that from scripture what God wants for us is something quite larger and more lasting even than a good marriage, a good job, the right house in the right neighborhood—so many of the things that we wonder about in God's supposed plan for our lives. God's greatest desire, that plan to which God is relentlessly moving us, is simply for God to be with us, now and for all eternity. I am uncomfortable when we cut that grand eternal plan down to a moment-by-moment, mundane, earthbound plan for each and every step that we are to take in our lives. That seems to me an incredible trivialization of the notion of God having a plan.

In my experience, when I have encountered or come to an awareness of God's plan for my life, that plan impresses me as always grander and greater than the plans that I have made for my life. Jesus looks at his disciples and he doesn't say to them, "I want your little light to shine forth before the people with whom you work in your office on Monday morning." Of course, he certainly implies that. But what Jesus says is, "You're the light of the world." That is Jesus's plan for us, which is large, cosmic, and considerably grander than most of our ideas of discipleship.

And yet, there is something that seems very faithful about the statement "God has a plan for my life." For one thing, it implies that the life you are living is not your own. For another thing, it certainly suggests that life is more than simply finding personal fulfillment, a sense of satisfaction, or a sense of meaning that makes sense to you. (Remember today's Gospel and epistle lessons if you think that!) Life is also about obeying God, working with God, having your little life caught up in some larger purpose than your life. And that seems to me very biblical and very faithful. In the larger sense, that is one reason we come to church. You are here this morning on a quest; this is part of the unending discernment process in which Christians engage, in which Christians try to figure out what it is that God wants them to do with the lives that God has given us.

While that may involve some step that you are to take tomorrow morning, I would think that more often it involves a larger framework, some more panoramic vision that somehow God is managing to use your life in good ways, and you are going to do all you can to move in step with the larger purposes of God.

A high school commencement speaker stood at the podium and in his address urged the graduates to have a dream, to follow their dream, and to let no one or nothing deter them from their life's dream. This sort of talk is fine, but it is not particularly Christian. Christians are people who are attempting to live out God's dream, to live their lives in such a way that God may get what God wants.

So I meet with a young woman who tells me that she is in a time of turmoil in her life because, in her words, "I am just trying to find myself and discover who I really am and what I want to do." And that is fine. That is a rather conventional modern project. I am who I discover I am, and whom I decide to be.

But the Christian story keeps telling us that we are who we are, not only through our knowledge and choices, but also through God's plans for us. In this sense, I think that it can be a very faithful thing to believe that—though you may have no idea of the specifics, and though you may not be certain of the next step you are to take in your life journey—"God has a plan for my life."

Which leads me to think that one of the problems with asking, "What has God planned for my life?" is that the question may not be large enough. We ought more frequently to ask, "What might be God's plan for this nation? What might be God's plan for this congregation? What might be God's dream for the whole world?"

Relating the text

A number of years ago, I remember talking to a business person, proudly telling him that my congregation was getting organized and we were working on a long-range plan.

The businessman responded, "In business, long-range planning is dead."

This came as quite a shock to me. I thought it was the church that was unorganized, working without goals, without plans.

"We didn't even know that the Berlin Wall was coming down. Nobody planned for that!" he explained. "Things are moving too fast. The future is too unpredictable. The trouble is if a business goes through all of that effort to come up with a long-range plan, people come to love the plan more than they love results. They just keep following and sticking with the plan, despite the results."

I remember seeing the bumper sticker that proclaimed, "God has a plan for your life. And it is very, very difficult!"

If you can figure out God's plan for your life, then go worship that plan and don't bother with Jesus. Following some plan is easier than following a living, speaking God who is free and sovereign, and greater than any plan we can conceive.

A pastor wrote me to tell me that he appreciated something that I had written, and then he said to me that he had always enjoyed my writing. This pleased me. And then he told me that he had recently been fired from his church. He was now working in a factory and doubted that he would ever be called to another church to preach.

This is what comes from reading what I write!

In my letter back to him I told him to stay away from my writing. But I also told him that I had a certain amount of envy for him. I have always felt somewhat inadequate as a preacher because I have never been fired from any church. From what I know of the gospel, people get into trouble for faithful preaching. I've never gotten into serious trouble, because my sermons were too faithful.

As I read the gospel, it implies that God has a great plan for our lives, and that plan is that one day we should be as vulnerable as a little child, that we should end up on a cross with Jesus.

Sunday between September 25 and October 1 inclusive

[Proper 21, Ordinary/Lectionary 26]

Esther 7:1-6, 9-10; 9:20-22

Psalm 124

James 5:13-20

Mark 9:38-50

Don't Go to Hell

Selected reading

Mark 9:38-50

Theme

Jesus warns us about the perils of treating as refuse that which God has lovingly given and created. Hell, that place of utter separation from the presence of God, is to be avoided. We are not to treat as garbage that which God has created, the ones for whom Christ has died.

Introduction to the readings

Esther 7:1-6, 9-10; 9:20-22

The story of Esther comes to a dramatic conclusion as wicked Haman is punished by the king, and Esther and her people are saved.

James 5:13-20

The epistle of James urges the early church to pray for those who are sick and to care for the unity and concord of the congregation.

Mark 9:38-50

Jesus warns of the need for decisive action in accord with the demands of God's kingdom.

Prayer

Lord Jesus, we pray for those who have wandered or have been cast into situations of bleak despair.

We pray for those who have lost hope.

We pray for those who have encountered so much prejudice and hate that they no longer are able to love.

We pray for those who lie on beds of pain, spend their nights in agony, and have no relief from their suffering.

We pray for those who have stopped believing in themselves, who have lost sight of their God-given gifts.

O great savior of the world, great seeker of the lost, seek and save, we pray, all those who dwell in the land of darkness and despair. Stir in us compassion and concern for those who think that they are beyond hope and help.

Protect and keep each of us from the snares of hell and restore in us a sense of the value and potential of our lives when lived in gratitude for your good gifts and in service to your kingdom. Amen.

Encountering the text

This Sunday's Gospel depicts Jesus speaking of hell. The best known biblical image for hell relates to a deep, narrow gorge southeast of Jerusalem called *gai ben-hinnom*, "the Valley of Ben Hinnom," in which it was said that rebellious and unfaithful Israelites once offered up child sacrifices to the pagan gods Molech and Baal (2 Chron 28:3; 33:6; Jer 7:31-32; 19:2-6). Thus, it was forever condemned by Josiah as an eternally unholy place (2 Kgs 23:10).

Later the valley was used as a garbage dump by the inhabitants of Jerusalem. Thus the Valley of Ben Hinnom became known as the dump, the place of destruction by fire in Jewish tradition. The Greek word *gehenna*, "hell," commonly used in the New Testament for the place of final and eternal punishment, is derived from the Hebrew name for this valley.

This valley was also an image of hell because of its association with the place to deposit the bodies of those slain in battle by God's judgment. Jeremiah prophesied that the valley would be used as a mass grave for the corpses of the people of Judah killed by an invading army (Jer 7:30-34).

Hell is thus a place of rot, of mutilated bodies and revulsion. To this the Old Testament adds the image of burning. Perhaps the burning is related to the idea of purging, of sacrificial fire destroying something that is offensive to God.

In the New Testament, evangelism is defined as to "save some by snatching them from the fire" (Jude 23). Jesus speaks often of "fiery hell" (Matt 5:22). He sees himself as a rescuer from hell. Jesus is never depicted as one who condemns people to hell, but rather as one sent to urge people to avoid hell. His urgings are nowhere more urgent and dramatic than in this Sunday's Gospel.

Hell is a dump, *Gehenna*. Jesus is the one who seeks to save the lost, to rescue from the tragedy that is hell. That is one of the themes presented in this Sunday's Gospel.

Proclaiming the text

Stark, staggeringly bleak alternatives are put before us in today's Gospel. Jesus tells us to make a choice. Choose this day, where you will be. It is better to mutilate yourself, to cut off your arm, to pluck out your eye, and to throw these vital organs away, than to end up in hell. Why does Jesus speak in such a stark manner? Of course, the Bible scholars tell us that Jesus is speaking here in hyperbole—exaggerated overstatements designed to grab our attention. We are told that rabbinic teachers in that day often spoke in this fashion.

Jesus says it is much better to go into God's kingdom mangled, without an eye, without an arm, than to find one's whole body thrown into the fires of hell. A whole, healthy body is a great asset. But Jesus says that here is an asset worth sacrificing if the choice is between God's kingdom and hell.

In our church, we don't talk much about hell. Hell is not one of the more uplifting biblical themes. But here in today's Gospel, Jesus undeniably speaks about hell. He doesn't really call it "hell," but rather he uses the Aramaic name of a place called *Gehenna*. This was an actual place, just outside the walls of Jerusalem. He is not speaking of the place of the Italian poet Dante wrote about in *The Inferno*. He is talking about Gehenna. This is a place in the Hinnon Valley somewhat south of Jerusalem. Centuries before the time of Jesus, it had been a place of pagan idolatry and thus got a bad name. Maybe that is why, by the time of Jesus, Gehenna had become the town dump. Rubbish, bones, and decaying carcasses filled this desolate valley. Thus, Jesus says literally, it would be better to pluck out your eye and go into God's kingdom missing some part of your body than to have your whole body thrown on the rubbish heap of Gehenna.

I can't imagine much rubbish was thrown away in Jesus's day before the days of paper containers, plastic bags, and old tires. If Gehenna was a detestable, rotten-smelling, disgusting place in Jesus's day, I am sure it would pale in comparison with our town dumps. Each American produces something like a ton of rubbish every year. Our town began an earnest program of recycling aluminum cans, plastic, and other recyclable waste a few years ago. I read recently that our recycling program is in jeopardy because we produce so much waste for recycling that we overwhelm the recycling mechanisms. We are getting as large a mountain of recyclable material as nonrecyclable material. We have two great mountains just outside of town.

Years ago, Vance Packard, a social critic, wrote a book called *The Waste Makers*, and that we are. We are the throwaway society, a society that not only produces and consumes but also casts off.

As a teenager, my friends and I would sometimes drive to the town dump. There, when the wind was right, and we could stand the odor, we would wander amid the refuse of our culture. It is amazing what people throw away. We would delight in making some great discovery—a perfectly good bicycle needing only a chain or a stack of vinyl records.

Later, when I had a course in biblical archeology, we wondered what future archeologist would think of our civilization, digging through our piles of rubbish like contemporary archeologists dig through a Near Eastern tell. We learned in archeology that the most important artifact in a biblical archeology site is broken pottery. Pottery enabled the archeologist to date the various strata of a given Near Eastern city's refuse. What will future archeologists, digging through our garbage, think of us?

Perhaps even the thought of visiting a rubbish site repulses you, and perhaps that is why we desperately attempt to keep our piles of rubbish far from view. However, there is something fascinating to me about a garbage dump. Here is the end of the line, where everything finally comes. All of the objects of our affection, our household objects that are used daily, the cast-off old cars, the once-beloved bicycle. Everything ends up here, having lost any shred of dignity or usefulness. Everything ends at the garbage dump.

At the city dump, one may occasionally find something worth salvaging, but not often. Things go to the dump after they have outlived their usefulness to human beings, after they have become so mangled and broken that there is no longer any shred of dignity or beauty left to them.

Thus Jesus says, "Take care. Make your choices wisely. Choose this day where you are headed. It would be better for you to let go of some aspect of your body or soul, than to have both body and soul thrown into the garbage dump of eternity. Your life is precious. Don't let it be discarded on the trash heap of life. God doesn't make any garbage, and God made you."

I was recently in a once-beautiful section of a once-great American city. Old Victorian houses lined the streets. But they had long since passed their beautiful days. Now, with windows out, boarded-up doors, rotting cornices, and trashy yards, the houses that once made up a functioning neighborhood now made up little more than a garbage dump. How can we do this? How can we turn our own neighborhoods into such places? And what of the people who must live amid such ugliness? It was Gehenna all over again.

I remember visiting a church member of mine who was going through great emotional difficulty. She had been committed to our state's hospital for the mentally ill. I found her after walking down foul-smelling corridors, where, from behind doors, there periodically came terrible sounds. She sat in a room with nothing but a steel bed and one chair. When I forced a cheerful, "How are you doing?" she responded, "I have been dumped here for good."

Her expression filled me with utter pity. She had become a piece of refuse. The hospital was located in the eastern part of the capital city. But its address was Gehenna.

And I have been in nursing homes, in wards where the chronically ill were kept, in homes for the severely disabled, and in centers for the chronically addicted. They all have names like, "Northside Care Center" or something like that. But in the light of today's scripture, you could call them Gehenna. They are any hellish place where human beings are discarded, left to rot, treated as little more than refuse.

And Jesus says that no child of God's creation and love is meant for Gehenna. Jesus stares our hellish possibilities in the face and rebukes them. He speaks to us with words that are stark. But let's be honest. Life can have a stark, hellish side. And that is what Jesus challenges with his warning.

Remember that phrase in the ancient Apostles' Creed? We say that Jesus was "crucified under Pontius Pilate, dead, and buried. He descended into hell. He rose. . ."

Jesus was the one who constantly descended into hell. Not just when he died, in those three days before his resurrection, but throughout his ministry. He entered those places that we avoid, those places that we put out on the margins, out on the edge of town—the shoddy nursing homes, the pitifully ill-equipped places for those suffering from mental illness, the town dump. We have seen him throughout this year in the Gospel of Mark, confronting demons, rebuking the devils that possess people, healing, and driving out all that dehumanizes and degrades. He spent so much of his life with those who had reached the end of the line.

In Jesus, we are not permitted to resign ourselves, saying, "They have dumped me here; this is the end of the line." We can choose to treasure the gift that God has given us in our lives, our talents, and our responsibilities.

The church is to be made up of people who treasure their lives and are determined that we will not let our lives slide into nothingness and despair, simply because of some aspect of our lives that we find difficult to control. I know a man who grew up in a family that had wine with each special meal. From time to time, he enjoyed what we call a "social drink" at parties. But at midlife he realized that he was developing some addictive habits. He was showing some of the early warning signals for the inability to deal with alcohol.

He became what we call a "teetotaler." To this day, he will never touch alcohol. Even though he enjoyed fine wine and the pleasures that came with it, he discarded this aspect of his life, rather than risk having his entire life discarded.

Furthermore, the church is to be the sort of place that keeps entering hell, keeps attempting to salvage lives, to rescue people, to remind them that they are precious to God, that they are beautiful and not destined for the ash heap of the world. With Jesus, we ought to be instruments of bringing people back to life. We are those who are to embody the great gospel message, "God's kingdom is here. Turn around, come forward, be saved, and join a great kingdom!"

I once served a little church that had been built over one of the town's early dumping grounds. It was in a resort community. In the early days, when the community was only a little cluster of houses with summer residents, people began dumping refuse—mostly beer cans from the town bars—in a swampy area toward the edge of town. Eventually the town grew, and the city leaders prohibited dumping in this area. When it came time to begin a church there, the only land that the church could afford was at that site. So, they graded over the beer cans and other rusted refuse and built a church.

I always took that as a sort of parable, a metaphor for, not only that church, but also the whole church. The churches always take in the refuse of the world and build upon it, making something beautiful out of that which the world had discarded as beyond redemption. The church does that with people. No one is beyond God's ability to redeem. That includes you.

Choose this day whom you will serve. Decide right now to zealously guard the good life that God has so graciously given you. What do you need to discard in order that you may save and salvage your precious life? Is there someone to whom you need to go and tell this message? Is there some great Gehenna that you need to enter in order to bring out and redeem with God someone who has been lost?

Later, sometime after this teaching, Jesus himself would be put up on a cross overlooking Gehenna. He could see Gehenna clearly from Calvary. His own deepest experience of Gehenna was Calvary. Take that as a symbol for what Jesus does throughout his ministry. He goes to hell, that he might defeat hell and win for God a kingdom of the ones whom the world once regarded as mere refuse.

Relating the text

"The Devil himself had probably re-designed Hell in the light of information he had gained from observing airport layouts."

—Anthony Price, *The Memory Trap* (London: Grafton, 1989)

"Through me is the way to the sorrowful city. Through me is the way to eternal suffering. Through me is the way to join the lost people. . . . Abandon all hope, you who enter!" [Inscription at the entrance to hell]

—Dante, *The Divine Comedy*, 1472

"Hell, Madame, is to love no more."

—Georges Bernanos (1888–1948)

"The Body of Christ lives in the world on behalf of the world, in intercession for the world. . . . For lay folk in the church this means that there is no forbidden work. There is no corner of human existence, however degraded or neglected, into which they may not venture; no person, however beleaguered or possessed, whom they may not befriend and represent. . . . Christians are distinguished by their radical esteem for the Incarnation . . . by their reverence for the life of God in the whole of creation, even and, in a sense, especially, creation in the travail of sin.

"The characteristic place to find Christians is among their enemies.

"The first place to look for Christ is in hell."

—William Stringfellow, *A Keeper of the Word: Selected Writings of William Stringfellow*, ed. Bill Wylie Kellermann (Grand Rapids: Eerdmans Publishing Co., 1994), 164–65

Sunday between October 2 and October 8 inclusive
[Proper 22, Ordinary/Lectionary 27]

Job 1:1; 2:1-10
Psalm 26
Hebrews 1:1-4; 2:5-12
Mark 10:2-16

The Power of Positive Thinking

Selected reading
Hebrews 1:1-4; 2:5-12

Theme

Christians are those who, amid life's many setbacks, difficulties, and tragedies, trust God. We have a certain optimism about life and its prospects, not because we have faith in the goodness and potential of humanity, but rather because we have faith in the graciousness and power of God. In Christ, God has subjected all things unto himself. While we see many difficulties in life, we also see Jesus, and that keeps us positive about the ultimate direction of life.

Introduction to the readings
Job 1:1; 2:1-10

Job, a man who was "honest" and "of absolute integrity," is the victim of a terrible series of tragedies.

Hebrews 1:1-4; 2:5-12

The writer to the Hebrews recounts the story of the graciousness of God, a story that enables us to trust and to praise God, even in our sufferings.

Mark 10:2-16

Jesus's critics ask him a question about divorce and remarriage, giving Jesus an opportunity to teach about the nature of God's kingdom.

Prayer

Lord Jesus, when we read today's headlines, when we think about our present situation, when we consider the trials and tribulations that we face, we become overwhelmed, disheartened, defeated.

We confess that we have had far too much faith in ourselves. We have thought that we had it within ourselves to solve our problems by ourselves. Yet, in our better moments, we know that we have not the power to cure what ails us and our world.

Lord, show us your glory. Reveal to us your majesty. Confirm our faith in your rule, for what we need most is glory, majesty, and rule not of our own devising.

Lord Jesus, show us your glory, that we might take heart, be filled with confidence and hope, and take our place in the work of your kingdom. Amen.

Encountering the text

The letter to the Hebrews is noted for its determination to strengthen a band of struggling early Christians, using every metaphor, image, scriptural motif, and rhetorical means to encourage suffering believers.

The first part of this Sunday's lesson appears as a reading for Christmas. It serves as a great shout of joy and the triumph of God in the incarnation of Christ. The lesson opens with a contrast between the pitifully partial revelation of God in the past and the fullness of revelation in Christ. We are living "in these final days" when, in Christ, the world has shifted on its axis, a new world has begun. Christ is all-powerful—the Son, present with God in creation, the reflection of the glory and radiance of God, the one who "maintains everything with his powerful message." Heaping every image upon the person of Christ, Hebrews asserts a sweeping claim for the power of Christ, "at the right side of the highest majesty."

To me, a great challenge for us preachers today is to preach in a way that strongly asserts the power of Christ within a church that, in my judgment, has honed down Christ to something less than he is depicted in Hebrews. Jesus is our good friend, our companion, but is he God's Son, Lord, savior of all? Today's lection from Hebrews, so full of christological affirmation, invites us to a strong statement of Christology, a vivid affirmation of a God who acts decisively in Jesus Christ.

The writer to the Hebrews manages to be honest about the real tragedies and difficulties that we face: "we don't see everything under their control yet." There are many reminders that our world is not completely under the lordship of Christ, not by a longshot. But we do see Jesus. We are able to be positive about the future because, though we do not see the complete victory of God, as Hebrews says, we do see "the one who is now crowned with glory and honor because of the suffering of his death."

Many of our people are depressed, hopeless, and pessimistic about the world and their place in it. Today Hebrews gives us an opportunity to proclaim a savior who is able to turn our pessimism into God-inspired optimism. In Christ, we can be honest about present difficulties, yet at the same time have hope that we live at the dawn of a new age in which Christ will be all in all.

Proclaiming the text

Some of you are ancient enough to recall the legacy of Dr. Norman Vincent Peale who, for decades of ministry and dozens of best-selling books, pushed his book *The Power of Positive Thinking*. Dr. Peale's message was a simple one that always sells in a mother-I-can-do-it-myself, self-help economy, "You can if you believe you can."

I, unlike Dr. Peale, for decades of ministry and dozens of poorly selling books, have pushed another preachment: "You cannot, and I don't care how much you think you can."

Many years ago, I was bragging to a student from California that I had been asked to preach at the Crystal Cathedral, thinking he would be impressed.

"The Crystal Cathedral?" he asked in disbelief. "Where Dr. Schuller does his 'Possibility Thinking'?"

"Yes," I said, "and what of it?"

"When are you to preach?" he asked.

"January," I replied.

"Good," said the mellow Californian. "That gives you two months to work on your sermon. Surely by January you can think of something positive."

"I can be positive in a sermon," I said defensively.

He said, "I've been listening to you for three years and I've never heard you be positive."

Okay. I guess I'm just not the possibility, positive-thinking type.

It was not always so for me. Once, in my prophetic angry young man days, I thought better of people and their possibilities. "The change agent" was my model of ministry. I'm going to get out there and get those once racist-sexist-materialistic rascals to change for the better. And they can change, if they really want to change, and who better to tell them to change than me?

But that was long ago. As a pastor, I got my nose rubbed in the human condition, was made to stare at the sheer caughtness of people. We're trapped. In a particularly sober moment, St. Paul said of himself, "I don't do the good that I want to do, but I do the evil that I don't want to do. But if I do the very thing that I don't want to do, then I'm not the one doing it anymore. Instead, it is sin that lives in me tht is doing it" (Rom 7:19-20).

You just can't think your way out of your trappedness. Isn't that what psychology, sociology, and biology have taught us? We are constrained, to say the least, in a tight web of determinisms. "My genes told me to do it."

Sometime ago I was visiting in the town where I grew up, visiting some buddies from my high-school days. We piled in one of their cars to go somewhere and I heard, coming from his tape deck, "You are a good person, but sometimes people take advantage of your goodness. You mean well, but sometimes things don't work out as you intended. You want to do better, but . . ."

"What's that?" I asked.

"That's my motivational tape to help me deal with my anger at my second wife after our divorce settlement," he replied.

"I'd love to see Will do one of those motivational tapes," said another.

"There you go again. It's your own fault. What did I tell you, you've messed up again."

Okay. I flunked Norman Vincent Peale's "positive thinking 101." Which is my way of explaining my difficulty with this Sunday's epistle. Here is the positive thinker, writing to the struggling Hebrews: "The Son is the light of God's glory and the imprint of God's being. He maintains everything with his powerful message."

Elsewhere Paul speaks of Christ as the great "yes" of God (2 Cor 1:18-22).

Have we caught often dour Paul in a rare moment of positive thinking? I, who like Adlai Stephenson, can say, "I find Paul appealing and Peale appalling," and find Paul's Peale-like positivism perplexing.

When Bill Bradley was asked if he was reconsidering his run for the presidency after he lost badly in the 2000 Iowa primary, Bradley responded, "I learned as an athlete that you have got to think positively. I didn't go into this half-heartedly. I'm positive."

"Stiff upper lip, carry on, take courage and all that, that's what got us through the war," said the English Grande Dame.

"In business, if you think failure, you'll sure get failure," says management guru Ted Peters.

"Treat people as if they were what they ought to be and you help them to become what they are capable of being," said Goethe.

Or as Johnny Mercer put it, "You've got to accentuate the positive."

And nothing that this morning's scripture says here has anything to do with any of that.

Here, in this strong affirmation from Hebrews, is not some silly affirmation of the resolute human spirit, or faith in the possibility of human achievement, but a strong "yes" upon the forlorn early Christians, not because of them, but because of God. Jesus has been revealed to them as "the light of God's glory."

"We don't see everything under their control yet" (2:8). There really is tragedy among us, setbacks, aggravations, and all the big and little evidences of evil. We believe that Jesus Christ is Lord, though his lordship is not yet fully established.

But we do see Jesus. We have not seen the final vindication of God's gracious love. We have not seen the complete victory of the reign of God among us. But we do see Jesus. Think of Sunday morning as a time, not when we get together to put a happy face on everything, to lie about the realities of sin and death among us. Rather, Sunday is a time to get a vision. We don't see everything. But we do see Jesus.

People who know Jesus can dare to be so honest and pessimistic about prospects for human betterment because we are so daringly optimistic about the ultimate triumph of God in Jesus Christ. Hebrews says (1:2) that Jesus is the "heir" of God, which means that everything that God has, God has given to Jesus. Then Jesus is called the creator of worlds. When God was powerfully creating the world out of the void in Genesis 1, Jesus was there. Which means that Jesus is the creator of worlds, which means that Christ is the sign of the creation of a whole new world.

Which means that we need not despair; we need not give up hope. We can be positive about tomorrow.

Here is optimism that arises, not by referring to some alleged "indomitable human spirit," but rather in the work of the one who is "superior to the angels." Our hope for the future is based not in programs for human betterment but rather in our present experience of the reign of Christ here, among us now.

In the present, we have feuding, factions, setbacks, and grief, but we still see where it's all headed. We haven't yet seen the last scene of the play, but we have seen enough to keep us in deep hopefulness.

In the present, there are these setbacks, sorrows, sadness, life's big and little tragedies. We wonder, *Who's in charge? Has the great God gone on holiday?*

Atheism is not a product of college religion classes; it's the residue of a world that sometimes breaks the hearts of believers. But in Christ, we have a vision of who is in charge, where it's all headed, and who will win the war.

I know a man who is a pastoral counselor who specializes in the treatment of addictive disorders. He himself climbed out of the ravages of alcoholism to live a life in service to others. At table the other night he said to us, "You know, I've at last come to that point in my faith where I stop saying, when something comes my way in life, 'This is good,' or 'This is bad.' God has taught me not to be so quick to label life as a curse or a blessing. I have to wait to see what good God will make of it before I render a verdict. Because sometimes, those things that I first thought to be negative have, in the hands of a good God, turned out positive. Even the worst 'no!' turned out to be God's gracious 'yes!'"

To that, even this periodically pessimistic preacher says "Amen!"

Relating the text

Just before Christmas in 1924, Thomas Hardy, no great optimist on any occasion, wrote this bleak assessment of humanity's notion of "progress":

"Even when you spread human history across the ages, and take a long-term view, moral improvement is mighty hard to measure. We've improved the plumbing, yes, but we also designed gas chambers at Auschwitz. The Holocaust is scarcely an advertisement for kingdom come! How does the impudent jingle go?

"After two thousand years of mass, we've got as far as poison gas."

—Thomas Hardy, "Christmas, 1924," from *Winter Words* (1928) in
Complete Poems, ed. James Gibson (New York: Macmillan
Publishing Co., 1976), 914

After the great Lisbon earthquake, in which so many perished, an event that shook the confidence of the optimistic eighteenth century, Voltaire satirized the times in his comical novella, *Candide*. The title character is a sweet, dumb young man who is told by a half-baked philosopher that, "In this best of all possible worlds . . . all is for the best." The silly young man believes the philosopher's optimistic assessment of the human situation.

Then Voltaire takes the youth through the worst series of disasters ever to befall anyone. All the while, after each tragedy, the young man brushes himself off and tells himself, "Well, though this is bad, this is the best of all possible worlds."

The result is a devastating critique of the "power of positive thinking."

Nothing to do but work,
Nothing to eat but food,
Nothing to wear but clothes,
To keep one from going nude.

—Benjamin Franklin King, "The Pessimist," nineteenth-century poem

---

In *David Copperfield*, Charles Dickens described Mr. Micawber who, despite everything, always moved through life as if it might get better:

"I have known him come home to supper with a flood of tears, and a declaration that nothing was now left but a jail; and go to bed making a calculation of the expense of putting bow-windows to the house, 'in case anything turned up,' which was his favorite expression."

—Charles Dickens, *David Copperfield*, 1850

Sunday between October 9 and October 15 inclusive

[Proper 23, Ordinary/Lectionary 28]

Job 23:1-9, 16-17

Psalm 22:1-15

Hebrews 4:12-16

Mark 10:17-31

The Good Teacher

Selected reading

Mark 10:17-31

Theme

The gospel of Christ is good news. But sometimes the good news of Jesus sounds like bad news. Jesus is the teacher who tells us the truth. Sometimes the truth hurts before it can heal. Fortunately for us, Jesus, the good teacher, continues to teach us, continues to make possible that, even for people like us, faithful discipleship is possible.

Introduction to the readings

Job 23:1-9, 16-17

From out of the whirlwind, Almighty God at last speaks to Job, showing Job a great vision of the majesty and wonder of God's creation.

Hebrews 4:12-16

We continue our readings from Hebrews with an image of Jesus as the "Great High Priest."

Mark 10:17-31

Just as Jesus is leaving for a journey, a man comes up to him and asks about eternal life.

Prayer

Lord Jesus, we come to church in order to be with you and learn from you. Therefore, during our time for worship, help us focus; enable us to hear what you have to say to us. Teach us. Even when your teaching is hard to take, give us the grace to receive your word, to grow in our faith, and to deepen our discipleship. Amen.

Encountering the text

The question, put to Jesus by this man in Mark 10, is about the big, grand, difficult subject of eternal life. Rather surprisingly, Jesus, the good teacher, demands that the man give up his great possessions and follow him. Here we have a vocation story. Jesus is inviting someone to be his disciple. But unlike the earlier call stories in Mark, this one ends with the recipient of the call turning away and rejecting Jesus.

Yet we note that the pericope does not really end with the man's grief and his rejection. It ends with Jesus's affirmation of his disciples, those who have indeed left all and followed him.

The text thus raises an issue for us preachers. Should we take our cues from the first part of the text—the man and his rejection of Jesus's invitation—or the second part, in which Peter declares the disciples' allegiance to Jesus and Jesus praises them, promising them grand reward for their following?

As we have seen throughout Year B of the lectionary, the disciples are rarely put in a positive light in Mark's Gospel. Today may be one of those rare moments when the disciples finally get the Teacher's point. The story ends in affirmation and rejoicing. Our sermons on this text ought to end there as well.

Discipleship, following Jesus down his narrow way, is difficult and demanding. That is the bad news. Yet the good news is that with God "all things are possible." Therein is our hope.

Proclaiming the text

One of the things that I learned, after I had been a preacher for a while, is that sometimes it is hard to tell the good news from the bad. In scripture, it is sometimes difficult to know whether you are dealing with the good news of grace or the bad news of judgment. "Grace," said Martin Luther, "often wounds from behind." That which you thought was a harsh divine judgment, turns out, in the topsy-turvy world of the gospel, to be an act of God's love. Sometimes grace and judgment are the same things. Sometimes, the only difference between good news and bad news is where you happen to be sitting when you get the news!

Of course, you don't have to be a preacher to experience this phenomenon. You have had experiences in which some difficult word spoken to you that at the time you may have thought of as harsh judgment, turned out to be the most loving thing anyone ever said to you.

A student was describing a course he was taking: "It is taught by the most insensitive, arrogant professor I have ever had. He is sarcastic, always on the attack, always trying to make us look dumb."

Then he added, "I've never worked so hard for a course in all my life. In fact, this may be the best course I've ever taken. He's a wonderful teacher!"

Perhaps that's why Aristotle, in some of his thoughts on education, said that only a friend can teach you really important things in life. Why? Because, said

Aristotle, only a friend knows how to hurt you in the right way! Sometimes it's hard to tell the good news from the bad.

Take this morning's scripture from Mark. Now right off I note that one of the troubling things about this story is that Mark does not tell it exactly the same way that it's told in the other Gospels. One other Gospel calls this man "young," and another Gospel calls him "rich." Mark just calls him "a man." I would rather him be a "young" man or a "rich" man, since I am neither. That way I can reassure myself, "This is not my story. It is a story about some of you!"

I'm always grateful, particularly in the Gospel of Mark, when I can get a story that is about you and not about me. Mark says simply that he was a "man," that is, just a guy off the street, an ordinary person with no particular pedigree, one of us. Later in the story, we are told that he "had many possessions," but who among us doesn't fit that description? We may not be rich, or young, but we all have lots of stuff, a great many things. So right off the bat we have a sneaking suspicion that we may not be able to keep this story away from us. It may be a story about us.

Read Mark 10:35-45.

One day, on his way, Jesus meets a man. Mark casually mentions that Jesus was continuing "down the road." You know what that means. You know where this "road" is going to end in just a few more chapters. It leads to the cross. And as he begins this fateful journey, he is encountered by a man who has "many possessions," who addresses him as "Good Teacher." Jesus is a teacher, a rabbi, who is called good.

The man is religiously inclined and attempts to get Jesus into a discussion about eternal life. But Jesus isn't dealing. So, in an attempt to brush off the man (Jesus seems to have a short fuse for these well-fixed, inquisitive types), Jesus tells him to go and obey all of the commandments and then come back and they can talk.

The man surely startles Jesus by saying, "Oh, I've obeyed all the commandments, since I was a kid in Sunday school. I've never broken any of the commandments."

It turns out that this man is not only successful materially (he has lots of stuff) but also successful spiritually. Who among us would claim to have obeyed all of the commandments? Jesus has been confronted here with a man who is a high achiever, a great success.

So, maybe in one last attempt to really sock it to him, Jesus says to him, "I love you, and because I love you so much, I'm going to give you something I don't just give everybody. I want you to go, sell everything you've got, give it to the poor, and then come follow me."

With that, Mark says this man, slumped down, got real depressed, gets back into his Porsche, and leaves. He was shocked by what the good teacher told him. He went away "grieved." He dropped the course, lost interest in the subject, and went in a direction where the good teacher was not.

And with that Jesus says, "Man, it is hard to save these young rich ones."

"How hard is it, Jesus?" ask his disciples.

Jesus responds, "It is about as hard to get a fully loaded camel through the eye of a needle! Impossible! Of course, with God, I suppose anything is possible, even this."

What do we have here, good news or bad? Of course, what we have here is bad news. We are ordinary women and men, who have lots of stuff, who have come to Jesus to be taught. Each of us has gotten out of bed and come to church in order to be taught by Jesus. We come to Jesus asking, "Good Teacher, what must we do to be faithful followers of your way?" Or, "Good Teacher, how can I better understand the Bible?"

Here, a sincere seeker comes to the feet of Jesus to be taught, and the class ends in failure. In fact, I believe this is the only call story in all the Gospels in which someone rejects the call. Someone—a man, maybe young, maybe rich, maybe just a man—is being asked to come follow Jesus. But he was shocked and grieved by what Jesus taught him. So he refuses, and the reason was money. This is bad news, discouraging teaching about how our material attachments, our false loves and idolatries, keep us from following Jesus. The story ends in depression, in rejection; it's the bad news about that.

But the good thing is, though this may be bad news, it may not be your bad news. I'll be the first to admit that people who have "many possessions" do not always come off that well in the Gospels. Bad news.

But wait, where does this story end? Does it end with the young man's rejection and exit? No, Peter the premier disciple blurts out, "Lord, we have left everything—homes, family, friends—and we have followed you!"

In other words, we are not like the inquiring man who came up to you asking idle theological questions but was shocked and grieved by your strange answers. Unlike him, when you called us, we did not slink away in the other direction. We came forth. We let go of a lot, in order to be embraced by you, in order to join on with your movement. We stayed the course, kept attending class, kept taking notes, even when we were shocked by what you taught us, even when we were grieved. Some Sundays we wanted to walk away, go in the other direction, sleep in late, because that way would be easier than to be confronted by the sometimes-shocking words of this "Good Teacher." But we did not. We stayed the course. We kept at it. We're still here.

And then Jesus says, "Rejoice!"

The story does not end in depression, grieving, and rejection, but in Jesus's glad promise and in rejoicing. That's how this story ends, with rejoicing. Jesus tells them, "I promise you, for everything you have given up, I will give you much more. For everything you have turned your back on, I will give you ten times more. Rejoice!"

Sometimes, on Sundays, I look out among you and I see you as you are—contemporary disciples who are trying to follow Jesus. Jesus has set out on a journey, and even though you know full well where the road leads, you are walking with him. Even though you know that his teaching sometimes elicits shock and even grief, you still listen. You still follow. And for that, Jesus says, "Rejoice!"

I see you, who have forgone promotions in your job and upward mobility because you wanted to be a good father more than you wanted the money. I see the one who turned her back on a great opportunity at work because she wanted to stay home and look after her mother after her stroke. I see teenagers who may not be voted "Most Popular" in the school annual because they have values and commitments that are more determined by Jesus than by the fickle crowd.

In the ending of this story, Jesus doesn't say to you, "It is impossible to save any early twenty-first-century North American types." Impossible! Rather he says, "Rejoice!" There are many odds set against following me but rejoice. With God all things are possible, even the fidelity of ordinary folk like us.

The story seems to imply, if you want to feel bad, be grieved, then grieve for those poor souls who have little more to live and die for than their stuff, their possessions, their own selfish selves. You get to give your lives for Jesus! You get to follow me where I'm going. You get to swim against the stream. You get to be part of the revolution! Rejoice!

"When Joe was born," she said, "we thought it a piece of incredible bad luck. It seemed at first so unfair. Our first child, and with a severe disability. Sad to say, Tom and I considered putting baby Joe up for adoption or just placing him in an institution. I asked my dear mother what she thought I ought to do. She told me right upfront. 'I know you,' she said. 'You are not going to be happy if you don't accept this child as the gift of God that he is. Do what you need to do to be a good mother. God has given you lots of gifts and resources. God means for you to use them for this baby.'

"What my mother said wasn't easy to hear. Wasn't what I thought I wanted to hear. But it was what I needed to hear. She was right. Joe has changed our lives, enriched our marriage. He has been a gift to me. I thought that he was the worst thing that happened to me. Turned out, he was the best thing in my life."

Sometimes it takes a teacher, a really good teacher, to bring out the best in us, to tell us not what we think we want to hear but what we need to hear. And when we dare to listen, dare to follow, then we are able to rejoice. Rejoice, despite all the difficulties, Jesus has told you the truth. He has stripped you down of all the meaningless stuff to which you cling. He is drawing you through that narrow needle's eye toward the way that leads to life, and that eternal.

With God, all things really are possible.

Relating the text

"*Leviathan* is about an underwater mining crew that uncovers a dangerous disease. It consumes the crew one by one, joining and blending them into a horrific sea creature. At a climatic point, one crew member (a doctor) decides that if they escape from the monster by getting to the water's surface, they will expose the world to the threat of this horrible beast.

"The doctor concludes that it would be better for the half dozen to die and save the world. In the film, this fellow is seen as deluded, a servant of the beast. Two others manage to overcome the doctor's desires and escape to the surface. In so doing, they risk exposing the world to Leviathan.

"In some societies, the doctor would be a hero. He practiced self-sacrifice for the wider good. But in our culture, the two escapees are heroes. One man and one woman are rugged, self-interested, selfishly heroic, and courageous individuals. They are brave and daring. At the end of the movie, the man slugs a female corporate executive. This monster-slaying woman-basher is the hero of the film.

"But I still think the real hero was the martyred doctor. He has more to teach us than the survivors of the terror. For according to the Bible (and re-echoed in the first word of the Lord's Prayer), self-sacrifice is more important than self-interest, community is more vital than status, and fellowship is better than success."

—Arthur Paul Boers, *Lord, Teach Us to Pray* (Waterloo, Ontario: Herald Press, 1992)

"I never give 'em hell. I just tell the truth, and they think it's hell."

—Harry S. Truman (1884–1972)

The great African American preacher and teacher Samuel D. Proctor, pastor of Abyssinian Baptist in New York City, my colleague at Duke Divinity School, and great teacher of preachers, wrote a book in which he joined with the great Gardner C. Taylor to give advice to fellow pastors. Proctor expended a large part of the book on the pastor as teacher:

"Theology never comes alive in abstract debate. It is best understood when it is lived. A good pastor will take the time to show the people how life should be lived, given such a great God as we are privileged to know, and given how marvelously we are made. From this wonderful knowledge comes an awareness that our purpose is to cultivate our gifts in God's honor and to God's glory, and to live all our days in loving obedience to God. It means finding joy in pausing to praise God and to find fellowship with others. . . . It means lifting up the life stories of others who have done so well in walking with the Lord, learning and hearing the music and the poetry that edify our lives in obedience and joy. It means finding our highest fulfilment in following Christ in service to others. Celebrating the lives of victorious Christians is a great opening for good teaching."

—Samuel D. Proctor and Gardner C. Taylor, *We Have This Ministry: The Heart of the Pastor's Vocation* (Valley Forge: Judson, 1996), 21

Sunday between October 16 and October 22 inclusive

[Proper 24, Ordinary/Lectionary 29]

Job 38:1-7, (34-41) or Isaiah 53:4-12
Psalm 104:1-9, 24, 35c or Psalm 91:9-16
Hebrews 5:1-10
Mark 10:35-45

Christianity: Following Jesus

Selected reading

Mark 10:35-45

Theme

To be a Christian means simply to be someone who is trying to follow Jesus. It doesn't necessarily mean that we understand everything about the Christian faith or that we have achieved perfection in following him. It means that we are disciples, those who are following behind Jesus in our daily lives.

Introduction to the readings

Job 38:1-7, (34-41)

From out of the whirlwind, God finally speaks to Job.

Hebrews 5:1-10

Christ is our great high priest, says the writer to the Hebrews, a priest who intercedes for us.

Mark 10:35-45

While walking along the way, Jesus instructs his disciples in the nature of true leadership.

Prayer

Lord Jesus, help us to hear your call in our lives, and when we hear, help us say yes.

Give us the grace to see the tasks to which you call us as your disciples. Then give us the gifts we need to accomplish those tasks for you.

We marvel that you have placed us within your inbreaking kingdom. At times we feel inadequate, unequal to your vocation of us. Nevertheless, help us delight in your will, walk in your way, and enjoy the privilege of serving you in this time and place. Amen.

Encountering the text

We believe that Mark invented the Gospel form as a means for communicating the truth about Jesus. No previous literary form—biography, poem, letter, history, news release—would carry the weight that is the gospel. Therefore, Mark, in an inspired burst of divine creativity, invented the Gospel as the means of speaking about Jesus.

Note that the Gospel form is organized around a journey. It has a beginning, a middle, and an end. Like many journeys, those who embark on it do not know where the way leads, where the road will end. Furthermore, they do not even know all that much about Jesus. He calls them to "follow me," but where are they going? Who is the "me" that they are to follow?

All that will be revealed on the journey. Today we see Jesus with his disciples and, as usual, revealing himself and his way to them during the journey. Today he speaks to them about the ways in which leadership among his followers is different from leadership among the Gentiles.

We will preach on the passage as a whole as an episode that reveals what it is like to be in relationship with Jesus. To be with Jesus is to be with him on the way. As with any journey, there are surprises, twists and turns, and growth and change.

To believe in Jesus is not to stay in one place for your whole life.

Proclaiming the text

I have sometimes poked fun at sermons that seem to have as their theme: "Nine reasons you are not really a Christian even though you may have thought you were one when you came to church." But it's no laughing matter how sometimes church seems to be about all the ways you fall short in your discipleship rather than about all the ways in which you are a disciple. I want to say something today about following Jesus.

I can't recall any moment when Jesus said to his disciples, "Believe the following five things about me."

No. What Jesus said was, "Follow me."

It is more important to be a disciple, a follower of Jesus, even than to be a Christian. Christianity is not a set of beliefs, first principles, propositions. It is a matter of discipleship, following. Faith in Jesus is not beliefs about Jesus. It's a willingness to follow Jesus. The faith is in the following.

We make a mistake to turn this into some sort of mystery. Jesus did not demand that we swallow a dozen philosophical absurdities in order to be with him. He asked us to follow him. Faith in Jesus is not first of all a matter of having felt something, or having had an experience. It is a simple willingness to stumble along behind Jesus, a willingness to be behind him. The faith is in the following.

There is, therefore, no need for anybody to be befuddled when asked, "Are you a Christian?" It's a freebie. Easy.

The answer is not a matter of having your head straight about the meaning of the atonement. The scripture is not a demand that you cite some inner psychological validation. The answer is simply to say, "Yes, I'm trying my best to follow Jesus. I'm his apprentice, his disciple." The faith is in the following.

If you ask someone, "Are you a carpenter?" there would be no need for hesitation. You may not be the world's best carpenter or the most experienced worker in the world. You may have been a carpenter for only two weeks, or for as many as twenty years, but the evidence that you are or are not a carpenter is simple and self-evident. Are you or are you not disciplining your life (discipline = disciple) to the skills, insights, and practices of carpentry? Case closed.

If you asked, "Are you a really good carpenter?" then there might be more hesitation. You are growing as a carpenter, but you are not perfect. The hesitation does not indicate that you are not a real carpenter. Rather, your hesitation shows that you are a true disciple of carpentry, that you are still growing, still on the way, still being perfected in the tools of the trade. A beginning carpenter is still a carpenter.

How often, in all the Gospels, do you hear Jesus criticizing and chastising his disciples? He is often exasperated that they don't get the point, that they fail to follow, or that they misunderstand.

Jesus's criticism of them does not mean they are not real disciples. It means that they are still on the journey. They are on the way. If they had not committed themselves to follow Jesus, if they were not linked to him and his way, there would be no need for correction. Faith does not mean they have arrived; it means that they are on the way.

A person who wants to be a carpenter must apprentice to a carpenter, minding the moves, absorbing the practices, being attentive to the principles of the trade, willing to be criticized by the master until the apprentice becomes what the master is and does what the master does. That's surely what Jesus means when he says simply, "Follow me."

I recall participating in a discussion in which people were asked, "When did you become a Christian?"

People took turns sharing some rather dramatic accounts of how they had been converted into the Christian faith. Some recalled soul-stirring moments when their lives were dramatically disrupted by an infusion of the grace of God, and they decided to follow.

But one man, with more than a bit of hesitation in his voice, said, "I can't remember when I wasn't a Christian. I was a Christian when I was a child, from the first."

My point is that the imitation of our apprenticeship—the way we got on the journey with Jesus—is not the crucial matter. The crucial matter is that we are on the way. To be on the way means to be, as a disciple, imitating the moves of the master in all we do.

Some years ago, I read a book of meditations for Christian college students. The book began, "As a Christian, who is also a student, your task is to be an excellent student. Your discipleship means that you should study conscientiously and thoroughly."

Wherever you are, whatever you do, you are a disciple of Jesus. That's one reason why I can't stand that phrase "full-time Christian service" as a way of distinguishing between clergy and laity. Following Jesus is not a matter of learning to do a few religious things on top of the things we do, but rather it is a matter of doing all that we do, not for ourselves, but for Jesus.

That's surely why Jesus's parables are stories about real life and his teaching is about matters like anger, forgiveness, ordinary injustice, disappointment—

the stuff of real life. He surely meant us to follow him now, in this life, not some other.

I know a barber who, after a day of cutting people's hair for money, goes out to a hospital for the mentally challenged and cuts hair for free. A friend of his is an accountant who, after a long day of serving people's financial interests for money, goes out at night to cruise local bars, to pick up women for one-night stands, and to enjoy himself as much as possible.

Both men, the barber and the accountant, are apprentices, people attached to some larger vision of what life is about, why we were put here. One is attached to Jesus. The other is attached to American consumerism and selfish hedonism. So the most interesting question to ask them is not the abstract, "What do you believe in?" but be more concrete, "Whom are you following?" Faith is in the attachment, the following.

The world is right in judging Jesus on the basis of the sort of lives he produces. The only "proof" we have, the acid test for the validity of the gospel, is whether or not it is capable of producing lives that are a credit to the master to whom we are apprenticed.

Relating the text

Flannery O'Conner once remarked that "most of us come to the church by a means the church does not allow." We think of being Christian as something we do, or something we decide. No, church begins with Jesus, with his simple words, "Follow me."

One often has the feeling, when reading the Gospel of Mark, that Jesus made some sort of mistake, that he has called the wrong people to be his followers. His disciples never seem to get the point, rarely seem to fully understand. But then we see that's just the sort of people Jesus seems to call. Martin

Luther reminds us, a crucified God seems to be attracted to the weak, the lowly, and the needy:

"Thus, God is the God of the humble, the miserable, the afflicted, the oppressed, the desperate, and of those who have been brought down to nothing at all. And it is the nature of God to exalt the humble, to feed the hungry, to enlighten the blind, to comfort the miserable and afflicted, to justify sinners, to give life to the dead, and to save those who are desperate and damned."

—Martin Luther, "Lectures on Galatians" [1535] [on Galatians 3:19] (in Luther's Works, 26:314)

I have long been uncomfortable with some of the ways we sometimes speak of our relationship to Christ.

People say, "Since I accepted Jesus . . ." "Accepted Jesus" makes it sound like you have received something that is fixed, stable, a onetime decision, and then it's over.

Or they say, "When I was saved . . .," as if it is some past event, over and done with, as if in that moment your relationship was sealed forever in stone.

Might it be more accurate to say something like, "When I started walking with Jesus," or "When I began my journey with Christ"?

The earliest name for followers of Jesus, according to the Acts of the Apostles, was "the Way."

Jesus comes and invites us with a simple, "Follow me." Some heed his invitation and follow, yet some fail to respond. Graham Greene tells of an old priest, mostly noted for drinking whiskey and having a string of failures, who finds himself in the last morning of his life: "What an impossible fellow I am," he thought, "and how useless. I have done nothing for anybody. I might just as well have never lived."

Then Greene offers this haunting verdict:

"He felt only an immense disappointment because he had to go to God empty-handed, with nothing done at all. It seemed to him, at that moment, that it would have been quite easy to have been a saint. It would only have needed a little self-restraint and a little courage. He felt like someone who has missed happiness by seconds at an appointed place. He knew now that at the end there was only one thing that counted—to be a saint."

> —Graham Greene, *The Power and the Glory*
> (New York: Penguin USA, 1995)

Christians are not those who are morally better than other people, or more perceptive and intelligent (look at the disciples in Mark!). We are those who have heard our names called, who have a sense that a party was about to begin, and we wanted to be part of it. We are those who know what the poet Auden meant when he said, "I know nothing, except what everyone knows—if there when Grace dances, I should dance."

I have watched lots of smart, brilliant people come to Jesus. From what I can observe, their conversion was not the result of some reasoned journey. It was a matter of being encountered in the depths of their being, more emotional than rational. More than that, it was a matter of taking up a Christian life, adopting the habits and practices of discipleship, like going to church, reading the Bible, praying, serving those in need. That makes me believe that Pascal was right. If you would be a believer, he said, just go and do the things that believers do:

"You desire to attain faith, but you do not know the way. You would like to cure yourself of unbelief, and you ask for remedies. Learn from those who were once bound and gagged like you, and who now stake all that they possess. They are men who know the road that you desire to follow, and who have been cured of a sickness of which you desire to be cured. Follow the way by which they set out, acting as if they already believed, taking holy water, having masses said, etc. all this will naturally cause you to believe."

—Blaise Pascal, *Pensées*, Section 233

In a number of places in the Gospels, Jesus urges us to "take up your cross and follow me."

I have a friend who is "taking up" painting, watercolor painting to be exact. To master an art, one must learn a whole range of skills, insights, facts, and techniques. For the past six months, my friend has been working at learning that wide array of skills needed to be a good watercolor painter.

But my friend has also learned that, while you are "taking up" an art like watercolor painting, it is also taking you. While one is mastering the art of painting, the art of painting is at the same time mastering you.

Meaning? Painting is a physical act. One cannot simply know some ideas about the craft; one must get it in the body, down to the tips of the fingers. It must move from the head to the hand. Therefore, much of the time is spent attempting to master the body, trying to get the fingers to move when they are supposed to move, mastering the right gestures in the arm, and so forth.

Time must be set aside each day to practice painting. One begins to organize one's life around the painting. Now, when my friend looks out a window on a fall day in October, she realizes that she is unconsciously composing the scene into a painting. She is beginning to see the world in watercolor. It is as if this painting thing has lodged itself in her soul. Her knowledge of painting has moved from the head to the heart, to the hands and back again. She has been changed.

Thus she can say, not simply that she has "taken up watercolor painting." She can also say, "watercolor painting has taken me."

I think today's Gospel implies that it's much the same with Jesus. When we take up the cross and follow him, he takes us places. The disciplines of discipleship—daily prayer, Bible reading, worship, service, and evangelism, witness—form us while we practice them. In the very acts required to follow Jesus, we become transformed. We don't master discipleship; rather, discipleship involves a willingness to let the Master have his way with our lives.

Sunday between October 23 and October 29 inclusive

[Proper 25, Ordinary/Lectionary 30]

Job 42:1-6, 10-17 or Jeremiah 31:7-9

Psalm 34:1-8, (19-22) or Psalm 126

Hebrews 7:23-28

Mark 10:46-52

On the Way

Selected reading

Mark 10:46-52

Theme

Jesus calls us to himself, not only to heal us of what's wrong with us, but also to make us his disciples. To stress only the benefits of Christ, without also stressing his demands and commands, is to have a perverted gospel. Jesus calls us not only to believe in his way but also to walk with him on his way. Jesus is on the way; will we follow?

Introduction to the readings

Job 42:1-6, 10-17

This reading comes from the end of the book of Job when, after all of his afflictions, God restored Job's fortunes.

Hebrews 7:23-28

Jesus, the Christ, is compared by the letter to the Hebrews with the high priest of the Hebrew scriptures.

Mark 10:46-52

On their way into Jericho, Jesus and his disciples are confronted by a blind beggar who asks for healing.

Prayer

I want Jesus to walk with me.

I want Jesus to walk with me . . .

Lord Jesus, you have called each of us to walk with you. Thank you for all the times when you have joined us and walked beside us. There are so many times in our lives when we couldn't have made it without you walking with us.

Lord Jesus, traveler along the way, give us the courage to walk with you where you lead us. Still our anxious fears of being led into places we think are too tough for us to go. We promise to walk with you, knowing you continue to walk with us. Amen.

Encountering the text

Some have said that the Gospel of Mark is one long passion story, one long account of Jesus on his way to the cross. And that would be a somber enough thought for us, if it were true that Jesus walks toward his cross alone. Here walks among us God's very Son (Mark 1), and we crucified him.

Yet the Gospel of Mark becomes even more somber. Jesus also invites others to walk with him toward the cross, disciples on their way to suffering and death along with a Lord who moves toward suffering and death.

Mark's key phrase for the gospel is "the way." Time and again, ordinary folk are asked to walk with Jesus on "the way." To believe in Jesus is to follow Jesus on "the way." Mark's whole Gospel is structured as a journey. Jesus does all of his teaching in this Gospel on the run, on the move. In Mark, if we are going to be taught by Jesus, then we'll have to stay on the way with Jesus, on the move.

And that insight sheds light on today's Gospel, the story of Jesus's healing of the blind Bartimaeus. It's not unusual to have a healing story in Mark's Gospel. What's unusual in this healing story is that we know the name of the man who is healed—Bartimaeus. This suggests to many commentators that this man who was healed was still known within the early Christian communities. He is remembered by name, unlike all the other nameless people whom Jesus healed. He is remembered because he, unlike the others, "began to follow Jesus on the way."

This man was not simply healed; he also followed. He becomes one of the first disciples. He becomes a model for true belief in Jesus; he followed along the way.

Proclaiming the text

He had been blind his whole life. He had never seen the sun rise or gazed into the face of his children or been able to support himself by the labor of his hands. He was blind. "Blind Bartimaeus"—that's what they called him—was the son of Timaeus. His whole life was named by his disability.

Most of his friends and family stayed in their little village, even though they heard that Jesus was passing close by. But Bartimaeus made his way to the roadside, hoping to get near Jesus, because he had heard that Jesus was a healer, a doctor who could cure him of his disability.

Most of his friends and family stayed home that day. After all, they were in reasonably good health, reasonably well fixed. Bartimaeus was desperate. He desperately needed something that only Jesus could give. He badly needed a healing touch.

And miracle of miracles, Jesus saw the blind beggar standing by the roadside and healed him. In a wonderful instant Bartimaeus was given his sight. In a moment, he saw the world that everyone else had been seeing. Jesus, the worker of wonders, healed him.

Why did Jesus perform healing miracles? I asked that of a Bible study group one evening. Most people answered that Jesus performed miracles because that was the way that Jesus got people to believe in him.

Then someone said, "If that's why Jesus healed people, then it didn't work. How many of the people whom Jesus healed followed him? How many do we never hear of ever again?" It was then that this particular healing story opened up for me and became more than a healing story; it became a discipleship story.

Jesus told Bartimaeus to go on back home and begin living his life as a "normal" person. And a man like Bartimaeus sure deserved to live the rest of his life in peace and tranquility after living the first part of his life in blindness.

And if he had gone back home to begin his new life, then we would know no more about him than we do of the dozens of others whom Jesus miraculously healed.

Bartimaeus must have followed Jesus, become a disciple, and been known and remembered whenever Mark wrote this Gospel. Why else would this healing story, unlike all the rest, have remembered Bartimaeus's name? We know his name—Bartimaeus.

"Bartimaeus? Sure, we remember him. He used to teach at First Church Galilee. He met and was healed by Jesus and was never the same. We remember him."

Bartimaeus, though he had been blind, really saw. He saw that Jesus was about more than simply healing. Jesus was about discipleship. Bartimaeus saw that Jesus, in healing him, had invited him to follow along the way.

Bartimaeus followed on the way. And that's why we remember his name, even today. He really saw who Jesus was.

To know, to see, and to believe in Jesus, is to follow him on the way. His way is not meant simply to be praised, to be admired, and to be adored. His way is meant to be walked.

Bartimaeus is remembered by us as the one who "got it." He followed on the way.

Relating the text

"In 1957 Gene Davenport, a college student in his teens, was assigned to pastor a small Methodist church in a then-segregated community 25 miles outside of Birmingham, Alabama.

"One Sunday night, named 'race relations Sunday,' Gene was preaching from Ezekiel's vision of a valley filled with dry bones when a procession of robed Klansmen entered the church and marched down the center aisle. Each dropped an offering on the communion table. The young preacher stepped over the communion rail and said, 'We don't want your money.' As the robed and hooded men continued their ritual without reply, the pastor scooped up their offering, held it above his head, and tore the bills to bits. They exited in formation, and he called after them, 'I wish I had not torn your money up, I wish I had sent it to the NAACP.'

"Several days later, he answered a call in his college dorm.

"'Are you Reverend Gene Davenport?'

"'Yes, sir.'

"'Pastor of Pelham Methodist?'

"'Yes, sir.'

"'Were you preaching last Sunday night when visitors made an offering?'

"'A threat is not an offering,' he replied. 'But who are you? The joke is over.'

"It was not a joke. The caller was a U.S. Secret Service agent summoning him to the federal courthouse to be charged with defacing currency.

"Although he was never indicted or tried, it was clear that defacing currency was a punishable crime, a violation of the Constitution. But mocking morality and profaning the church apparently were not.

"Davenport's courage to witness authentically meant leaving the safety of the pulpit and stepping across the communion rail."

—David Augsburger, *Dissident Discipleship: A Spirituality of Self-Surrender, Love of God, and Love of Neighbor* (Grand Rapids: Brazos Press, 2005), 189–90

Sometimes the greatest challenge, in the spread of the gospel, is not to get our mouth moving but to put our feet in motion. In my church, when someone is going through a tough time, that person sometimes says to me as a pastor, "You are the only person I've heard from at the church." That's sad.

So whenever people say to me, "I'm so sorry for the trouble that Mary is going through, but I just don't know what to do for her," I say, "Go!"

Just go. God will give you the words to say. And sometimes, you don't need to say much of anything. Just go. Be there. Make yourself vulnerable to her need. Be present. Go.

Show me if somewhere Jesus said to his followers, "Talk to others about me." What he said repeatedly was, "Follow me!" Put your beautiful feet in motion. Go!

I was at a workshop on evangelism in the local church. The leader, an expert in evangelism, said, "The toughest part in evangelism is simply walking into the room." Evangelism is not so much what is said but what is done, the feet being as important as the mouth.

What the women were told, when they went out to the tomb on the first Easter, was not simply, "Tell!" They were commanded by the angel to "Go! Tell!"

Chapter Nine

Sunday between October 30 and November 5 inclusive

[Proper 26, Ordinary/Lectionary 31]

Ruth 1:1-18
Psalm 146
Hebrews 9:11-14
Mark 12:28-34

Ordinary People

Selected reading

Ruth 1:1-18

Theme

The story of Ruth is the story of two ordinary women, Ruth and Naomi, who befriend each other and look after each other. Ruth dares to make Naomi's people her people. They rise above the tragedies in their lives and survive. Ruth thus becomes a parable of the way that God Almighty blesses the world, working through ordinary people to work God's wonders of salvation and preservation.

Introduction to the readings

Ruth 1:1-18

The widow Naomi's two sons die, and she bids her daughter-in-law Ruth to go back to her people. But Ruth refuses, vowing to stay with Naomi, saying, "Your people will be my people, and your God will be my God."

Hebrews 9:11-14

Christ came as the great high priest, says the writer to the Hebrews, the one whose blood purifies us.

Mark 12:28-34

A scribe asks Jesus, "Which commandment is the most important of all?" Jesus answered that the two greatest commandments are to love God and to love your neighbor. And "after that, no one dared to ask him any more questions."

Prayer

Lord Jesus, most of us gathered here today are not spectacular saints. We are ordinary Christians. Most of us will not be noted for our heroic feats of fidelity; we will be remembered, if at all, for our ordinary, everyday fulfillment of our duties. Few of us will know the blessing of spectacular revelation and dramatic, divine visions; we will know you through the ordinary means of grace—reading scripture, listening to a sermon, singing a hymn, and getting up on a Sunday morning and coming to church.

Thus we, ordinary Christians though we are, are bold to approach you in worship, are brash enough to ask your aid in our daily living, confident that you save the world by working through ordinary people to perform your extraordinary acts of mercy.

Use us, ordinary people, we pray. Amen.

Encountering the text

This is one of the few Sundays in the church year when our text is from the book of Ruth. Ruth's is a charming story, not only because it is a well-conceived biblical narrative, but also because it is a story in which the hero is a woman. Ruth is depicted as an ordinary person who deals with the difficulties and vicissitudes of life in a wonderfully faithful way. That ought to connect with many of the people to whom we preach because most of the people to whom we preach are ordinary people just trying to get by, serving God in rather unspectacular ways. Yet their unspectacular, ordinary faithfulness is also something beautiful for God.

Ruth is also noteworthy because she is not an Israelite. Ruth decides to join her fate with the destiny of the people of God and thus becomes someone who reminds the church of its mandate to reach out to all of God's people, stepping over traditional human boundaries in order to be faithful to God's expansive grace. Ruth is thus not only an ancestor of Jesus Christ but also a precursor of Jesus's expansive, boundary-breaking love.

If your church celebrates All Saints' Day on this Sunday, you can easily adapt today's proclamation to apply to All Saints' by focusing on Ruth and Naomi as two saints from the Hebrew scriptures who show us the way, the way that is embodied in its fullest with the coming of Jesus Christ. On All Saints' Day we celebrate the saints, all of them. All Christians, by virtue of our baptism, are "saints." That is, saints are ordinary, everyday, run-of-the-mill Christians.

If you would prefer not to preach on Ruth this Sunday, that is if your lectionary does not include this selection from Ruth, you can adapt much of this week's material as response to Jesus's critics' question, "Which commandment is the most important of all?" One might have expected Jesus, as a son of Israel, to respond with reference to the Sabbath laws or to the ritual practices of the temple. Instead he reaches into Israel's tradition and makes a stunning summary of Israel's faith—love of God and neighbor. The story of Ruth, in our interpretation, is a charmingly simple story of love and loyalty between two women from two different cultures. What would our world be like if Christians, in our lives and particularly in our interactions with other cultures, practiced our faith simply as love of God linked with love of neighbor?

Proclaiming the text

I've got a charming story for you this Sunday, a story of two women, two ordinary women who are survivors—the story of Ruth and Naomi. A famine in

Judah had driven Naomi, her husband, and their two sons to Moab. Naomi's husband died there, and her two sons married Moab women, one of whom was Ruth. Then the two sons also died without leaving any children behind. Surely you understand what that meant, in that day, in that part of the world. Naomi and Ruth and the other daughter-in-law were without much hope. No husbands and no children to care for them in their old age. A woman who was husbandless and childless in that day was referred to as "barren." And that stark word sums up their prospects for the future: barren. Now alone and vulnerable, Naomi tells her two daughters-in-law, "I have no more sons to offer you. You had better go live with your own people. Goodbye. I will go back to my people in Judah."

The other daughter-in-law leaves, but Ruth says something to Naomi, maybe the only thing you have ever heard out of the book of Ruth. Ruth says to Naomi, the younger woman speaking to the elder, "Don't urge me to abandon you, to turn back from following after you. Wherever you go, I will go; and wherever you stay, I will stay. Your people will be my people, and your God will be my God." It's a thought that is put into music and often sung at weddings. Though in this context it is a younger woman speaking to an older woman, it is often used to express the beauty of marriage in which a person, in marriage, takes on the family and the name of another person. My people will be your people.

For Ruth to say this to Naomi was rather amazing. Remember Ruth was a Moabite. Here we see someone of another race, another religion and nationality, and another generation, saying, "I will stick with you, I will be with you; where you go, I will go. Your people will be my people."

Thus the book of Ruth is also a story of two tough, resilient women who, after life has dealt them a couple of bad breaks, cling together and with clinch-fisted determination attempt to make it in the world. It wasn't easy for women in their day, particularly unmarried, childless women.

And survive they do. After returning to Judah, Naomi spots an old, fairly well-to-do man, Boaz, at his threshing floor. He needs a wife. So Naomi rushes to tell Ruth to put on her best dress and meet Boaz at the threshing floor.

Ruth meets Boaz, marries Boaz, and the rest is history. They have children, and those children go on to have other children, and they become part of the glad story of the perseverance, even the triumph, of God's chosen people. It's more than a story of mere survival; it's a story of human creativity and savvy resourcefulness. Maybe it's also a story of faith, faith that God means for us to have a future, faith that God has given us what we need in order to make the most of our circumstances. Ruth meets Boaz and marries Boaz, and they make a life together, at a place called Bethlehem.

I note that your ears perk up at the mention of this little town. The story of Ruth is a story that takes place in the little out-of-the-way village of Bethlehem. It is a story about two resilient women, who against all odds make a good life for themselves, make a future where there has been none, and triumph. You may now recall that Ruth, at Bethlehem, was the great, great, great-grandmother of Jesus.

The story of Ruth and Naomi is inspiring and charming. It is an everyday story. It is a story without any miracles or visions. There is not much mention of God in this story. It is mundane and everyday and ordinary and human. And yet that is part of this story's glory. In a mundane, ordinary, everyday place, named Bethlehem, two ordinary women become part of the purposes of God. Their stories are woven into the story of what God wants to do for the whole world. Presumably God couldn't have blessed the world through the advent of Jesus (which we will be celebrating here at the end of next month) without the resourcefulness, the faithfulness of Ruth.

Preaching is often an opportunity for high-sounding poetry. But a sermon also ought to be a time for great prose. The book of Ruth is a prosaic, mundane vision of how God deals with us. If we want to meet God, we need not go up to some mountaintop, some aloof, heavenly situated place. We need to be living in a place like Bethlehem, an ordinary and everyday place, where women have to get by on their wits and do the best they can in bad circumstances, where the cards that life deals us are not always what we want but we must play them as they are.

Do you want to get close to God? Then the story of Ruth, as well as the Gospel story of the babe at Bethlehem, suggests that we will meet God in our times of grief, when people leave us in untimely ways, people on whom we are dependent. We will meet God in times of vulnerability. When we have issues with our in-laws, when we are worried about what is going to become of us tomorrow, that's when God comes to us and dares to give us, even in our circumstances, something to do to help God save the world. Because of Jesus Christ, we believe that God is as much with us on Monday morning as on Sunday morning.

God loves us ordinary people in ordinary ways, thank God.

Relating the text

The book of Ruth and its story of two brave, though ordinary, women is often the Bible's way with the divine. The extraordinary arises within the ordinary. The heavenly breaks out amid the earthly. What we tend to call earthly and ordinary the Bible wants to depict as the realm of God's amazing work among us. If you want to meet God, then the Bible implies that you don't have to go off on some mountaintop. You don't have to rummage around in the recesses of your ego or move to some high spiritual summit. You just have to be in a place like Bethlehem, trying to make your way in the world, attempting to make ends meet, getting along as best you can with what you've got.

This is a counter view of "spirituality" that is abroad today. Many people have noted a dramatic outbreak in "spirituality" in America. Increasing numbers of Americans are becoming interested in spiritual matters. Most of this tends to be rather fluffy stuff, vague, ethereal, an attempt to inflate one's spirit and rise above the messy mundane quality of life. Spirituality is when we float above the grubbiness of the stuff of everyday life. But if you happen to live in an unspectacular, out-of-the-way place like Bethlehem (and that's where most of us live), don't believe it.

Archbishop William Temple once said, "Christianity is the most materialistic of all the world's religions." Or as C. S. Lewis said somewhere, "God likes matter, he invented it." Or, as one of my Jewish friends puts it, "Any God who won't tell you what to do with your pots, your pans, and your genitals, is not worth worshipping."

My wife conducted a weekly Bible study for graduates here at the university. They worked through the entire Bible in a year.

When they got to the book of Leviticus, one of the members of the Bible study opened up their discussion by saying, "I have been dreading this night. I have been dreading when we got to the book of Leviticus. Because I had heard that the book of Leviticus is down on people like me. I had heard that Leviticus has some nasty things to say about people of my sexual orientation. Well, what I learned this week is that Leviticus is down on lots of things! Leviticus has negative opinions about how we eat, how we treat livestock, how we make dinner, and how we make love. It isn't that Leviticus is opinionated about homosexuality; it's opinionated about just about everything! Maybe the way to deal with Leviticus is that you should only read Leviticus if you read all of it!"

Then another member of the Bible study group asked, "Why does God care about all of that stuff? I can't believe that God would have enough time to form an opinion about how we behave in the kitchen, how we behave in bedrooms, in living rooms. Why on earth does God care?"

Yet another member of the group responded, "But that is kind of great, when you think about it. God cares. God cares even about the stuff that happens in the kitchen. The pots and the pans and everything are religious."

Take that as a good definition of incarnation. Now that God has come into the world, through people like Ruth and Naomi, or a couple like Mary and Joseph, in a place like Bethlehem, now even the pots and the pans are religious.

What a God we've got. Or, more to the point of incarnation, what a God has got us. Now, after what happened in Bethlehem, with Ruth and Naomi, and with Mary and Joseph, if we are going to meet God, we need not climb up to the top of some mountain or rummage about in our psyche; we can meet God right here. Or better, God meets us here. In mundane ways God meets us—in something as common and everyday as a bit of bread or a sip of wine, in common things like people such as Ruth and Naomi or ordinary people like us.

Now, the word has been made flesh and dwells among us. Made flesh. Our flesh.

Wisdom of Solomon 3:1-9 or Isaiah 25:6-9

Psalm 24

Revelation 21:1-6a

John 11:32-44

Talking to the Dead

Selected reading

John 11:32-44 (Epis/RC, see the end paragraph under "Encountering the text")

Theme

In the church, we learn from, live by, and receive encouragement from the saints. We are not the first to walk the path of the cross. The saints have walked before us, and, if we will dare to listen and learn, they will show us the way.

Introduction to the readings

Isaiah 25:6-9

Isaiah foretells that day when God "will swallow up death forever" and will make a great feast for all the poor in which all will "be glad and rejoice in his salvation."

Revelation 21:1-6a
John, on the Island of Patmos, sees a stirring vision of "a new heaven and a new earth" where there is no weeping or mourning.

John 11:32-44
Jesus raises the dead brother of Mary and Martha, crying out, "untie him and let him go."

Prayer

Lord Jesus, we give you thanks for those who have preceded us in following you. We are grateful that we were not the first to venture forth in discipleship. We did not have to summon up the courage to serve you all on our own. You gave us the saints.

By their example, their prayers, their witness, their stories, and all the other ways they encouraged and instructed us, we give you thanks.

Enable us to profit from their examples. Give us grace to walk with your saints, to follow down the courageous way that they beckon us, to allow these noble examples to prod us to lives of greater faithfulness. Amen.

Encountering the text

We are preparing for another Sunday, that day when we talk with the dead. Although you might expect me to refer to the departed on All Saints' Day, truth to tell, every Sunday is an opportunity for Christians to be with the dead. Such talk may sound morbid or very odd. But only if you are unaccustomed to the Christian way of regarding those who have gone before us in this faith.

For instance, this Sunday, like almost any other Sunday, we will again be taking our cues from the literature of dead people—the prophet Isaiah, John on Patmos, and the Gospel of John.

In today's Gospel, Jesus raises his dead friend Lazarus. "Untie him and let him go," Jesus commands when he gets to Lazarus's tomb. In a way, that is a parable of what happens in your church every Sunday. We come into the presence of the dead—people like Isaiah, John, and Lazarus—all people who are entombed in the dead past. And then, by the action of the Holy Spirit, through the inspiration of Jesus, these long dead figures walk among us, speak to us, point us to the way.

We live in a culture that has been called "ahistorical." "History is bunk," said Henry Ford. Our memories don't go much further than what we had for lunch yesterday.

All Saints' Day is therefore a grand opportunity for us to be reminded of the gift of the saints, the peculiar wonder of a community (the church) that moves forward by looking back, that lives through talk with the dead. We do not have to make up our faith as we go. There are trustworthy guides who have walked before us—people like Isaiah, John, and the others who form the "communion of the saints." They will show us the way, if we have the courage to listen.

Epis/RC: Matthew 5:1-2 is your assigned Gospel. You will find that all of today's material is easily adaptable to Matthew's Beatitudes. Jesus describes our honored dead, the saints who have walked before us in meekness, peace, and righteousness. Since today's proclamation is a thematic sermon on the theme of the saints who have lived the faith before us, it can be adapted to almost any of today's lessons.

Proclaiming the text

I once served a church where my predecessor told me a strange story. Like many older churches, this one was surrounded by a huge cemetery where members of the church had been buried for generations. He was visited by some relatives of one of those who had been long buried there. They asked his permission to bring in a professional "medium" whom they were going to hire to stand beside their relative's grave and attempt to contact him. They wanted to seek the departed's advice on various family financial matters.

My predecessor refused. He told them that we were Christians and that "we didn't believe in stuff like that." Was he right to turn them away? We do not believe in the use of mediums, and we may not expect to receive specific directives from those who are now buried in the cemetery, but still, in a way, we do communicate with the dead. Maybe those who have left us in death cannot hear us; I do not know. But we do believe that we can hear them.

After all, this is All Saints' Day, that time of the church's year when we think about the saints, all of them, all those baptized who have lived this faith, walked the way of discipleship before us, and who now rest from their labors.

Yet not only this Sunday, but nearly every Sunday, we communicate with the dead. What have we done before this sermon? We have opened the scriptures, we have read from the testimony of those who have been dead for many centuries. We have engaged in a rather amazing act, amazing for folk in our culture. We have acted as if these ancient people with names like Isaiah, John, Lazarus, Mary, and Martha, know more about God than we do. We have believed that they have something to teach us that we could not learn any other way.

Christianity is an inherently "traditionalist" faith. Among the disciplines of discipleship is a willingness to listen to the dead, to give them a privileged place in our conversation. G. K. Chesterton said that democracy is that willingness to listen to someone's opinion and take it seriously, even if that person happens to be your groom. Tradition, Chesterton said, is that willingness to listen to someone's opinion even if he happens to be your father.

In today's Gospel, Jesus visits a family in grief. Lazarus, after a short illness, has died. His sisters, Mary and Martha, have already had the funeral and buried him. Jesus is deeply grieved by the death of his friend, Lazarus. Yet he comes out to the cemetery and, with a loud voice, commands him to rise. While this sounds like a resuscitation rather than a resurrection, we are right to hear in John's story a kind of echo of Easter. Jesus is Lord of life. Whenever he comes among the dead (even on the first Sunday in November), the dead begin to rise. Let that be a lesson for you.

In our world, the dead remain that way. We come to a dead end, the last chapter in the story, the end. What can be done? Give up and accept our fate, and all the other ways that we reconcile ourselves to death.

But here comes John and his Gospel, and Mary and Martha, to tell us the story of their brother, Lazarus, and how Jesus graciously brought him back to life. Now that Jesus has come into the world, things are not as fixed, final, finished as we once thought. Sometimes, by the strong work of Jesus, there is a way when we thought there was no way. Sometimes, even though it's November, Jesus can make it seem like Easter.

We would not know this truth had not John, Mary, and Martha and all the other saints told us this story and others like it. We would not know the gospel good news, would not know Jesus if a saint had not loved us enough to tell us that good news and to live it in such a way that we eventually heard it as our good news. None of us would be here without the saints.

So, we gather on Sunday, we open up the Bible, and we sing songs that none of us, or even anyone we know, created.

Sometimes we speak of the need for Christians to be givers. But on this Sunday, let us speak of our need to be receivers. We are to be the sort of people who are willing to listen, to receive what the saints have to teach us, to have our contemporary discipleship judged by their example.

The saints—those blessed dead who have gone before us—graciously show us the way.

Relating the text

"You shall no longer take things at second or third hand, nor look through the eyes of the dead, nor feed on the specters in books."

—Walt Whitman, "Song of Myself," 1855

"Heaven is not only about the future, but it is also about the past and the present. It is a means of connecting Christians now alive with all who went before them. Whatever else eternal life is, it is 'the communion of saints'—the bond of grace between all Christians living and dead. The loss of the concept of heaven is also the loss of a companionship we rightly feel with all who have preceded us in the faith."

—Laurence Hull Stookey (1937–2016)

"The saints have no need of honor from us; neither does our devotion add the slighted thing to what is theirs. Clearly, if we venerate their memory, it serves us, not them. But I tell you, when I think of them, I feel myself inflamed by tremendous yearning."

—Bernard of Clairvaux (1090–1153)

"*Saint*, n. A dead sinner revised and edited."

—Ambrose Bierce, *Devil's Dictionary*, 1911

Sunday between November 6 and November 12 inclusive

[Proper 27, Ordinary/Lectionary 32]

Ruth 3:1-5; 4:13-17 or 1 Kings 17:8-16

Psalm 127 or Psalm 146

Hebrews 9:24-28

Mark 12:38-44

Money and How to Manage It

Selected reading

Mark 12:38-44

Theme

Money is a gift of God. Like any of God's good gifts, money may be abused by us, made an idol, given ultimate homage that ought only be given to God. God has given us money so that we might show praise through the generous offering of our gifts to do God's work in the world as a sign of God's inbreaking kingdom among us.

Introduction to the readings

Ruth 3:1-5; 4:13-17

After the death of her husband, Ruth is in a vulnerable position. Her mother-in-law, Naomi, urges her to marry Boaz.

Hebrews 9:24-28

The writer to the Hebrews speaks of Jesus as the great high priest who bears the sins of the whole world.

Mark 12:38-44

At the temple Jesus watches people offering their gifts and notes a poor widow who gives all that she has to God.

Prayer

Most merciful God, from you comes every good gift. Your goodness created us, your bounty has daily sustained us, and your Son has forgiven and saved us. To you we owe all that we are and all that we have.

Enable us to show our gratitude through our cheerful, exuberant service to you and to others. Inspire in us that honest vision that sees our possessions, not as our achievements, but as your gifts. Give us the grace to give to others in the same fashion as we have been blessed by you—generously and graciously, happily and thankfully. Amen.

Encountering the text

Today's Gospel, Mark 12:38-44, has always been a threat to me. For one thing, Jesus begins by criticizing the religious leaders who crave public acclaim, who offer "long prayers," and who enjoy prominent positions at big banquets. I wear a "long robe" on Sundays. I like respect. I have been known to go on and on in prayer occasionally. Thus, this passage makes me nervous.

Moreover, then Jesus observes "rich people" offering gifts to God at the temple. Even though I don't like thinking of myself as rich, compared with the majority of the world's people, I am rich.

Jesus notices a poor woman whom most of the crowd overlooks, the poor widow who offers all that she has, even though it is only a modest coin: "All of them are giving out of their spare change. But she from her hopeless poverty has given everything she had, even what she needed to live on."

We see a couple of themes here that are dear to Mark's Gospel. For one thing, there is a rather constant barrage of criticism of the powerful and the influential. Then, there is note of the poor and the vulnerable. Moreover, there is the theme of the inbreaking of God's kingdom.

When God's kingdom comes near to us, the world breaks forth into various kinds of praise and thanksgiving. One way that we praise God is through offering money. The poor widow, it would seem, gave from more than a sense of duty or legal obligation. Her generous, effusive self-giving strikes us as an overflowing of gratitude and praise. Her gift is perceived by Jesus, not as a harsh sacrifice, but as a noteworthy expression of the kingdom. When God's kingdom comes, there is healing, exorcism, and joy. We need to be healed of our love of and worship of money. We need to be exorcised of the demon of materialism that holds so many of us captive.

In the fall of the year, many churches have their yearly church stewardship campaigns in which people are asked to give to the church. Therefore, this Sunday seems a good time to preach about money, about the way that the advent of Jesus and God's kingdom overturns our natural inclinations to hoard and accumulate and transforms even possessive people like us into generous givers.

In today's Gospel, Jesus bids us to notice this poor woman, a person we might have overlooked in our inclination to notice only the rich and powerful. Let us see her as a parable, a model for exuberant Christian generosity.

There is much material in today's "Relating the text" section. I urge you to use it, adapting it to your congregation to help them think this Sunday about managing money in a specifically Christian way.

Proclaiming the text

There is a wealth of illustrative material in today's "Relating the text" section. With your congregation in mind, use this material to order a sermon on the theme of money. How ought Christians look at and use money?

You might start with the passage from William Stringfellow as a pattern for a sermon on money. The quote from Allen Verhey provides a good biblical overview of the gospel attitude toward wealth and those who have it. The quote from Richard John Neuhaus could be put to good use as a clergy confession of how difficult it is to keep money in its place, even for us (especially for us?) clergy.

A possible sermon outline is the following:

A. Today's story of the widow's coin reminds us that Jesus had a great deal to say about money: where our money is, where our heart is.

B. The widow models a Christian view of money. Money is to be exuberantly given as a sign that Christ has made possible a new management of money that is gracious, giving, and glad.

C. What are some specific ways that we ought to show forth our faith by the way we manage our money? Here speak of the joy—yes, the joy—of giving, the way Jesus gives us the means to let go of our possessions, to give in a way that is carefree and joyful. The quote from Stringfellow could be helpful here.

We preachers probably don't speak as much about money as the Gospels speak of it. This Sunday is a great opportunity for us to speak about money in a way that is faithful.

Relating the text

"Money is the fruit of evil as often as the root of it."

—Henry Fielding (1707–1754)

In today's Gospel text, Jesus turns his disciples' attention away from the discussion of the prominent and the powerful (the scribes discussed in the first part of today's Gospel) and toward the poor widow. It isn't the size of her gift that Jesus recognizes or romanticizes. Rather, Jesus seems to indicate her utter self-abandonment in giving. She gives all. All.

Here is a woman whom we would label as a victim. Her husband has died, so now she is the victim of the economic and social injustices of the world.

But note what she does. She turns the whole system of accumulation and acquisition on its head. She gives all. In so doing, she becomes a judgment upon the cautious, miserly, grasping culture where most of us live and shows a way to a very different world. Jesus, being a representative of that other way, that alternative world, praises her.

"The [United States] is among the wealthiest countries in the world, and yet it is filled with people, rich and poor, who are anxious about their future and who feel they don't have enough."

—Sarah van Gelder, "Real Wealth: Redefining Abundance in an Era of Limits," *Yes! Magazine* (May 2, 1996)

"*Philanthropist*: a rich (and usually bald) old gentleman who has trained himself to grin while his conscience is picking his pocket."

—Ambrose Bierce (1842–1914)

"The carefree attitude toward riches forms in Jesus's followers a disposition, a readiness, to give generously to help the poor. Such action is the other side of the response to the eschatological blessing of the poor. The concrete command is 'sell your possessions and give alms'. . . . With such generosity one welcomes the coming kingdom and its present impact in Jesus. Jesus calls for such a response to the great reversal in this command; he is not to be understood as legislating. That the concrete command is not intended as legislation is made clear by the cognate command to lend to the poor (Luke 6:34-35), which presupposes continuing possession, by the example of Zacchaeus (Luke 19:1-10), and by the commendation of the costly 'waste' of ointment (Mark 14:3-9)."

—Allen Verhey, *The Great Reversal: Ethics and the New Testament* (Grand Rapids: Wm. B. Eerdmans Publishing Co., 1984), 18

"Freedom from idolatry of money, for a Christian, means that money becomes useful only as a sacrament—as a sign of the restoration of life wrought in this world by Christ. The sacramental use of money has little to do with supporting the church . . . the church and the church's mission do not represent another charity to be subsidized as a necessary or convenient benevolence, or as a moral obligation. . . . Appeals for church support as charity or for maintenance commonly end up abetting the idolatry of money.

"Such idolatry is regularly dramatized in the offertory, where it is regarded as 'the collection' and as an intermission in the worship of the people . . . the offertory is integral to the sacramental existence of the church, a way of representing the oblation of the totality of life to God. No more fitting symbol of the involvement of Christians in the everyday life of the world could be imagined, in American society at least, than money . . . the offering always implies a particular confession that their money is not their own because their lives are not their own but, by the example of God's own love, belong to the world."

—William Stringfellow, *A Keeper of the Word*, ed. Bill Wylie Kellermann (Grand Rapids: Wm. B. Eerdmans Publishing Co., 1994), 248–49

We clergy ought to make clear that the mismanagement of money is not only a problem for the laity! Richard John Neuhaus speaks of the dilemma of clergy mismanagement of and idolatry to money:

"For many people, Sinclair Lewis' Elmer Gantry still casts a shadow of suspicion over Christian ministry. Journalists relentlessly press the Gantry syndrome in connection. . . . There are very few decisions that a young pastor or pastoral couple make that are more important than the attitude toward money. One should as early as possible determine the top income one would ever want or strive to have. Of course, there has to be a degree of flexibility in such a decision, but the question of money and the dangers it poses should be kept under the closest scrutiny. Otherwise the desire ineluctably grows, avarice feeds upon itself, and one ends up as the victim of an appetite that is in fact insatiable and consumes by worry, guilt, and discontent the hours and days that were once consecrated to ministry."

—Richard John Neuhaus, *Freedom for Ministry* (New York: Harper & Row, 1979), 191–92

As a young minister, I was an associate pastor at a large church that hired a church fund-raiser to help us with a large capital-funds campaign. At the initial meeting, the fund-raiser asked the board about our goals for the campaign.

"You have to understand that we are a church that has a high percentage of older people, mostly widows on fixed incomes. So we really can't expect to raise too much money."

The fund-raiser asked to see a list of our major givers. He took the list with him at the close of the meeting.

The next meeting, he told the board that he had done an analysis of our congregation's giving.

"Please note," he told us in his report on his analysis of the church's giving patterns, "that the majority of your top fifty contributors are 'widows on fixed incomes.' Please note that, according to my calculations, those 'widows on fixed incomes' pay about 60 percent of this congregation's annual budget. I'd say if you want to improve the giving in this congregation, you need to talk to those women first, find out why they give, then try to infect the rest of the congregation with the faith of these 'widows on fixed incomes.'"

Sunday between November 13 and November 19 inclusive
[Proper 28, Ordinary/Lectionary 33]

1 Samuel 1:4-20
1 Samuel 2:1-10
Hebrews 11:14, (15-18), 19-25
Mark 13:1-8

Our Future with God

Selected reading
1 Samuel 1:4-20

Theme
God intervenes, steps in, and makes a way when we thought that there was no way. God has been with us not only in the past but also in the present, enabling us to be with God in the future.

Introduction to the readings
1 Samuel 1:4-20
Hannah, after years of barrenness, prays desperately for a child. She vows to dedicate the child to God. This child will grow up to be one of God's most powerful prophets, Samuel.

Hebrews 11:14, (15-18), 19-25
Hebrews looks at the Christ from the standpoint of the faith and expectation of Israel. Jesus is our great High Priest, the one who makes an offering on our behalf.

Mark 13:1-8

Walking past the beloved, massive temple, Jesus makes a stunning prediction: this great temple will be destroyed amid war and destruction.

Prayer

Lord Jesus, help us discern your will in all the events of our lives, good and bad. Give us the wisdom to seek not only your gifts but also your vocation. Transform the gifts that you give us into service for someone other than ourselves. Use our lives in your service. Amen.

Encountering the text

Our story is that of an old woman who is childless—and therefore, in that time and that place, also futureless. Children are our future, and here is a woman who has aged out of the possibility of children.

Then God shows up and Hannah is given the unimaginable gift of a child. Recognizing that her baby is a gift, Hannah immediately dedicates him to the Lord and names him Samuel, and the rest is history.

It is a story about a woman who is given a child and she in turn gives her son back to God. Hannah thus turns her good fortune into a vocation. Her child will not simply serve her needs in her old age; her child will serve God and be a part of God's loving work in the world.

In scripture, gift is often related to vocation. God not only blesses us but also gives us assignments. Thus our future becomes intertwined with God's future, our lives count for something as they are caught up in the loving purposes of God.

If your denominational lectionary does not include today's first lesson from 1 Samuel, you could adapt much of today's material to the Gospel from Mark 13. The story of God's promise to Hannah is a promise of a future. The episode of Jesus's prediction of the destruction of the temple is also a look into the future. Admittedly, the future, as Jesus foretells it, is a destructive time of suffering and loss. However, Jesus is here being an apocalyptic prophet who links God to the future. The horrendous events that he predicts are also part of God's providential care for creation. We don't always know what the future holds. It's a safe bet that the future will include both joy and sadness. However, in Jesus Christ, whatever the future holds, we know who holds the future. God is with us not only today but tomorrow as well.

Proclaiming the text

I was teaching the course "Introduction to the Ordained Ministry." I had the students introduce themselves by writing a couple of pages of autobiography, titled "My Life with God."

"How does God help to explain your life?" I asked them. "Tell me how God accounts for who you are."

I loved reading those papers. Most of us are skilled in explaining ourselves on the basis of ourselves. Our lives are the products of our desires, our choices, and our efforts.

Scripture attempts to teach us to narrate our lives as part of God's work with us. The life I'm living is not necessarily my own: God has desires, choices, and efforts that help to make my life something that God wants.

Well, the best paper in the batch was one that began, "I was a teenager from hell. I made my parents' lives miserable. They weren't surprised when, only after a year, I flunked out of the University of Texas, drinking and partying my way into oblivion."

I knew I was in for a treat of an autobiography and I wasn't disappointed.

"I hung around Austin for a while and strangely, got involved in a nearby United Methodist church. I thought I was rebelling against church, but I loved this church, adored the pastor, and got more and more involved. Then one Sunday afternoon I drove back to my little town in Texas to tell my parents the astounding news that I was going back to school, that I was going to become a Methodist preacher.

"When I sat my parents down and told them the incredible news, I was shocked when my mother immediately broke into tears and said, 'I'm so embarrassed. I'm so ashamed.'

"Embarrassed? Ashamed? I thought. What did my mother mean? Then she spoke, 'Do you remember that I had two miscarriages before I was pregnant with you? When I got pregnant with you, I prayed to God that if he would only help me bring this baby to term I would dedicate him to the Lord. And I would call his name Samuel, just like in the Bible.'

"And I said, 'You did what? You sure could have saved me a lot of trouble if you had told me that story sooner!'

"'I didn't know it would work,' she confessed. 'We're Methodists! We don't take this stuff literally.'"

I tell you this story to warn you, just in case you think you are hearing ancient history when I read you the story of Hannah and Samuel, that stories like this still happen. That is, God continues to give people unimaginable gifts. In Hannah's case, God gave her a child in her old age. In so doing, God gave Hannah a future that she thought impossible.

But there's more. Hannah knows enough about the way God works to know that God's gifts often entail God's assignments. When God intervenes, God also often calls. Hannah didn't just get a baby boy; she also gave the boy to the service of God.

Rarely does God give us gifts that are solely for our personal benefit. God gives us gifts so that we may be better givers to God and our neighbors.

On Sunday morning we pray: God, give me better health. God, please give my family some peace and stability. God, help me be faithful in my marriage. God, enable me to achieve the goals that I have set for myself.

But if we are to pray faithfully, then our prayers must be not only about what we want but also about aligning our lives to what God wants. We must therefore also pray: God, prod me to use my good health for someone other than myself. God, give my family a meaning greater than my family. God, help my marriage to be in service to the needs of others. Lord, help my eagerly sought goals to also be your goals.

The Germans have an expression, "Every gift (*gabe*) entails an assignment (*aufgabe*)." I think that is what Hannah embodied. I think that's the lesson of this ancient, beloved story for us today.

Relating the text

In the Gospel of John, Jesus said that he goes "to prepare a place for you." Is that good news? Consider the places that Jesus prepares for us here—places where there are different, sometimes demanding, difficult people, places where there are huge needs to be met. Maybe the good news is that Jesus precedes us and prepares a place where we can do good work in his name.

The high school commencement speaker stood at the podium and in his address urged the graduates to have a dream, to follow their dream, to let no one or nothing deter them from their life's dream. And this sort of talk is fine, but it is not particularly Christian. Christians are people who are attempting to live out God's dream, to live their lives in such a way that God may get what God wants.

In *Ethics*, Dietrich Bonhoeffer spoke directly to the question of whether the task of the church is to offer solutions to the world for its problems:

"It is necessary to free oneself from the way of thinking which sets out from human problems and which asks for solutions on this basis. Such thinking is unbiblical. The way of Jesus Christ, and therefore the way of all Christian thinking, leads not from the world to God but from God to the world. This means the essence of the gospel does not lie in the solution of human problems, and that the solution of human problems cannot be the essential task of the church."

—Dietrich Bonhoeffer, *Ethics*, 1949

Years ago Fred Craddock, professor of preaching at the Candler School of Theology in Atlanta, was on vacation with his wife in the Smoky Mountains in Tennessee. It was the last day of vacation, and they'd stopped at a favorite little café called the Blackberry Inn. They didn't want to be bothered.

Well, this old country fellow walked in, just talking to everybody (you know the type). Fred thought, *curses*, as he hid behind the menu. Sure enough, the old guy came to Fred's table:

"You folks on vacation?"

"Yes."

"Having a good time?"

I was, thought Fred.

"Gonna be here long?"

"No, not at all."

"What do you do?"

That was the question Fred had been waiting for, because he could shut people down with his answer: "Well, I'm a professor of homiletics and theology." The old man lit up and said, "You're a preacher man! Well, I got a preacher story for you!" He pulled up a chair and sat down.

"Yeah, I was born back in these mountains. My momma wasn't married. We lived in a shack outside of town. The other women in town used to spend their time guessing who my daddy was. And I didn't know who my daddy was. That was a real problem back then.

"My momma worked a lot. Other kids weren't allowed to play with a boy like me. I would hide in the weeds at recess, and I ate my lunch alone. They said I wasn't any good and I'd never amount to anything.

"Kids used to call me Ben the Bastard Boy . . . Ben the Bastard Boy . . . I thought Bastard Boy was my last name."

The old man was weeping now, but he collected himself.

"Well, anyway, there was a church in Laurel Springs. It had this preacher. His voice was big like God. I knew church wasn't a place for boys like me."

(We know at church they wouldn't call him Bastard Boy; they'd find other ways to say the same thing.)

"Sometimes I'd sneak in and sit toward the back so I could sneak out before the service ended. But this one day, I just got lost in what the preacher was saying. Before I knew it, church was over. The aisles got all jammed up. Folks were looking at me. I was making for the back door quick as I could when all at once I felt this big hand on my shoulder.

"This big voice boomed, 'Boy!' It was the preacher man himself! He said, 'Boy!' I froze. He talked so loud everybody heard as he said, 'Boy, who's your daddy? Boy, I know who your daddy is.' That was a knife in my gut, and I wondered did he know who my daddy was. He said, 'Boy, now let's see . . . why, you're a child of' . . . he paused and everyone listened, 'Boy, why you're a child of God, and I see a strikin' resemblance!' Then he swatted me on the bottom and said, 'Now you run along and go claim your inheritance.'"

Fred looked at the old guy. He seemed familiar, so Fred asked, "Sir, what's your name?" The old guy said, "Ben Hooper." Fred replied, "Ben Hooper . . . Ben Hooper . . . Oh Yes! I remember my daddy telling me about you, the illegitimate boy elected twice the governor of Tennessee."

Old Governor Hooper looked up at Fred and with tears in his eyes said, "I was born that day."

—Fred Craddock, *Preaching Today* (audio), as recounted in a sermon by Tony Campolo at Bel Air Presbyterian Church, Los Angeles, CA, January 1988

Reign of Christ or Christ the King
Sunday between November 20
and November 26 inclusive
[Proper 29, Ordinary/Lectionary 34]

2 Samuel 23:1-7 or Daniel 7:9-10, 13-14
Psalm 132:1-12, (13-18) or Psalm 93
Revelation 1:4b-8
John 18:33-37

Overwhelmed

Selected reading
Revelation 1:4b-8

Theme
Jesus Christ is Lord and king. His reign, begun from the cross, will be brought to fruition. It's great grace, particularly during times of stress, distress, and chaos, to know who sits on the throne. The pretended rulers of this world do not have the final word. They will be overwhelmed. Jesus will reign.

Introduction to the readings
2 Samuel 23:1-7
As King David nears death, he praises the greatness of God.

Revelation 1:4b-8
The vision of John begins with glorious praise to the Almighty God.

John 18:33-37

Pilate questions Jesus during his trial, asking him, "Are you the king of the Jews?"

Prayer

Almighty God, who gave unto your Son, Jesus Christ, a realm where all peoples, nations, and races might worship and serve him, help us see your reign among us.

Give us the courage to acknowledge your lordship amid the competing and conflicting claims to loyalty that other principalities and powers make upon us.

Alpha and Omega, beginning and end, come among us in power and glory, still our anxious hearts, give us renewed confidence in the ultimate triumph of your will for the world. Give us the gifts we need to be loyal citizens of your kingdom and no other. Amen.

Encountering the text

The Revelation to John begins with a great shout of joy. This, the last book of the Bible, celebrates the triumph of God, the realization of God's justice in a world filled with injustice and suffering. Here is no distant, uninvolved deity. In Christ, God has decisively entered the world, reclaiming lost territory as God's own.

The note of joyful triumph that begins this vision, continues throughout. Even when the letter moves from celebration and doxology to criticism of the church and the present order, all of that criticism is predicated on the initial affirmation of the triumph of God in Jesus Christ.

Today's text is poetic and hymnic in quality. It seems to sing what it says. Therefore, detailed, verse-by-verse explication of the poetry seems beside the point. Rather, we are meant to enjoy this hymn of praise, this great shout of victory. In our sermon, it will be our task to explore the implications of the hymn rather than to dwell on various details.

Here, at the end of the church's year, we end with focus upon the reign of Christ and joyous acclamation of God's ultimate victory.

Here is a word that needs to be sounded in the contemporary church. When we gather for church, we are apt to be overwhelmed by all of the ways in which we fail at being the church. When we look at the headlines in today's news, it is quite understandable when we ask, "Where is God?" In the light of today's somber headlines, it seems more logical for the church to be speaking about defeat rather than victory. However, in the church's peculiar logic, a logic that is engendered in us through our confrontation with scripture, we dare to acclaim, all evidence to the contrary, that Jesus reigns. God has met the seemingly overwhelming forces of evil with the overwhelming force of God's grace and love.

Proclaiming the text

The newscaster had just reported the death, in England, of a little girl who took her own life, saying that she could no longer bear to live. She was simply overwhelmed by the cruelty of her classmates who ridiculed her and made fun of her because of her weight problem. The little girl said in a suicide note that she had nothing left to do but to take her own life.

After the newsperson had read this report from England in businesslike, unemotional words, she looked up from her script, stared into the camera, and said, "Isn't that the worst thing you have ever heard? Just overwhelming in its sadness."

I thought her comments rather remarkable. Here was a newscaster who made her living, day after day, week-in, week-out, reading reports of assorted tragedy and heartache. It was amazing that she still had any feeling left. It was wonderful that she still could be moved to great pity despite her daily diet of assorted heartache and tragedy. Pity is no small achievement in an age in which we are overwhelmed by tragedy.

That is why the British theologian David Ford has called our age the "age of overwhelmed-ness." Ford says that in our age, we have been so exposed, principally thanks to the media, to assorted evidence of tragedy, heartbreak, and despair, that we are overwhelmed. The occasional natural disaster, which humanity hears from vague reports of long after the fact, has become our daily diet on the evening news.

There are people who spend their entire lives compiling statistics of the pain: the number of deaths on the highway each year; the number of infants who die from Sudden Infant Death Syndrome; the carnage due to cancer, AIDS, or other epidemics. In fact, they don't even call it an epidemic anymore. We call it a pandemic because the results are so massive. Little wonder that vast numbers of us are overwhelmed.

Some of us attempt to defend ourselves from being overwhelmed by the pain. We turn off the evening news when it begins, or else we become numbed. We lose ourselves in engagement with the sports of the daily news rather than the current events.

And yet, in our better moments, we know that this numbness, this psychic turning away, is an inappropriate response to the problem. We must face the tragedy. Tragedy is a fact of modern life, and we must face facts. If we are going to do anything about the problems that beset us, we have to confront the problems honestly.

During an age of overwhelmed-ness, however, it is difficult to look at things honestly.

In Shakespeare's *Hamlet*, the young prince muses to himself, asking what he ought to do in response to the sin of his mother and his uncle who had killed his father and now have married each other. Young Hamlet wonders if it is better to take up the sword against "a sea of troubles," or whether it is better to simply pull the covers up over his head, to end his life, to sleep, perhaps even to dream, and to end it all. Young Hamlet is faced by a sea of troubles that has become a veritable flood. He is overwhelmed.

Presently, there are many people who feel they lack the capacity to even talk about the problems of our world. As a new century begins, how do we feel? Do we feel exuberant, confident about what lies ahead? Or do we feel overwhelmed? Our problems seem so large, so intractable, so resistant to our little actions. What can anybody do? Like Hamlet, we wonder if the most prudent force is simply to quit, to anesthetize ourselves in some fashion, to sleep, to dream. Where on earth would we get the strength to take up arms against a "sea of troubles" when that sea has become an overwhelming flood?

Here, at the end of the church's year, when we traditionally celebrate the reign of Christ, our text is from the Revelation to John. The Revelation, the last book of the Bible, arises out of a troubled church. Rarely does the writer turn aside and give us a hint of the troubles that these fledgling congregations faced, but we know, reading between the lines, that here was a church clinging for its life on the fringes of the Roman Empire. You can almost see them there, a little band of Christians, surrounded in the pagan cities. They seemed so small, so overwhelmed. What are they to do?

Where on earth might one find hope for the future in such circumstances?

Interestingly, Revelation begins with great shouts of praise. One might expect the vision to begin in despair. After all, the church is in trouble, and the empire is stepping up its persecutions of Christians. What hope is there in that?

However, despite all evidence to the contrary, Revelation is noted for its sustained outbursts of exuberant joy and praise. The vision begins, not in despair, but in doxology, in praise, in cadences that scholars believe were derived in great part from some of the hymns of the early church. They certainly sound like hymns. Listen to today's scripture again. (Read a portion of today's lesson from Revelation.)

John, who should have been overwhelmed by the great sea of troubles that faced him and his beloved churches, responds by an overwhelming affirmation of the grace and triumph of God in Christ. In Jesus Christ, God has decisively entered the world and is busy reclaiming a lost world. Revelation begins with poetry that evokes images of invasion, of cosmic battles, then of decisive victory by Almighty God.

John on the island of Patmos responded to the overwhelming-ness of the present evil with affirmation of the overwhelming-ness of the victory of God in Jesus Christ.

Sweeping claims are being made here. What happens in Jesus is not something that is personal or private, as we sometimes pervert the Christian faith. It is all very public. Political even. Cosmic even. Matters of vast importance are being addressed. Seemingly intractable problems are being defeated. There is no corner of creation that is immune from this sweeping influx of grace.

British theologian David Ford finds an analogy here to the Wesleyan revival in England during the eighteenth century. In the mid-eighteenth century, John Wesley began his ministry in an England that seemed overwhelmed by social problems. The gin trade had led to huge problems with alcoholism. The industrial revolution had lain waste the rural English countryside, resulting in a vast influx of people seeking employment in the cities. Child labor was the scourge of the land. There was vast social dislocation and chaos. Things seemed overwhelming.

Eventually, John Wesley countered these problems, not necessarily with a new social program for human betterment, but rather with a revival that, in Ford's words, "responded to the problems of the day with an overwhelming affirmation of Divine grace." The Wesley brothers responded to the problems of their day with singing, with hymns. Among the great legacies of the Wesleyan revival are some of our most beloved hymns such as "O for a Thousand Tongues to Sing," "Hark the Herald Angels Sing," and "Love Divine, All Loves Excelling."

What good do hymns do? Do they put food on the table? Do they solve any of our economic or social problems? What good did the hymns of Charles Wesley do for England? Or for that matter, what good do the opening hymns of Revelation do?

I think they respond to the overwhelming-ness of evil with an affirmation of the power of God. And that is the place to begin. If we lack confidence in the ultimate triumph of the will and purposes of God, then we will never have courage to honestly face our situation. We have to have someplace to stand, some great foundational affirmation that will enable us to be truthful about our circumstances. Only secure, confident people can be truthful.

Therefore, Revelation begins with a great shout of joy, a great, exuberant, confidant affirmation of the power of God.

Therefore, this morning, if we really want to face our problems squarely, if we really want to stride into the future with confidence, the best thing we could do is to sing. We need to sing some exuberant hymn about the triumph of the grace of God.

You have undoubtedly experienced this yourself here on Sundays. You come here and, despite my best efforts in the sermon, despite the clear reading of God's word in scripture, what really moves you, what really fills you with power to go on, is the singing. When we join our voices together in some great hymn of praise, then you know, in the very depths of your being, that Jesus Christ reigns, that he will rule until all things have been put under his feet, that the enemies of God will ultimately be defeated, that good will have the last word over evil, and that all will be well.

You know this, not in some rational, intellectual way, but rather in the deepest, most profound depths of your being. Worship enables you to go on.

May I suggest that that is the major reason why you are here this morning? You are looking for strength to go on in an "age of overwhelmed-ness." The only way to go on is to counter the seeming overwhelmed-ness of evil with a counterbalancing affirmation of the overwhelmed-ness of the power of God.

Our God is not some distant, aloof, uncaring deity, some empathetic but essentially powerless being. Our God not only cares but also acts. Our God has power to heal the brokenness among us.

And that's why we sing.

Relating the text

The distinguished Yale scholar Robert Jay Lifton used to write about "nuclear numbness." Lifton, a psychologist by trade, said that in the face of nuclear proliferation and the possibility of a nuclear disaster, people simply become numb. Their ability to reason, to plan ahead, and to take in information shuts down. They become overwhelmed. The nature of nuclear threat is such that our ability to conceptualize the threat is overwhelmed by the nature of the threat.

Some feel that the nuclear threat has dissipated, but there have been plenty of other threats behind the nuclear threat. "Psychic numbness" may be an apt distinction of many people in our age.

Several years ago, I was involved in a meeting concerning racial problems in our city. The meeting was long and rather depressing. It was difficult to find a common theme, other than that we had racial problems and no one knew exactly what to do about them.

On the way out of the meeting, a man who was a lifelong activist during the Civil Rights Movement said to me, "It makes you long for the '60s, doesn't it?"

I asked him what he meant.

He continued, "Back in the '60s, when it came to racism, we knew exactly what we needed to do. We had a clear goal—the passage of new legislation.

We could organize accordingly and move toward our goal. When we achieved our goal, we could celebrate and feel good here. But today, the problems are subtler. The conflict is deeper. There is no clear picture of what we need to do, no consensus on what comes next. It is all very depressing. We just feel overwhelmed."

We certainly do.

A student group had invited me to speak on any subject of my choosing. Having heard this before, I talked with the president and he said, "Any topic of my choosing? What if I spoke on the topic, 'Current problems on campus that must be addressed'?"

There was a long silence. The student then responded, "Dean Willimon, I don't think so. Frankly, we are just overwhelmed with problems. We are exhausted from discussion. What I think we would like to hear about are solutions. Do you have any good news? Is there anything constructive and positive that can be said about the climate on campus?"

Good news, indeed. There is a sense in which good news must precede any discussion of bad news. Only after we have been convinced that there is a possibility of grace, a possibility of good news, a possibility of the triumph of good, are we able to speak of what needs fixing.

Let today's sermon, delivered on the Sunday when we focus upon the reign of Christ, be an occasion for unadulterated, exuberant, joyous good news.

Today's "Proclaiming the text" notes the hymnic quality of the opening of Revelation. The current hymns of praise to the church are also referred to. It would, therefore, be most appropriate to select some strong, exuberant hymns of praise for today's service. You might also consider selecting three or four hymns of praise that relate to themes of the sermon and then interspersing these hymns throughout the sermon.

For instance, after beginning the sermon, noting that we live in an "age of overwhelmed-ness," you might have the congregation sing a couple of verses of "A Mighty Fortress Is Our God." Then resume the sermon for a few paragraphs and have them sing another hymn like, "Joyful, Joyful, We Adore Thee." In other words, by the time you got to the end of the sermon in which you affirm the power of music to respond to the overwhelming-ness of the world's evil, you would have demonstrated your point in the worship of the congregation.

PREACHING
WORKSHOPS

Preaching Miracles

This being Year B in the Common Lectionary, you will note that we have had many miracles to preach. Mark majors in a depiction of Jesus as worker of miraculous signs. Furthermore, for a number of Sundays this summer, we have been in the Gospel of John, which also contains a number of "signs" that are said to point to the true significance of Jesus.

In his article on miracles and preaching in the *Concise Encyclopedia of Preaching*, Professor Ronald J. Allen says,

> We might define a miracle as an event which manifests power in an extraordinary way. The purpose of the miracle is to effect change (normally positive) in the affairs of the human or cosmic communities and to demonstrate the power of the agent responsible for the miracle. The miracle worker hopes to win or confirm the trust of those who witness the miracle. A miracle story narrates a miracle. The purpose of the miracle story is ordinarily to win or confirm the trust of those who hear or read the story in the power that performs the miracle in the narrative. The miracle story also reveals possibilities for the human and cosmic realms which result from the presence of the power in the world. The miracle story does not present details which explain the miraculous happening as such but simply presumes its occurrence.

We might more simply think of miracles, particularly those of Jesus, as testimony that something is afoot in the affairs of humanity. We live in a world in which we are drawn to the predictable and the certain. When something happens more than once, we assume it to be a pattern, a "law of nature" that is predictable and demystified. Miracles intrude into this settled arrangement and imply that there is, in the words of Hamlet to Horatio, "More things in heaven and earth than are dreamt of in your philosophy." In scripture, God is ordinarily the power who performs miracles, but not always. Jesus works miracles as a sign of the inbreaking of the kingdom of God. However, people unrelated to God can do miraculous works (Acts 8:9-13; 13:4-12), and even Satan and Satan's representatives can work miracles that parallel those of God (Rev 13:11-15).

Miracles and miracle workers appear to have been commonplace in many cultures of antiquity. So the primary New Testament question is not, "Did this miracle really happen?" but the theological, interpretive question is, "Is this miracle a work of the true and living God, or is it something that detracts us from God?" Jesus appears, in many places in scripture, to be ambivalent about miracles and signs. He seems to have criticized those who clung to the miracles without seeing them as pointing to the presence of God. Apparently, miracles can be an idolatrous substitute for God and any wondrous sign demands some.

In the European Enlightenment, miracles suddenly became a problem for propagators of the Christian faith in a way that they had not been before. The Enlightenment split of the world into the "natural" world and the "supernatural" world caused problems for the biblical witness to miracles. Furthermore, when the natural world was conceived of as a place of unbreakable "laws," miracles seemed to be an upsetting disturbance in the way the world was designed.

In the premodern view of the biblical writers, the cosmos is a single sphere in which the divine presence and power is manifested in many ways, of which miracle is one.

This suggests that biblical readers did not think of a miracle as an outside intrusion, an overturning of nature, but rather as a kind of uncovering, a revelation of what was really going on in the world.

Preachers today ought not to be concerned over the modern quandary of whether the biblical miracles occurred as described; there is no way for contemporary research to confirm or deny the occurrence of such events. Some people in our congregations, however, are often troubled about these matters. Rather than enter into a dubious debate over whether or not a miracle happened, we ought instead to encourage our hearers to ask, What does this event reveal about the nature of God? Who is the beneficiary of this miracle? Who would be hurt by the miracle? What did this miracle do for the believing community? What does it do for us? Once we have answered those questions, we preachers can then ponder the ways in which we can effect the same function within the sermon.

Biblical scholar Antoinette Wire identifies four kinds of miracle stories that stress the "political," power implications of miracle. A miracle is God's way of opening closed, oppressive systems that dehumanize and degrade people, says Wire. Among the functions of a miracle that she identifies are, first, provision miracles (e.g., the manna in the wilderness), which portray divine provision in the midst of want. A sermon on this type of miracle might ask how God provides similarly today. The second function of a miracle is exorcisms (e.g., the Gerasene demoniac), which represent God's displacement of arbitrary, restrictive, even violent powers with freedom for the possessed. So a sermon on these miracles enquires into the ways that powers bind people today and the ways in which God defeats those oppressive powers. Third is controversy miracles (e.g., the healing of the withered hand on the Sabbath), which picture God's work in releasing people from a variety of social and moral restrictions. The preacher might ponder ways in which God is releasing today's society from arbitrary social and moral laws. Fourth is request miracles (e.g., the woman with the issue of blood), which are initiated at the request of someone who feels bound but who shows faith in Christ by requesting a miracle. When the request is granted, potency is restored.

I am drawn to the insights of contemporary literary criticism that stresses that the miracle stories must be interpreted with reference to the total narrative in which they occur. For instance, the Gospel of Mark certainly enjoys portraying Jesus as a powerful force who works deeds of power for good. When Jesus arrives, the power seems to break forth, and there is new possibility for people who are trapped and bound.

Literary critics stress that miracle stories create a "world," a narrative environment in which we come to see our received world in a different way.

Sometimes the miracle story itself can offer a way of presenting our sermon. Into our human caughtness and sense of despair, Jesus intrudes and works newness and wonder-evoking power. Miracles are a constant reminder that our world is not closed, fixed. The future of the world, the fate of human life, is not all within our hands. Particularly for the impotent and the dispossessed, Jesus offers life and power for God. Every miracle is therefore a sort of Easter, a sign that God is determined to work his will in the world, despite all the forces arrayed against the will of God.

(I have been helped in these thoughts by Ronald J. Allen's *Our Eyes Can Be Opened: Preaching the Miracle Stories of the Synoptic Gospels Today* [Lanham, MD: University Press of America, 1982].)

On *Not* Reaching Our Culture through Our Preaching

Recently I led a group of pastors in a discussion about our preaching. When I asked the pastors, "What areas would you like help with in your preaching?" most of them responded with, "I want help in making connection with my listeners, relating the gospel to their everyday lives."

"I want to preach sermons that really hit my people where they live." "I want to preach in a way that is real, that addresses the real-life concerns people really have."

In sum, these pastors wanted to preach in a way that addressed their culture. There was a time when I would have agreed that this was one of the primary purposes of Christian preaching—to relate the gospel to contemporary culture. However, I have come to question this way of construing the task of Christian preaching.

Most of the preaching I have heard in my own church family really tries hard to relate the gospel to the modern world. I have come to believe that that is our weakness rather than our strength. In leaning over to speak to the modern world, I fear that we may have fallen in! When, in our sermons, we sought to use our sermons to build a bridge from the old world of the Bible to the new modern world, the traffic was only moving in one direction on that interpretive bridge. It was always the modern world rummaging about in scripture, saying things like, "This relates to me," or, "I'm sorry, this is really impractical," or, "I really can't make sense out of that." It was always the modern world telling the Bible what's what. I have come to see that this way of preaching fails to do justice to the rather imperialistic claims of scripture. I don't believe that the Bible wants to "speak to the modern world." Rather, I think the Bible is after bigger game. The Bible doesn't want to speak to the modern world. The Bible wants to change and convert the modern world.

We, who may have lived through the most violent century in the history of the world—based on body counts alone—ought not to give too much credence to the modern world. Not only is the modern world the realm of the Internet, the telephone, the telegraph, and allegedly "critical thinking"; but this world is also the habitat of Auschwitz, two of the bloodiest wars of history, and assorted totalitarian schemes that have taken the lives of millions. Why would our preaching want to be comprehensible to that world?

The modern world must be made to understand that it is nothing more than that—just a "world." By that I mean the modern world is an ideological construct. The modern world is an idea, an intellectual fabrication, a way of construing reality that has lasted for about two hundred years, mainly in northern Europe and some of its colonies, which now may be ending. Modernity, which held sway over human imaginations in the industrialized West for about two centuries, is now losing its grip.

Unfortunately, too often Christians treated the modern world as if it were a fact, a reality to which we were obligated to adjust and adapt, rather than a point of view with which we might argue. Modernity has arrogance built right into itself. That is, modernity, which began as a search for certain and irrefutable knowledge, a quest for the "facts," likes to think of itself, not as a point of view or way of construing the world, but simply as the facts. Therefore, all other ways of construing the world must converse with modernity on modernity's terms. Any other way of construing the world is labeled, by modernity, as being "primitive," "narrow," "tribal," or "provincial."

Fortunately, modern ways of knowing and thinking are gradually losing their privileged status in Western thought. We are realizing that modernity is only one way of describing what is going on in the world. Modernity has been a good ride in many ways. Humanity has received many gifts from modern, scientific, technological ways of thinking. However, as we move through the first quarter of the twenty-first century, we are realizing that modernity was not without its losses.

Moreover, when we speak of reaching out to our culture through the gospel, we must be reminded that the gospel is also a culture. This is only one of the problems with the attempt to "translate" the gospel into the language of the culture. As we often say, "Something is lost in translation." We are learning that you have not said "salvation" when you say "self-esteem." To have "a positive self-image" is not at all what Christians mean when we say "redemption." To invoke "the American way" is not equivalent to "God's kingdom."

One reason this sort of translation is doomed to failure, one reason why it inevitably ends up with our preaching something much less than the gospel of Jesus Christ, is that Christianity is a culture. Just as you cannot learn to speak French by reading a French novel in an English translation—you must sit for the grammar, the syntax, and the vocabulary and learn it—so you cannot know Christianity by having it translated into some other medium like Marxism, the American way, or the language of self-esteem. Christianity is a distinct culture, with its own vocabulary, grammar, and unique practices, just like any other culture. Too often, when we reach out to speak to our culture, we merely adopt the culture of modernity at the moment, rather than presenting the gospel to the culture.

Rather than reaching out to speak to our culture, I think our time as preachers is better spent enculturating modern, later twentieth-century Americans into a culture that is called church. When I first walk into a class on introductory physics, I do not expect to understand the vocabulary, terminology, and concepts. Why should it be any different for modern Americans walking into a church?

This is why the concept of "user friendly churches" leads to churches getting used. There is no way that I can crank the gospel down to the level at which any American can walk in off the street and know what it is all about within fifteen minutes. My Lord, one can't even do that with baseball! You have to learn the vocabulary, the rules, and the culture in order to understand it. Being in church is something at least as different as baseball.

Therefore, rather than worrying a great deal about "reaching our culture," I think that we mostly ought to worry about speaking to the church, forming the church through our speech, laying on contemporary Christians the stories, images, and practices that make us disciples.

The other day someone emerged from Duke Chapel and had the audacity to tell me, "I have never heard anything like that before. Where on earth did you get that?"

Fortunately, I had the presence of mind to respond. Where on earth would you have heard this before? After all, this is a pagan, unformed, uninformed university environment. Where would you hear this? In the philosophy department? Watching *Mr. Rogers' Neighborhood* on TV? Give me a break. No, to hear this, you've got to get dressed and come down here on a Sunday morning.

It is an anachronistic, strange assumption for a contemporary American to feel that he or she already has the equipment necessary to comprehend the gospel, without any modification of lifestyle, any struggle, in short, without being born again.

When you join Rotary, they give you a handshake, a lapel pin, and a membership card. When you join the church, we strip you down, throw you in the water, and half-drown you. This is our way of saying, "Welcome to discipleship. Be prepared for the shock of moral regeneration and intellectual reorientation. Here is a way of life that is more than simply a different way of construing the human condition. Here is something that is nothing less than a counterculture to the one in which you have been."

The point is not to speak to the culture. The point is to change it. God's appointed means of producing change is called church. God's typical way of producing church is called preaching.

Poetic Preaching

W. H. Auden is reputed to have once said, "You don't have to be a poet to be a Christian, but it really helps." Biblical literature tends to be highly metaphorical, imaginative speech pushed to the limit—and that's not a bad definition of poetry itself.

I dearly love those moments in scripture when a biblical writer is plodding along in prose, just reporting what has happened, just telling about an historical event, and then it is as if the prose cannot contain what the writer is saying. The writer breaks forth in psalm, hymn, doxology, or acclamation. Only poetry will do.

So paraphrasing Auden, I'll say that you don't have to be a poet to be a preacher, but it really, really helps if you are!

Poetry says to us things that we are unable to say to ourselves. A good poem writes in the oddness of human life, whereas most of the time, most of us regard the oddness of human life with perplexity.

I remember hearing a poet describe the function of poetry as that of a "speed bump" in our thinking. Poetry slows us down. And as Flannery O'Connor once complained, "Modern people don't take long looks at anything." We are accustomed to rushing along, not stopping to pay attention or to "take long looks at anything."

Poetry helps us to be attentive.

One of the most challenging lessons I had to understand in learning how to read a poem was to get over my modern notion that poetry is a reflection of my experience. I had the impression that a poet has some experience and then writes to share the experience with others—experience connecting with experience.

Poetry, I discovered, is not so much a reflection of someone's personal experience but rather poetry is the creation of human experience. The greatest poems have an alien quality about them. They are artifacts, a word from the outside, a word not self-derived. So many of our best poems are words that we cannot speak to ourselves, a word from another. However, sometimes when we are reading a poem we hear a thought that we have had but perhaps didn't even know that we had. The poet's thought uncovers our deepest thought. Thus Alexander Pope famously described poetry as, "What once was thought but never so well expressed."

All of this makes it a challenge to use poetry in our preaching. I remember the great preacher Elizabeth Achtemeier saying that bad poetry is immediately comprehensible whereas good poetry usually takes time to comprehend. So many of our best poems require work, repetition, and time before they give us their meaning. In a sermon there is little time to ponder the meaning of the words. Thus, only bad poetry can be used in a sermon. Who wants to use bad poetry? So Achtemeier says, "In other words, don't use poetry in sermons."

Good poetry demands to be read slowly and repeatedly. Even then, we know there is a surplus of meaning, layers of meaning yet hidden from us. I discovered that undergraduate students were annoyed—sometimes even angry—when they failed immediately to comprehend a poem I used. "I just don't get it," they said. They had been schooled into thinking that the purpose of education is to give one the skills whereby one "gets" everything. They were under the democratic fiction that everybody ought to be able to get everything, regardless of training, character, or effort, and they were therefore offended by a hard-to-understand poem and its opaque quality.

One more quality of poetry: poetic phrases stick in the brain long after straightforward prose statements have been forgotten. Poetry helps words to sing—to become memorable music. Surely this is why so much important biblical literature is poetry, so as to stick in the mind and burrow in the soul forever.

I marvel that Jesus appears not to care if his hearers do not immediately "get" his peculiar truth. The gospel is strange news that makes the accustomed, received word seem odd and makes those who "get it" seem odd as well. The gospel is the word defamiliarized. Jesus seems willing to let his truth take time with us and to demand of us that we take time with his truth. Something about the gospel—perhaps its irony, its strangeness—requires a medium no less metaphorical, no less demanding and odd than the parable.

I then realized how I had been trained—through a lifetime of the liturgy and hymns, listening to sermons, and preaching sermons—to engage in poetic, metaphorical thinking.

I give thanks that I have had at least a living experience in a mode of thought that does not expect truth to be immediately accessible. The truth that is Jesus Christ, the truth of the gospel, is that sort of deep, strange truth that requires not my application of an astute methodology, but rather my open, imaginative receptivity—my humility. Here is truth that comes not as an astute, personal epistemological achievement but rather as a divine gift.

So as I stood at the door of the church one recent Sunday, a person came out and whined, "I am sorry. I was confused by your remarks. I just didn't get it."

"Oh, yes you did," I responded in love.

Postmodern Preaching: Peculiar Truth

In one of his aphorisms, Nietzsche, father of all things postmodern, asks, "What if truth was a woman?" The question sounds sexist, and Nietzsche had some terrible things to say about women, but my Christ-conditioned ears hear more. What if truth was not detached, objective, freestanding, unconditional, and all the other things that modern, Western folk have been taught to think? What if truth was more personal, relative, intuitional, corporeal, and personified? In short, what if truth were a crucified and risen Jew named Jesus?

In John's Gospel, one of the few biblical texts where "truth" is mentioned, Jesus says, "I am the way, the truth, and the life. No one comes to the Father except through me" (John 14:6). Note that he does not say that he has come to talk about truth, or that he has some interesting truth to share with us. He simply says he is truth. Further, he says that he is the way, implying to my ears that his truth is not only a person, personal, but also a way, a journey, a movement to somewhere we would not have gone had we not been encountered and called by Mr. Way, Truth, and Life. Note that we sometimes call such biblical texts "passages."

Postmodernity has wonderfully exposed the way that our epistemologies have been corrupted by Western, modern, democratic, capitalist (that is, godless) ways of knowing. We take difficult, thick, bubbling scripture and boil it all down to "Four Spiritual Laws" or "Six Fundamentals," a few abstract, detached ideas about "what Jesus really said." Biblical fundamentalism and the Jesus Seminar are the two last gasps of modernity's attempt to contain Jesus. Francis Bacon was clear that his methodology sought truth for purposes of control. Truth is what we discover, through our modern methodologies, in order that we might run the world as we damn well please, so that we can control the world in such a way that we never need recourse to God either to explain the world or to make the world work.

Christians are currently in a process of rediscovering how very odd our peculiar notions of truth are in a world that has been dominated, at least the Western industrial world of the last two centuries, by essentially atheistic ways of knowing.

Postmodernity asks modernity to admit to the political caughtness of its ways of thinking and knowing. Many of the ideas that I think I thought up on my own are, in truth, relative to the sort of car that I drive and my annual salary. Most of my thoughts are only those permitted by a violent, consumerist culture.

I cannot figure out why some Christians consider this discovery of "relativity" to be the great threat of nonfoundational postmodernity. As Christians we have long believed that all truth is completely relative—relative to this Jew from Nazareth who died violently and rose unexpectedly. We do not know how to think about ourselves or the world until he reveals to us what is going on, who is in charge, where we are all headed, for what purpose we were created, and all the rest. "I am the way, the truth, and the life."

How to reach a world that is now postmodern? What will preaching be in postmodernity? I have hunches (in postmodernity, sweeping generalizations and final statements are suspect). When I began preaching, somehow I had the notion (I graduated from Yale Divinity School) that the modern world was my greatest homiletical challenge. All these skeptical, critical, modern people; what can we say to them from an old, culturally conditioned, Jewish book like the Bible? Now I feel (referencing Walter Brueggemann) that postmodern proclamation will be preaching that is less troubled over submitting itself to the now-discredited canons of modernity (reason, objectivity, universality, scientism, historicism, and the others) and more open to the claims that originated in a time other than our own among a people other than ourselves—that is, scripture.

Too much of modern preaching saw a sermon as an attempt to elicit religious sentiments from individual hearers. Postmodern preaching will be more about formation than evocation, the formation of a countercultural linguistic community called "church." Postmodern preaching will delight in the acknowledgment of the political significance (power configurations) of all speaking; therefore it will be speech tied to the distinctive linguistic community of the gospel. It will take Acts 2 as its model, a word from heaven meant not just to speak to the world but rather to expose, unmask, and then to change the world through the generation of a countercultural community who now know something they could not possibly have thought up on their own. The promise is of the evocation of a new people, a counterpolity offered "for all who are far away—as many as the Lord our God invites" (Acts 2:39).

More important than even this, it will be preaching that admits it is derivative from and frighteningly dependent upon steady traffic between here and heaven. All faithful preaching begins as an act of a determinedly self-revealing God: Yahweh who loves to talk, who delights in argument, declaration, epistemological conflict, assertion, and promise, who loves to create something out of nothing through nothing more powerful than words.

Christians know something about God only because we have been addressed by a self-revealing God. All of our knowing is miraculous, a gift of God from outside the limits of our experience, even so determinative an experience as the experience of women or of the oppressed. Preaching has something to say to the world only because of the grace of God. Preaching is heard, not because the preacher has succeeded at last in making common sense contact with modern people, but rather because of a miraculous intervention of God. Karl Barth says that if you will always think of preaching as you are told to think of "manna" in Exodus 16, you will not be far from the kingdom.

I remember an old preacher saying that at least two miracles happened that day at Pentecost. The promised Holy Spirit descended with power. Yes. Equally miraculous was that Peter preached. Peter, who could find nothing to say in the courtyard when confronted by the maid just a few weeks ago (Luke 22:54-62), stood up, raised his voice, and preached (Acts 2:14).

Preaching is still sign and wonder (Acts 2:43). It is a gift, a miracle, irrefutable evidence of a sound from heaven, the only way this creative God creates new worlds.

Prophets All

A little tattle-tale comes running to Moses, "Daddy Moses, Eldad and Medad are prophesying in the camp" (Num 11:27). Earlier the Lord, after speaking to Moses, took a notion to spread a little Spirit on some of the elders, Spirit that the Lord had previously disbursed mainly to Moses. Now, having received the gift of the Spirit, Eldad and Medad get downright loquacious and begin speaking up for God. Joshua doesn't like this effusive spirit. "My master Moses, stop them!"

We can't have ordinary, uncertified people prophesying, speaking for God—today Medad and Eldad, tomorrow my son or daughter. Joshua asks Moses for a prophetic restraining order.

Moses's response: "If only all the Lord's people were prophets with the Lord placing his spirit on them!"

Moses, who had been none too adept at speaking the truth to power himself until God gave him a spirited shove (see Exod 3–4), is not miserly of spirit. Would to God that all of God's people were prophets! There are never too many spirit-gifted prophets.

The Common Lectionary on Pentecost uses this obscure episode from Numbers 11 as a setup for an even more effusive, more prophetic spiritual breakout in Acts 2. At Pentecost, we were all gathered in one place. Then there was a rush of wind, tongues of fire, Holy Spirit. And everyone began to speak, "declaring the mighty works of God in our own languages" (Acts 2:11). As in Numbers 11, the Spirit's gift is the gift of speech, prophecy. As in Numbers 11, the Spirit's creation of a multitude of preachers results in communal bewilderment (Acts 2:6). Amazed and astonished, we ask, "What does this mean?"

In reply to the mocking of the mob, Peter speaks. Only a short time before, we left Peter with the maid in a courtyard (Luke 22:54ff.). Peter could find nothing to say when she charged that he was also with the Galilean. Now Peter is the spokesperson for the church, the major interpreter of the miracle of Pentecost. Apparently, Pentecost has enabled Peter to find his tongue. Peter explains the ruckus in the upper room by reference to the prophet Joel. In earlier days, the Spirit was poured out on a few gifted individuals called prophets. But there will be a day, according to Joel 2:28-32, when God's Spirit will be poured out on all. All. Even among the typically voiceless—old women and old men, young people out of work, underpaid maids, janitors—God's Spirit will descend in the later days bringing things to speech.

Later the world would marvel that such "uneducated and inexperienced" people like Peter (Acts 4:13) were speaking, each telling in their own words "the mighty works of God" (Acts 2:11). The holy wind at Pentecost is power unto speech. The gift of Acts 2 is the gift of prophecy. That day surely somebody remembered Moses's swaggering, "If only all of God's people were prophets!" That day is now, those prophets are us. When we are baptized, we are baptized into the ministry of preaching the truth. We're all prophets now.

And what makes a person a prophet is not the possession of unusual courage or insight but rather the prophet's subservience to the truth. The purpose of our preaching, the test for a "good" sermon, is its ability to be enlisted by God as part of God's prophet-making process. God intends to have a people who speak the truth, who testify to the world of God's great, loving assault upon the world. As Moses put it, "If only all the Lord's people were prophets with the Lord placing his spirit on them!"

The Acts 2 Pentecostal test for prophesy is not how outrageous we preachers have managed to be in the pulpit, but rather how many people we have produced who are able to say no: people who can speak the truth to power, people who can go up and stand before the Pharaoh and impudently tell him that he is not fully in charge of the world, people who have visions and dreams and who don't mind telling the world about them.

From my reading of Acts 2 and Luke's account of the birth of the church, I derive a few principles for prophecy: The Spirit has given the world a prophetic community, not simply a few outspoken social critics. The goal of the Spirit's descent is the creation of a *polis*, a people who look, speak, and act differently from the world's notions of community. The goal of our pastoral care, preaching, visitation, prayer, and praise is the production of a whole gaggle of prophets who will let God use them to get back what God owns.

The prophetic community is composed of those who have not had much opportunity, in the world's scheme of things, to speak. In other words, the Holy Spirit produces uppity speech. When I asked an African American friend of mine, "Why does African American preaching tend to get loud and raucous?" he replied, "Because my people have been told so often, for so long, that we ought to be seen and not heard, or better, invisible and quiet. We are to stand politely on the margins while the majority culture does its thing. So the church gathers my people and enables them to strut and shout, to find their voice, to stand up and be heard." The Acts of the Apostles is the story of how a bunch of ignorant and unlearned people (Acts 4:13), with the empowerment of the Holy Spirit, got too big for their britches and by the power of the risen Christ disturb the peace (Acts 17:6).

Fortunately, when these prophets speak out and speak up, they do not have to come up with something to say on their own. Jesus promises that the Holy Spirit will give them the right words.

"When they bring you before the synagogues, rulers, and authorities, don't worry about how to defend yourself or what you should say. The Holy Spirit will tell you at that very moment what you must say" (Luke 12:11-12).

The pastor as prophet is the one who keeps reminding the church of how God has chosen ordinary people to help take back the world, that God has chosen "what the world considers foolish to shame the wise. God chose what the world considers weak to shame the strong. And God chose what the world considers low-class and low-life—what is considered to be nothing—to reduce what is considered to be something to nothing" (1 Cor 1:27-28).

Therefore our prophetic preaching has as its goal the evocation of prophetic schoolteachers, shopkeepers, nursing home residents, and sixteen-year-olds who can speak the truth to power. Not everyone is called to be a preacher to the congregation. As Ephesians 4 says, "He gave some apostles, some prophets, some evangelists, and some pastors and teachers" (4:11). What is the chief purpose of all these divinely bestowed gifts? "His purpose was to equip God's people for the work of serving and building up the body of Christ" (4:12). Paul is not talking about an established order of clergy but rather the way that God gives baptismal gifts to all for the good edification of the church. Ordained clergy preach to the church so that the church might preach to the world.

First Peter is speaking to all Christians, all the baptized, not just the church's leaders or clergy in saying,

"But you are a chosen race, a royal priesthood, a holy nation, a people who are God's own possession. You have become this people so that you may speak of the wonderful acts of the one who called you out of darkness into his amazing light" (1 Pet 2:9).

Luther says that all Christians, by virtue of their baptism, are called to declare the wonderful deeds of God, to preach. Yet not all are called publicly to preach to the church. "Although we are all equally priests, we cannot all publicly minister and teach. We ought not to do so even if we could" (Martin Luther, "The Freedom of a Christian," in *Martin Luther: Selections from His Writings*, ed. John Dillenberger [New York: Doubleday, 1961], 65). Husbands are to preach to wives; wives are to preach to husbands; parents are to preach to children; all of us are called to preach to the world. But because we can't all preach at the same time when the church gathers, the church selects some to preach to the church on Sunday so that the whole church can join Jesus in preaching to the rest of the world all week long. Those selected are called pastors, preachers, and servants of the word.

The real test of preaching that is done by an ordained pastor is not the praise of the public, nor even its faithfulness to the original Greek of the biblical text, but rather the ability of the pastor's sermon to evoke a prophetic people.

(Portions of this article are taken from William H. Willimon, *Pastor: The Theology and Practice of Ordained Ministry* [Nashville: Abingdon Press, 2000], chap. 10.)

Taking the Truth

In his Yale lectures on preaching in 1877, celebrated Boston preacher Phillips Brooks gave American preaching its most durable definition. Preaching is "truth through personality." Brooks spent more of his lecture on the second half of the equation—the personality of the preacher—than on the first half—the truth of preaching.

"Truth through personality is our description of real preaching. The truth must come really through the person, not merely over his lips, . . . through his character, his affections, his whole intellectual and moral being" (Phillips Brooks, *Lectures on Preaching* [New York: E. P. Dutton & Company, 1907], 5).

Brooks's definition of preaching stresses at least part of the nature of incarnational truth. Here is truth that must be embodied in order to be received. The definition is not only congruent with an incarnational faith in the Word-made-flesh but also fits nicely in the burgeoning science of psychology and personality development in late nineteenth-century America. Brooks's characterization of preaching was congruent with William James's philosophy-as-psychology that was to capture the American intellectual imagination. Today, when asked, "What do you want in a preacher?" most congregations of my acquaintance will say "a warm personality" or "a real and genuine person" before they say "biblical fidelity" or "theological substance."

Brooks tended to stress the personality of the preacher more than the nature of the truth communicated through the personality. And so do most contemporary homileticians. Modern Americans live in what one commentator has described as "the psychological society" in which psychological problems are the only problems that concern us. Modernity has a way of detaching us from the world and pushing us ever deeper into ourselves. We tend to think of the world as internal before it becomes external. We think that we think inside out. We have these innate ideas, these stirrings within us, and preaching evokes and provokes them, projects them out upon the world, and this we call "reality." It's all inside.

The Roman orator Quintilian defined a good speech as "a good person speaking well." The character of the speaker is vitally important for the audience's reception of the speech. Thus Brooks stood in an ancient tradition in characterizing preaching as "truth through personality." Today I hear a great deal of talk about the personality of the congregation too, truth communicated through a personality to a group of personalities. The modern congregation's "felt needs," modern prejudices, limitations, and possibilities are the major concerns of contemporary homiletical thought.

It is my judgment that current preaching is in great need of theological refurbishment. We desperately need something from the outside. We must recover a sense of preaching as something that God does—a theological matter before it is an anthropological matter—preaching as the business of God before it is our business. In other words, if Brooks were lecturing at Yale on preaching today, I hope that he would expend most of his effort on truth—specifically, the one who is "the way, the truth, and the life"—rather than on the preacher's personality.

The personality of the preacher is noteworthy mainly as the person of someone who has seen and heard something, a messenger who has been grasped by a message, someone who has been addressed. Otherwise, in my experience, the personalities of preachers are not that interesting. Good preaching, said theologian Karl Barth, is like a person standing on a street corner pointing upward into the sky. Of course a crowd gathers, craning their necks upward, attempting to see whatever it is that the person who is pointing upward sees. Theology reminds us preachers that the crucial matter is not so much that we eloquently point upward but rather that we see something that merits drawing a crowd.

Preaching, to be truly Christian preaching, must be reflexive, responsive. Something has happened to us and to our world, therefore we speak about it.

Martin Luther characterized the gospel as the *verbum externum*, the "external word," a word that is not self-derived, a word that comes to us from outside of our personal experiences or interior ruminations. Perhaps this is why "faith comes from hearing." The gospel, that gives rise to faith, comes to us from the outside. It must be spoken to us, told to us, rather than arising out of us. Preaching, in this Lutheran characterization, is truth assaulting, forming, reforming personalities rather than truth merely being expressed through a passive person.

In 1537, Luther began a series of sermons on the Gospel of John. It is clear that Luther undertook this task not because he wanted to get something off his chest, not because he had something welling up from within him that he wanted to say, but rather because he had been confronted with a Word that lay outside his world, a Word that created in him and his hearers a new world. He comes to the Gospel of John as one might be met by a stranger. The stranger must be encountered in all of his strangeness, in his sheer otherness, allowed to have his say, or one has not really met the stranger. This Luther does with the Fourth Gospel.

Luther says that the preacher who would introduce so strange a Gospel as the Gospel of John to a congregation must first immerse himself in the peculiar way that the Bible talks and then cultivate the courage to say what has been heard, regardless of the reactions of the hearers. The preacher

> must remain conversant with this evangelist; to this end we must familiarize ourselves with his way of speaking. Therefore we propose to consider his Gospel in the name of the Lord, discuss it, and preach it as long as we are able, to the glory of our Lord Christ and to our own welfare, comfort, and salvation, without worrying whether the world shows much interest in it. Nonetheless, there will always be a few who will hear God's precious Word with delight; and for their sakes, too, we must preach it. For since God provides people whom He orders to preach, He will surely also supply and send listeners who will take this instruction to heart. (Quoted in Hughes Oliphant Old, *The Reading and Preaching of the Scriptures*, vol. 4 [Grand Rapids: Eerdmans, 2002], 20)

Note how different this statement is than the approach of contemporary homiletics. We tend to think that the test of a sermon is the effect upon the listeners. Have they heard what is said? Do they consent to the argument? Are they emotionally moved? Have their lives been enriched?

Luther says that the challenge is not in the listeners but in the Gospel. We are to preach, not for the hearers, but "to the glory of our Lord Christ . . . without worrying whether the world shows much interest in it." We are to love the text more than we love our congregational context. We preachers are to worry more about what is being said, and how well we can replicate that word, than we are to worry about whether or not what is being said in the Gospel is being heard in the world. Thus in a sermon on Matthew, Luther said that the test of our ministry as preachers is "not whether many or few people believe or do not believe, are damned or saved" but rather "fidelity to the Word of God" (the Sermon on Matthew as cited in E. Plass, ed., *What Luther Says: An Anthology,* vol. 3 [St. Louis: Concordia, 1959], 1208).

In a world of "seeker services" and "user friendly" churches, I submit that Luther's view of preaching is countercultural as well as counterecclesial in the extreme. Before preaching is communication, exhortation, admonition, comfort, or motivation, it is prayerful listening for God's word. A good sermon begins with the biblical text, with reflection upon and listening to the text before there is any reflection on congregational context. In other words, a good sermon begins by being confronted by the truth, the truth that is revealed in scripture, the truth who is Jesus the Christ.

Preaching can be said to be "effective" only because it is true. It is not through psychology, sociology, or skillful rhetoric that we reach people but rather through theology—and what God said. Without hearing that word, preaching has nothing to say. Otherwise preaching is but a blasphemous attempt to speak in the place of God rather than to speak for God. Thus prayer is the first step in sermon preparation; and all subsequent steps of biblical study, sermon construction, and even sermon delivery are aspects of prayer. Prayer is listening to God more than prayer is talking to God. The humility, admission of emptiness and need, and the expectant attentiveness that are the disciplines of prayer are also the disciplines of sermon preparation. Preachers are to say what we have heard, whether the congregation hears or refuses to hear.

It is a joy to be with you in this ministry of listening to and speaking from the word.

The Biblical Word

When theologian Karl Barth gave his lectures on preaching under the gathering cloud of Nazism, with thousands in the German church casting their lot with Hitler, Barth said the only thing that could save the church now was strictly, exclusively, determinedly biblical preaching. Barth also said that if there is one thing worse than being a nonbiblical preacher it was being a boring one. What is the remedy against boredom, that bane of homiletical existence? Barth said that the remedy was to be biblical:

> Preachers must not be boring. To a large extent the pastor and boredom are synonymous concepts. Listeners often think that they have heard already what is being said in the pulpit. They have long since known it themselves. The fault certainly does not lie with them alone. Against boredom the only defense is again being biblical. If a sermon is biblical, it will not be boring. Holy Scripture is in fact so interesting and has so much that is new and exciting to tell us that listeners cannot even think about dropping off to sleep. (Karl Barth, *Homiletics* [Louisville: Westminster John Knox Press, 1991], 80)

Today's preaching is derivative of yesterday's scriptural word. In preaching, the written word returns to its original form as the spoken word as scripture again becomes proclamation. Preaching is public speaking that strives never to be original. Preaching is Christian only when it is biblical, obviously derivative of, submissive to, and controlled by the biblical word. Therefore, the most important disciplines required of a preacher are those associated with the preacher's subservience to scripture. No preacher speaks without having first prayerfully allowed scripture to speak.

We have a sketch of a remembered sermon by Moses in Exodus 19:3-6. This is the sermonic prelude to the ten commandments: Then Moses went up to God; the Lord called to him out of the mountain saying, "This is what you should say to Jacob's household and declare to the Israelites: You saw what I did to the Egyptians, and how I lifted you up on eagles' wings and brought you to me. So now, if you faithfully obey me and stay true to my covenant, you will be my most precious possession out of all the peoples, since the whole earth belongs to me. You will be a kingdom of priests for me and a holy nation. These are the words you should say to the Israelites."

Note that Moses's sermon begins in remembrance (Exod 19:4). From memory ("You saw") the sermon moves toward exhortation ("So now, if you faithfully obey me"). This is a typical biblical move, a typical homiletical move from recollection to performance, from memory of what God has done to statement of our present responsibility before God. Israel never tired of remembering the exodus as the basis for its life with God. The "people of God" exist as a creation of God, as a response to something that God has initiated. We look and live differently from other people because we recall our salvation, how we were created out of nothing by a God who "lifted you up on eagles' wings and brought you to me."

Thus scripture is not merely a helpful resource for preaching, it is the genesis, rationale, substance, and means of preaching. When we preach from the scriptures the Bible is living in its native habitat and functioning as it was intended. When the Bible is given over to scholars of religion who are subservient to the academy rather than to the church, it is often made to answer questions that are of little interest to the originating intentions of scripture itself. Favorite historical-critical questions—"How can this statement be credible to modern, scientific, Western minds?" "Are these the genuine words of Jesus?"—are not as relevant as scripture's originating homiletical question: "Will you come forward, be part of a new, countercultural people of God, and follow Jesus where he leads you?"

Sometime during the mid-fifth century BCE Israel returned from exile. Their beloved Jerusalem lay in ruins. A decision was made to rebuild the walls, a first step toward reclaiming Israel's identity as a people. During the reconstruction, a scroll was found, the book of the law of Moses, which the Lord had given to Israel. Before the Water Gate, from morning until midday, in the presence of all the people, the priest Ezra read and "all the people were attentive to the book of the law." Ezra stood upon a wooden platform and read. Ezra's fellow priests "gave the sense" of the words being read, "so that the people understood the reading" (paraphrased from Neh 8).

The people wept when they heard the words read and interpreted. They wept for joy at finally having recovered words lost to them in exile and for sadness at how far they had strayed from God's appointed way.

Ezra told them not to weep. He proclaimed the day a great holiday, a holy day, telling them to go and have a great party, "because the joy from the LORD is your strength" (Neh 8:10). They celebrated greatly "because they understood what had been said to them" (8:12).

Here is a portrait of Israel at its best—a snapshot of what would become Israel's tradition of the synagogue. The word is read and interpreted in worship, the people weep, and then they celebrate and align their lives accordingly. Israel is constituted, corrected, resurrected, and redeemed by words. As Walter Brueggemann says in his commentary on Nehemiah 8 in *The Church as Counterculture*: "This peculiar community is not self-generated, but understands itself in terms of a special authorization in a script available for steady and regular, attentive reiteration" (Albany, NY: Suny Press, 2000). Christian clergy stand in that place once occupied by Ezra as public readers and interpreters of scripture. Like Israel, the church is gathered, not as the world gathers, on the basis of race, gender, nation, or class. These words of scripture are not spoken merely in order to elicit agreement or noble feelings among the hearers, but rather to form, reform the hearers. It is the nature of scripture to be "political," that is, formative. It is the nature of scripture to want power over our lives. It is the nature of scripture not so much to want to speak to our world but rather to absorb our world into the biblical world. In reading the Bible, God is not merely being revealed to us but is allowed to have God's way with us.

Our earliest detailed account of a Sunday service in the early church is that provided in Justin Martyr's *Apology* (c. 150): "And on that day called Sunday, all who live in cities or in the country gather together to one place, and the memoirs of the apostles and the writings of the prophets are read, as long as time permits: then, when the reader has ceased, the president verbally instructs, and exhorts to the imitation of these good things."

Here we see all the elements of the Christian service of the word: the church gathers its scattered people, the church reads from scripture and engages in acts of narrative and remembrance, and then the church hears instruction, exhortation—that is, preaching—in order that Christians may embody what they have heard read and proclaimed.

As preachers, it is our peculiar service to the church, as its lead biblical interpreters, to lay the story of Israel and the church, as recorded in scripture, alongside our present modes of church. Ezra did that at the Water Gate. Jesus did it in his hometown synagogue in Luke 4. It is my prayer that, this volume is helpful to you in this demanding vocation as servant of the word. In exilic conditions, the word gathers a people. This is Israel in diaspora: the people listen, aligning themselves to the word, singing the songs of Zion, naming the name, telling the story, and thus surviving as God's people.

(Some of the preceding material was taken from William H. Willimon, *Pastor: The Theology and Practice of Ordained Ministry* [Nashville: Abingdon Press, 2000], chap. 5.)

The Theological Significance of Preaching

Eugene Peterson says the challenge of preaching is that we are sinners preaching to sinners. He says that members of the congregation are like a friendly dog; they show up, listen to what you say, wag their tails, rub against you, and then they go back to living their same old dog-like life.

Some years ago, Bishop Ken Goodson was asked to go to the airport and pick up the first surgeon ever to do an open-heart transplant. Bishop Goodson picks him up and as they ride together the surgeon goes on at length about his work, saying to Bishop Goodson, "You have no idea what it is like to reach into a man's chest and hold his beating heart." Bishop Goodson responded, "Yes, sir, I do. I'm a preacher, and we preachers do that every week."

As someone who joins you in reaching into people's hearts every week, I have a few observations about the theological significance of the homiletical task.

1. We are a people formed by words. God speaks words and the world comes into being through words. In the beginning God creates the heavens and the earth, separates day from night and land from water, and forms humanity from the earth. In the opening of the Gospel of John we're told that Jesus is the Word, the divine logos. The beginning of everything that is, is the word. Jesus is the Word made flesh. At the core of the Christian faith is this word-derived mystery of the creative, fecund word.

2. Preaching is a gift of God. Preaching is not something that we offer to the church, but rather it is something that God does through us. Preaching is a

gift that God offers to the church and does it through us. God speaks sometimes through us, sometimes in spite of us, and sometimes through someone else. Clarence Jordan was a PhD in Greek New Testament back in the 1940s and he read the Bible, especially that part in Acts where all held everything in common. He decided to do what he had read about in the Bible, so he founded Koinonia Farm. Jordan said that preaching is like a Trojan Horse . . . looks harmless enough, just words, a few stories and then, BANG! It got you.

3. Preaching is about the collision of powers, God's word being brought to bear on a world that is in rebellion against God. The first sermon that Jesus preaches in the Gospels, Mark 1:15, is not a long sermon, but it is explosive and full of political implication: "Now is the time! Here comes God's kingdom! Change your hearts and lives, and trust this good news!"

Again, Peterson says somewhere that a preacher should pretend to be an undercover agent. The world is in fact a world in rebellion against God. You know it; nobody else knows it. What you have to do as a pastor, as a preacher, is to blend in. For the most part you like the surrounding culture. You dress like most other people dress, you eat the same sort of food that most people eat, but you always keep before you the knowledge that you are a spy, an undercover agent for God's kingdom. Then once a week you stand up on Sunday mornings and say, "I've walked around in your shoes, but I'm really a gospel-spy, and this is what I've discovered this week about how our world and our lives are out of line with the gospel." You subtly tell folks what you as the undercover agent discovered throughout the week. You can't give them all the gospel at once. It's like guerrilla warfare—shake a bit of gospel here, throw some over there, plant some subtle seeds from time to time, and there you have it. If you tell them the gospel all at once, if you give them the whole truth, they won't just fire you; they will kill you. So go undercover, blend in, gather data, but always know which side you are really on. You are a preacher. You are an agent of the revolution, an instrument in the reclaiming of the world for God.

4. Christian preaching is biblical preaching. While we preachers are, as Augustine says, peddlers of words, the word from which we start, and the word

that controls our sermons, is the Bible. We go to the Bible looking for a word to speak, praying that our people will not only meet the Bible, but will be met by God. The preacher primarily serves a congregation by serving them the biblical word. This is what Leander Keck called "priestly listening." We listen to the text in order to discover what to say. We listen to the text, work with it, allow the text to work with us, pray over it, consult commentaries, consult this book, in order to make some fresh discovery in the word and then we share that discovery with our congregation on Sunday.

What a joy, and what a daunting task, to be engaged with you each week in the ministry of preaching!

The Wonderful Thickness of the Text!

Some summers ago, I attempted to read the Koran. Despite my earnest efforts, I didn't make it through the entire volume. For one thing, Mohammed, the prophet of the one true God, has an opinion on everything: how to weigh grain, how to cut meat, homosexuality (he was against it). It really is amazing how many issues there are about which Jesus appears to have had absolutely no interest.

Mohammed never tells stories. Ask him a question, he gives you a straight answer. "I have three things I want to say about how to run a government," he will say. Quite a contrast with Jesus. Mohammed always answers every question; Jesus, almost never. The Koran has a low tolerance for ambiguity, narrative, enigma; the Bible wallows in it.

When one reads the Koran, one knows immediately how a reader could derive a "fundamentalist" understanding from it. Yet it is more difficult to understand why there are those who read, for instance, the Gospel of Luke and find therein "fundamentals." Luke is "thick," the literature is polyvalent, predominately narrative, almost never propositional, open to multiple interpretations, defying reductionistic reading. The thick, impenetrable nature of these texts may be by conscious design. A hard-to-understand text begs for attention, engages our natural human inclination to figure things out. However, the texts may be difficult, obscure, and distant simply because they are talking about what is true whereas most of what we live is false. A living, righteous, prickly God tends to produce difficult scripture.

For instance, many of us struggle with John 20. John first does the story of Easter as a footrace between the disciples in which they came, then they "saw and believed" (John 20:8). Believed what? John says that "they didn't yet understand the scripture that Jesus must rise from the dead" (20:9). Presumably, they believed that the body had been stolen. At any rate, whatever they believed was not yet quite Easter. Easter ends with everyone going back home (20:10) and that was that. At least the men go home. Mary stays behind to weep. She is confronted by the risen Christ, whom she regards as either the gardener or a body snatcher, or perhaps both (20:15).

Then, just to keep things interesting, John 20:19 begins Easter all over again with the story of Thomas and his doubts. Defying resolution or simple understanding, the risen Christ appears again in John 21 in a complex, utterly enigmatic appearance that becomes quite convoluted with details of fish, fishing nets, Peter, and feeding sheep.

We have a "problem" with this literature. Our problem is not, as we sometimes flatter ourselves into believing, that we are modern, critical, and skeptical whereas the text is naive, primitive, and credulous. That was historical criticism's reading of our interpretive dilemma.

No, I have come to believe that our problem is that we have become tone deaf to a text so thick, so opaque, so rich as John 20–21. We are ill-equipped to hear the Easter text. After all, we are modern, Western folk who have taught ourselves to be content with a flat, well-defined, and utterly accessible world. Our world has become "user friendly," for we can imagine no world worth having that is not subject to our utility. Our ways of knowing are positivistic, historicist, and inherently reductionistic.

Robert Alter says somewhere that, until the parables of Kafka or James Joyce's *Ulysses*, there is a sense in which we modern people had lost the skills necessary to read the Bible. Only after artists were again determined to write reality on a number of levels, exploring the complexities of human consciousness, the mystery of time, the polyvalence of words, were we able to ask the right questions of 1 Kings.

William C. Placher makes the evocative suggestion that the very messiness of the biblical texts—the way they parallel each other, conflict, repeat, and fail to connect—is an embodiment of the God that they try to bring to speech: "The narratives of this God who eschews brute force were not edited with the brute force necessary to impose a single, clear framework." Just as this God, according to a number of the parables of Jesus, is willing to live with wasted seed, a net full of good and bad fish, and a garden in which the weeds mix with the wheat, eschewing violent, coercive purification and harmonizing, so the willingness of the biblical writers and canonizers to live with the messiness of the texts is a testimonial to their faith in a God who chooses to suffer, to embrace human messiness, and to love us in our inconsistency rather than to force us to make sense.

The interpretive skills that many of us learned in seminary invariably took a superior stance toward the text; modernity is inherently arrogant. We have been conditioned to feel that we moderns are privileged to stand at the summit of human development, uniquely equipped to stand in judgment upon any idea or anyone who preceded us.

We cut apart the text, split it up into its smallest units, sever it from the community that produced it, lop off that which offends our modern sensibilities—my verbs are intentional. We are doing the same violence to the text that we do to any culture or people who are strange to us, who don't fit into the categories that we received from the enlightenment, who refuse to produce the commodities we value.

Much of our violence begins with our modern lust for the one "right" interpretation, the one official reading. All interpretation, including historical-critical interpretation (especially historical-critical) serves some configuration of power, some social arrangement. I once thought it shameful that "uninformed" laypersons were busy interpreting biblical texts in all sorts of ways, without the benefit of academic training. I now honor such diversity of reading—particularly when they occur among folk who are seeking not only to understand the text but also to embody and perform the text as ecclesial resistance against the powers-that-be who serve the academy rather than the church.

What I am pleading for here is an interpretive approach to our scripture that is true to the form of the scripture itself. Just as the Koran, by its very form, renders certain kinds of readers, so the Bible, by its form, is more congenial to certain interpretive strategies than to others.

The text itself encourages, provokes uncentering, dislocation, and dislodgement. The very thickness of the text may be part of the text's strategic assault upon our received world.

I think we need to condition our people to expect interpretive difficulty on Sunday morning, to relish the multiplicity of messages, to love the thickness of the text, to come to church expecting to have their present reality subverted by the demanding text. Too many of us preachers say, after reading a troublesome text, "Give me twenty minutes and I will explain this for you." Even to read a troublesome text and then to say, in a well-modulated voice, "Now I have three things I want to say about this," begins to defuse the text, make it make sense without allowing the text time to make us make sense. To be baptized is to be willing to let the text stand in a superior interpretive position to us, not the other way around. Rather than treating the text like a cadaver to be dissected, we ought to pray with the psalmist, "Thou has searched me and known me, oh Lord."

Easter is true because the text says it is true, because what the text says is true to the church's continuing engagement by the living Christ. It requires not certitude, the sure fixing of truth, but rather trust, a playful willingness to let the strangeness of the text have its way with us. The text has subsumed us into itself, rendered unto us a world that would have been unavailable to us without the world having been constructed (as most worlds are) by the text. Yet that does not mean that the world rendered thereby exists only in the imagination of the text. Every time the church gathers, breaks the bread, and drinks the wine, we proclaim to any who dare to listen, that what the text says, is. The text, we believe, has the power to evoke that which it describes.

We have the text, we believe, as a gracious gift of a God determined not to leave us to our own devices. What happened on Easter—namely, Jesus coming back to us, refusing to leave us alone, intruding among us—is what happens each Sunday in the reading and preaching of the text. Scripture, read and preached, is Easter all over again. And, thank God, we never exhaust the significance of it, despite our most thorough interpretive efforts, for the text and the world it renders is thick. There is always a surplus of meaning, even after the longest of our sermons.

Thus John ends his account (at least one of his accounts) of Easter by preaching,

"Then Jesus did many other miraculous signs in his disciples' presence, signs that aren't recorded in this scroll. But these things are written so that you will believe that Jesus is the Christ, God's Son, and that believing, you will have life in his name" (John 20:30-31).

Scripture Index

**Page numbers in bold indicate the passages that
are the selected readings for each week.**

Exod 16:2-4, 9-15 101

Ruth 1:1-18 . . . . **225**
Ruth 3:1-5; 4:13-17 239

1 Sam 1:4-20 . . . . **247**
1 Sam 2:1-10 247
1 Sam 3:1-10, (11-20) **11**
1 Sam 8:4-11, (12-15), 16-20 23
1 Sam 15:34–16:13 33
1 Sam 17:(1a, 4-11, 19-23), 32-49 43
1 Sam 17:57–18:5, 10-16 43

2 Sam 1:1, 17-27 53
2 Sam 5:1-5, 9-10 63
2 Sam 6:1-5, 12b-19 71
2 Sam 7:1-14a 81
2 Sam 11:1-15 91
2 Sam 11:26–12:13a 101
2 Sam 18:5-9, 15, 31-33 111
2 Sam 23:1-7 255

1 Kgs 2:10-12; 3:3-14 121

1 Kgs 8:(1, 6, 10-11), 22-30, 41-43 131

1 Kgs 17:8-16. 239

1 Kgs 19:4-8. 111

2 Kgs 4:42-44. 91

Esth 7:1-6, 9-10; 9:20-22. 177

Job 1:1; 2:1-10 187

Job 23:1-9, 16-17. 197

Job 38:1-7, (34-41) 207

Job 42:1-6, 10-17. 217

Ps 1 167

Ps 9:9-20 43

Ps 14 91

Ps 19 157

Ps 20 33

Ps 22:1-15 197

Ps 23 81

Ps 24 . . . . 71, 233

Ps 26 187

Ps 29 1

Ps 34:1-8 111

Ps 34:1-8, (19-22) 217

Ps 34:9-14 121

Ps 45:1-2, 6-9. 139

Ps 48 63

Ps 51:1-12 101

Ps 54 167
Ps 78:23-29 101
Ps 84 131
Ps 85:8-13 71
Ps 89:20-37 81
Ps 91:9-16 207
Ps 92:1-4, 12-15. 33
Ps 93 255
Ps 104:1-9, 24, 35c. 207
Ps 111 121
Ps 116:1-9 157
Ps 124 177
Ps 125 147
Ps 126 217
Ps 127 239
Ps 130 . . . . 53, 111
Ps 132:1-12, (13-18) 255
Ps 133 43
Ps 138 23
Ps 139:1-6, 13-18. 11
Ps 145:10-18 91
Ps 146 . . . . 225, 239

Prov 1:20-33. 157
Prov 9:1-6. 121
Prov 22:1-2, 8-9, 22-23 147
Prov 31:10-31. 167

Song 2:8-13 139

Isa 6:1-8 1

Isa 25:6-9 233

Isa 50:4-9a 157

Isa 53:4-12 207

Jer 11:18-20 167

Jer 23:1-6 81

Jer 31:7-9 217

Ezek 17:22-24 33

Dan 7:9-10, 13-14 255

Amos 7:7-15 71

Mark 2:23–3:6 11

Mark 3:20-35 . . . . **23**

Mark 4:26-34 . . . . **33**

Mark 4:35-41 43

Mark 5:21-43 53

Mark 6:1-13 63

Mark 6:14-29 . . . . **71**

Mark 6:30-34, 53-56 81

Mark 7:1-8, 14-15, 21-23 139

Mark 7:24-37 . . . . **147**

Mark 8:27-38 . . . . **157**

Mark 9:30-37 . . . . **167**

Mark 9:38-50 . . . . **177**

Mark 10:2-16 187

Mark 10:17-31 . . . . **197**

Mark 10:35-45 . . . . **207**

Mark 10:46-52. . . . . **217**

Mark 12:28-34. 225

Mark 12:38-44. . . . . **239**

Mark 13:1-8. 247

John 3:1-17 1

John 6:1-21 . . . . **91**

John 6:24-35 . . . . **101**

John 6:35, 41-51 . . . . **111**

John 6:51-58 . . . . **121**

John 6:56-69 . . . . **131**

John 11:32-44 . . . . **233**

John 18:33-37 255

Rom 8:12-17 1

2 Cor 4:5-12 11

2 Cor 4:13–5:1. 23

2 Cor 5:6-10, (11-13), 14-17. 33

2 Cor 6:1-13 . . . . **43**

2 Cor 8:7-15 . . . . **53**

2 Cor 12:2-10 . . . . **63**

Eph 1:3-14. 71

Eph 2:11-22. . . . . **81**

Eph 3:14-21. 91

Eph 4:1-16. 101

Eph 4:25–5:2. 111

Eph 5:15-20. 121

Eph 6:10-20. 131

Heb 1:1-4; 2:5-12. . . . . **187**

Heb 4:12-16. 197

Heb 5:1-10. 207

Heb 7:23-28. 217

Heb 9:11-14. 225

Heb 9:24-28. 239

Heb 11:14, (15-18), 19-25. 247

Jas 1:17-27 . . . . **139**

Jas 2:1-10, (11-13), 14-17 147

Jas 3:1-12 157

Jas 3:13–4:3, 7-8a. 167

Jas 5:13-20 177

Rev 1:4b-8 . . . . **255**

Rev 21:1-6a 233

CPSIA information can be obtained
at www.ICGtesting.com
Printed in the USA
LVOW13s1115121017
551941LV00004B/7/P